THE AMERICAN TRADITION

Also by Clarence B. Carson

The Fateful Turn: from Individualism
to Collectivism, 1880-1960

THE AMERICAN TRADITION

by

CLARENCE B. CARSON

Professor of American History
Grove City College, Pennsylvania

The Foundation for Economic Education, Inc.
Irvington-on-Hudson, New York   1964

The Publisher

THE FOUNDATION FOR ECONOMIC EDUCATION is an educational champion of private ownership, the free market, the profit and loss system, and limited government. It is nonprofit and nonpolitical. Sample copies of the Foundation's monthly journal, *The Freeman,* as well as a list of books and other publications, are available on request.

To

Myrtice

Contents

Preface

THIS BOOK is intended for those who
believe or are open to the proposition that there was, or is,
an American tradition. It is an attempt to set forth the
main characteristics and tenets of that tradition. My
position, in contrast to some who have written about it, is
that it is possible to discern the definite patterns of an
American tradition in history, that it was not something
so intangible that it can be vaguely described as pragmatic, experimental, and democratic. Indeed, such char-
acterizations are notions about Americans and their history, not solidly founded in evidence and the penetration
of the superfice which shields us from American history.
Instead, the tradition was concretely embodied in institutions and articulated in practices. The following terms call
attention to its main outline: constitutionalism, government by law, representative government, federalism, individualism, equality, voluntarism, free trade, private property, natural rights, internationalism, moral order in the
universe, thrift, industry, and competition.

I have attempted to do several things in this book. First,

the main tenets of the American tradition have been
treated topically. This will appear from the chapter titles.
Second, most of the topics are treated historically. My
thesis is that the outlines of three traditions have appeared in colonial English America and the United States.
Those who came to America from Europe in the seventeenth and eighteenth centuries brought with them the
remains of a corporate and authoritarian tradition. It
broke down in America and was replaced by the tradition
which I have called both American and liberal. Since the
late nineteenth century, the trend toward collectivism has
considerably altered the earlier tradition, though I question that collectivist ideas and practices should be referred
to as a tradition. Collectivists may use the remains of a
tradition to accomplish their ends, but their programs and
practices depend upon government manipulation and coercion for their continuation. At any rate, this is the historical framework within which the account is made.

It should be said, too, that this book was *not* written by
an observer from another planet. In short, it may not be
entirely objective, whatever that may mean. It has been
my intention to keep the facts straight and to make interpretations that follow from the evidence. Beyond that,
I have attempted to follow the path of reason. Even so, I
have brought a viewpoint to the materials and may well
have incorporated it in the book. I believe that the central American tradition was one of the great achievements
of all time, and that much that was embodied in it was
timeless. In the last generation, it has been distorted, obscured, and forgotten. If things continue as they have for
the last fifty years, it will shortly survive only in such dessicated remnants as there were of the Roman Republic in

the time of the Empire. In short, I believe that much of
the tradition is still valid, could be restored and built
upon. This book is written with that end in view.

It gives me pleasure to acknowledge the assistance of
those who have helped to make this book possible. I am
grateful to all of the people at the Foundation for Economic Education who contributed in some way to the
completion and publication of the book, and in whose
monthly journal, *The Freeman,* these chapters appeared
as a series beginning in April, 1963. My particular
thanks go to Dr. Paul L. Poirot of the Foundation, whose
cheerful and encouraging letters kept me going during the
trying months, who rendered valuable editorial assistance,
and who oversaw the project from its inception to its completion. Mrs. Eleanor Orsini has made the task of correcting proofs less burdensome upon the author by doing
her job so well. I am indebted to Miss Vernelia Crawford
for her work on the index. The uniform courtesy and ef-
ficiency of all those people in the Foundation with whom
I have had contacts is to me a tribute to Mr. Leonard E.
Read who was its founder and is its guiding hand.

The publication of this book was made possible by a
bequest from the late James W. Clise, a bequest to the
Foundation for Economic Education for the development
of spiritual values. It is my hope that the book will serve
the purposes he had in mind.

My debt to others is considerable, but none of these
people or organizations are in any way responsible for any
errors in fact, invalid generalizations, or departures from
the truth which may occur herein. That responsibility is
mine alone. Nor should their assistance be construed as
endorsement of particular ideas or interpretations.

May I express more directly my gratitude to my wife, to whom this volume is dedicated, for her assistance in preparing correct drafts to be sent off, for her enthusiasm for the project, for her gentle reminders to get on with it, and for her tolerance of the vicissitudes which accompany living with one who writes.

CLARENCE B. CARSON
Grove City, Pennsylvania
October, 1963

1.

Introduction: Lest We Forget

IT IS A COMMON OBSERVATION that societies and civilizations decay from within before they are overcome from without. For some time, I have harbored the suspicion that this decadence results primarily from forgetfulness. Success should beget attachment to the ways that brought it to a people, confidence in the rightness of these ways, and devotion to the principles which describe them or from which they spring. So it often is at first, I suspect. But continued success engenders complacency; complacency sets the stage for forgetfulness. When men have forgotten what it was that made their success possible, they are subject to an overweening false pride in their own powers and abilities. That pride goeth before a fall is an adage whose truth is ignored at the pain of destruction.

Forgetfulness comes about in some such fashion as this. It can be likened to what could conceivably happen regarding some physical development, say the invention, development, spread, and use of electricity. At one time there was no electricity available in forms that could be used. Men learned something of its properties, how to tame it, to produce it, conduct it, and make it perform useful functions. There would come a time when almost every house was supplied with electricity, when people

1

had all sorts of devices and appliances for using it. At first, of course, men would know that it was an artificially created convenience, that it resulted from the labors and inventiveness of men, and that it would have to be kept coming and the means for using it maintained else there would be no electricity or appliances.

Suppose, however, that this electrical system had been perfected to a degree that no humanly developed system is likely to be. Suppose that all of the electricity came from hydroelectric dams which ran automatically, that it was brought to homes by underground wires which lasted a long time, that no repairs or maintenance were required for decade upon decade. It is quite probable that men would come to believe that they produced electricity by flipping a switch, that all one needed to know to use electricity would be how to replace a burnt-out fuse, that all effort and intelligence would come to be focused upon maintaining outlets and appliances. Electricity would be taken for granted. Men would come to accept its availability as a right.

Meanwhile, the roads leading to the plants would grow up, and the plants themselves would be hidden by trees and shrubbery. The location of the underground cables would long since have been forgotten. In such circumstances, if the power did fail, men would look for the cause of the trouble in the appliances; they would angrily replace one good fuse with yet another, supposing that they had been sold a bad lot at the store. In short, they would treat symptom after symptom, in the vain belief that by so doing they could cure the ailment.

By analogy, something resembling this is happening to America today. We have, as a people, well nigh forgotten the sources of our rights, our freedom, our prosperity, our domestic harmony and accord, and international peace. The source of our ways has been obscured by aberrant growths of ideas and habits over the years. The location of the roots to our system has been forgotten by many people. We have become engrossed in the details of making our system work and have lost sight of the obstructions which hinder the flow of power. Or again, we act as if the paraphernalia of our system were sufficient to make it operate, as if there were no hidden sources which provide the motive power.

Constitution Based on Higher Law

A particular example may serve to illuminate the point. When those who drew up the Constitution provided for a Supreme Court, they did so because they held certain beliefs. They believed that there is a Higher Law operating in this world, that it is prior and superior to man-made law, and that legislation is—or should be—only a particular application of this Law. Insofar as this Higher Law was believed to be available in any human document, it was supposed to be in the Constitution.

In the final analysis, though, Higher Law was conceived to be the law of God. Hopefully, they meant to record and live according to Divine law as it might be discovered in natural law or by revelation. However incompletely or inadequately the Constitution might mirror this Law, it derived its force and respect from the belief in an ultimate and higher source of authority. The role of the Supreme Court was to apply this Higher Law as it was to be found in the Constitution to particular cases and thus to insure a government of laws in the United States. Thus, the Supreme Court derived its reason for being and authority from the belief in a Higher Law.

This fact has long since been forgotten by the generality of the people, or by their descendants. In time, the very justices of the Supreme Court began to forget the sources of their authority. Some became so bold as to proclaim that the Constitution was what the court said it was. Historical treatises have even been written demonstrating that judges make law by their decisions, which become precedents for other rulings. The effects of this divorce from the sources of authority were not immediately felt. The people had developed habits of obedience to the decisions of the courts, and they continued for a time to accept them as if no change had occurred. Emboldened by their success, the courts have departed more and more from their earlier role. The day has come when many people no longer accept their decisions, when some of their judgments have to be enforced by brigades of marshals, and these have to be supported on occasion by the United States army.

The symptoms of the ailment presently are being treated in a variety of ways. Appeals are made to the observance of law and order. As if law and order were self-evident values, needing no deeper sanctions for men to adhere to them! The mass media of communication are used to try to arouse a sense of guilt in those who defy the "law." What they apparently do not understand is that the sources of transforming and inhibiting guilt lie deep also, that an ethos is not, or at least has not been, self-contained. Just as they did in the imaginary example of electricity, people attempt to restore a lost condition by

working on the receptacle: in this case, the people; in
that, the appliances. Obedience may be exacted by the
use of force, but willing adherence to the court decisions
depends upon the linkage of the courts and their decisions
to an ultimate source of authority. The Supreme Court
has no reason for being if there is no Higher Law.

In brief, we are forgetting or have forgotten the origin
and sources of our tradition. The tradition is with us
still in many institutions and forms derived from it, but
the pipes from the sources, to speak metaphorically, are
silted up with corrosion, and less and less energy gets
through.

Organized Loss of Memory

Actually, of course, the American tradition has not
been simply forgotten. It is true that a people tend to
forget the origins and meanings of anything the further
they are removed from it in time. But knowledge of and
attachment to the American tradition did not just slip
away because of defective memory. After all, American
history has been taught regularly in the schools for a long
time. The Constitution has been studied regularly by pupils over the years, and many documents such as the Declaration of Independence and Washington's Farewell Address probably are known to most Americans. On the
surface, it would appear that a massive effort has been
made to keep alive the American tradition. Even poorly
taught civics, history, American government, and political science should have left fresh deposits of understanding in the minds of those who would become political and
social leaders in the country, for presumably these would

be sharper of wit than the generality of students and would catch some of the deeper meaning that would not be apparent to a dull teacher.

If it were only a matter of memory, the schools should have supplied the remedy. Quite often, they have not and do not. On the contrary, students are innoculated regularly against an understanding of the tradition by the textbooks that are used in history, civics, and "democracy." The very courses which are supposed to be preserving it are rendering death blows to it by slanting, by misinterpretation, by the biases of writers, and by subtle perversions of it. Let me submit one example from among books that I have examined. My remarks are drawn from a review done for *America's Future*. The book is called *The United States of America; A History for Young Citizens*, was written by three college professors, and was published in 1963 by Silver Burdett. It is by no means a flagrant example of the distortions which are taught the young today. But it does serve to show how history is served up so as to leave students with a very unsure grasp of the tradition. To wit:

There are many ways to set the tone, which is quite often also the bias, of a textbook in history. It can be done by pictures, by headings, by the choice of words, by the materials selected and presented, and by omissions. There is a major and minor tone to this book, achieved by combinations of the above methods, and the two are blended in such a way as to produce a consistent, if dubious, impact.

The major tone may be called identification with America and American history. This tone is set, in the first place, by the use of attractive drawings, photographs, and sketches, frequently presented in striking colors. At the outset of the book, there are color photographs of mountain forests in North Carolina highlighted by flowering rhododendron, of grassy prairies in Kansas, of "rugged slopes" in the Rocky Mountains, of the "bleak but beautiful desert" in Arizona, of giant redwoods, and so on. The concluding pictures in the book, in vivid technicolor, are of tall modern buildings, of hydroelectric dams, of a cloverleaf intersection, of a beautiful modern school building, and of a national shrine.

Identification is promoted by the language as well. Before the book proper is reached, there are several pages devoted to "We believes." Some excerpts will show their character:

> We believe that the rich and beautiful land in which we live has been a major factor in shaping the American nation and the lives of its people. (p. viii.)
>
> We believe that Americans have created a way of life unsurpassed in excellence by any other nation of modern times. (p. 3.)
>
> We believe that the history of America forms an epic incomparable for its richness and variety. (p. 4.)

Another device, somewhat more cloying, is the "We did its" sprinkled liberally throughout the book. The following examples are taken from headings within chapters:

> We buy vast new territories. (p. 197.)
> We buy all of Louisiana. (p. 198.)
> We insist on Freedom of the Seas. (p. 199.)
> We add the Philippines. (p. 468.)
> We build good will in China. (p. 471.)

Presumably, the sense of immediacy as well as of identification is promoted by the use of the present tense in headings. For example, "British troops win a costly victory." (p. 118.) "Ethan Allen captures Fort Ticonderoga." (p. 119.) "Thomas Paine wins support for the Patriot cause." (p. 120.) There is much more of the same.

The minor tone is one of laudatory interpretation of what is now established. For example, a whole chapter is devoted to the discussion of the United States Constitution, much of which is perceptively done. But some of the commentary of the authors reveals a decided bias. For example, note this explanation of a passage of the Constitution. "Paragraph *a* gives Congress the power *to tax and spend for the general welfare.* Under this broad power, Congress can help the states improve the health and education of their citizens. Congress can appropriate money to build roads, dams, and do many other things that are good for the entire nation." (p. 164.) There should be no doubt that the government now does such things, but there is every reason to believe that the Constitution made no such grants of power. Indeed, President James Madison, who certainly should have known, in his veto of the "Bonus Bill" specifically denied that there had been any such grant of powers. He said, in part:

> "The power to regulate commerce among the several States" can not include a power to construct roads and canals, and to improve the navigation of water courses in order to facilitate, promote, and secure such a commerce without a latitude of construction departing from the ordinary import of the terms. . . .
>
> To refer the power in question to the clause "to provide for the common defense and general welfare" would be contrary to the established and consistent rules of interpretation, as rendering the special and careful enumeration of powers which follow the clause nugatory and improper. Such a view of the Constitution would have the effect of giving to Congress a general power of legislation instead of the defined and limited one hitherto understood to belong to them. . . . (Henry S. Commager, ed., *Documents of American History,* I [New York: Appleton-Century-Crofts, 1963], 212.)

Of course, these authors do not quote Madison to any such effect. Instead, they go on in the following vein. "Paragraph *c* permits Congress *to regulate interstate and foreign commerce.* Whenever goods or services are in-

volved in trade among states or between the United States
and other countries, Congress is able to set minimum
hourly wages for workers, limit the hours that children
may work, and establish other standards in the nation's
commerce and industry." (p. 164.) There is no hint here
of the distortions of the Constitution involved in such interpretations.

Their choice of words to describe developments in the
latter part of the nineteenth century serves to justify government intervention and regulation. In describing the
formation of the transcontinental railroads, they say,
"Later the Southern Pacific took over the Central Pacific,
forming the most *powerful* corporation on the Pacific
coast." (Emphasis added, p. 374.) Or note this description of John D. Rockefeller's methods:

> For years, railroads doing business with Rockefeller
> were *forced* to . . . (give back) part of the money they
> charged to carry oil for his company. The practice of
> giving rebates was a common one, but Rockefeller was
> able to *demand* higher rebates than his competitors. . . .
>
> These arrangements, of course, handicapped Rocke-
> feller's competitors. Many were *forced* to sell out to
> Standard, though some were unwilling to do so. Still,
> they often had no alternative, for Standard's growing
> *power* could *crush* them if Rockefeller gave the word.
> (Emphasis added, pp. 380-81.)

Whatever one thinks of the business ethics of that time,
these are not accurate descriptions of the practices. Such
words as "force," "power," and "crush" imply a use of
coercion which was not usual, and if it had been used
there were laws to punish it. Moreover, the use of such
language, falsely, sets the stage for justifications of the
use of force to contain and control businesses.

Similar biased language is used to describe the relation
of employers to their workers. For example, "Some employers forced workers to sign *yellow-dog contracts,* in
which workers promised not to join a union." (p. 387.)

Or, "Frick then hired *strikebreakers* to reopen the plant under the protection of the militia's guns." (Emphasis added, p. 390.) The authors follow a common practice here of adopting union terminology, which certainly colors the narrative and evokes a distorted picture of events. The above events alluded to could be accurately and neutrally described in the following way. "Some workers signed contracts (referred to by union leaders as *yellow-dog contracts*) in which they promised not to join a union. It is quite possible that some of them would have been unwilling to do so if it had not been made a condition of employment." "Frick hired other workers to replace those on strike, and these new employees were protected by the militia."

In contrast to their descriptions of the activities of industrialists, the authors treat reformers and their programs with the utmost tenderness and sympathy, despite the fact that reformers recommended and used the real *power* and *force* of governments to accomplish their ends. No hint of this is intruded into the narrative. Note this eulogy to two of the reformers:

> Though their crusade against poverty, ignorance, and poor housing must sometimes have seemed hopeless, Jane Addams and Jacob Riis never gave up. Starting alone, they eventually enlisted the aid of many people to improve living conditions in the slums. Tiny, frail Jane Addams and big, strong Jacob Riis showed what people can do when they work hard for a good cause. (p. 411.)

Progressives are accorded unmitigated praise:

> The progressives were firm believers in the intelligence of the average voter in America. They believed that decent people would act to remove the evils from American life if these evils were revealed to them. (p. 422.)

In short, "Though they had not solved all the problems

of industrialized, urbanized America, they had made America a better place in which to live." (p. 433.)

The reforms of the second Roosevelt are handled in a similar loving manner. For example, "Today the Tennessee Valley has bustling communities, thriving industries, and prosperous farms where once there was little but poverty. The TVA story is known all over the world as an example of one way a democratic nation can solve some of its problems." (p. 453.) Note, too, this description of Roosevelt's first Fireside Chat, and its results:

> He spoke for twenty minutes just as if the listeners *were* gathered around his fireside, his warm, reassuring voice explaining what was being done to make banks safe. . . .
>
> The first fireside chat was a tremendous success. On Monday, Roosevelt ordered most banks reopened, and the people accepted his words that the banks were safe. Almost as if by magic, their faith in the nation's banks was restored. (p. 450.)

There is more to the same effect, but perhaps I can draw my conclusions from what has been presented. Such history is an apology for and a eulogy to present-day America. This is history adapted to the broader purposes of "life adjustment." The pupil who has been taught from this book should be prepared to nod knowingly when the current clichés are used. He will have been rather consistently inoculated against an understanding of the major tenets of the American tradition. The book has consistently prepared him for the acceptance of ever-wider use of governmental power, for ever-broader extension of collective responsibility, and for an increasingly narrow sphere of operation for the individual and for voluntary groups. The pupil will have been acclimated to the use of force and power by governments and shielded from recognizing it by the smooth euphemisms by which it is covered up.

History Reconstrued

It would be jumping to conclusions, however, to conclude that the authors of the book referred to above, or of
others similar to it, were intentionally distorting the
American tradition or that they were consciously pro-
moting governmental power. On the contrary, they may
have been doing nothing more than presenting a simpli-
fied version of American history as they have been led
to understand it. Back of this book lie several decades of
intensive work by intellectuals in undermining, distorting, obscuring, and defaming the American tradition.
Base motives were frequently ascribed to those who drew
up the Constitution. The Constitution was described as an
outmoded document which may have been somewhat
better suited to an agrarian society. Businessmen were
made to appear to be predatory beasts. Governmental action, and its beneficial effects, was made the focus of attention, and private and voluntary group activity was
largely ignored. Individualism became attached to "rugged"
or "atomistic." European innovations were lauded and
things American were castigated as backward and unpro-
gressive. Individuals seeking private gain were "selfish,"
but those who would use the government to "help the people" were selfless.

In short, American history was reconstrued in such a
way as to make melioristic reform appear necessary and
inevitable. After such efforts, and these can be docu-
mented *ad nauseum,* it should not be surprising that textbooks for the schools should reflect these ideas.

It is tempting to ascribe base motives to the reformers
who used their research activities and literary skills to

undermine the American tradition. Would it not be accurate to account for the zeal of reformers by calling it a quest for power by frustrated intellectuals? After all, the descent upon Washington by intellectuals after the election of a reform President is now a familiar and recurrent phenomenon. Undoubtedly, these intellectuals often get more power than they could dream of possessing without the use of government.

Tempting as it is to charge the reformers with having base motives, and right as it might be in the case of some individuals, however, I doubt that anyone who would honestly attempt to study the earlier reformers would be convinced of the validity of such a thesis. There is no need to question the sincerity of Eugene Debs, of Ida Tarbell, of Henry Demarest Lloyd, of Charles A. Beard, of Vernon L. Parrington, of Walter Rauschenbusch, of Edward Bellamy, of Upton Sinclair, of Lincoln Steffens, and of Jacob Riis. For aught we know, they may have ached to help those in need, burned with a pure zeal for the fate of the underprivileged, thirsted to right all wrongs in the world, and believed with the force of faith in the programs that they advanced. Even many of those who distorted and obscured the American tradition may have been convinced that they were only correcting the record.

The Lost Tradition

For myself, I prefer to forego the questioning of motives. In the deepest sense, these men, and their intellectual descendants of today, had *forgotten* the tradition and the reason for its being. They had forgotten what our ancestors knew, that a government of men is usually ar-

bitrary and despotic, that a Constitution must be rigorously adhered to or it will lose its force and character, that
concentrated power is ever a dangerous thing to the liberty of a people, that power exercised by a majority can
be tyrannical just as that exercised by a minority, that
the ultimate meaning of human institutions rests in their
relationship to the individual, that government cannot act
positively to benefit selected individuals and groups without acting *un*equally upon others, that goods are produced
by the willing action of men who have incentives, and so
on. In short, they had forgotten—that is, did not believe
—the fundamental tenets of the American tradition. Seeing the abundance of America, they supposed that they
could redistribute it at will, without deleterious effects.
Seeing the freedom in America, they supposed that they
could pick and choose among its components. Seeing
how much had been done by taking thought, they imagined they could do all things.

No one has yet told the story of the twentieth century
of America in terms of the pride and presumption of intellectuals. But there is much material for such a history.
Just before World War I, the Federal Reserve system was
set up. It was advanced as the final cure for depres-
sions! World War I was supposed to be the war to end all
wars. Yet, in little more than twenty years the world was
embarked upon another catastrophic struggle. No little
contribution was made to this turn of events by the "experts" who attempted to redraw the boundaries of Europe.
Intervention in the affairs of people around the world, by
governments at the prodding of intellectuals, has produced domestic and international discord on a titanic
scale. One might suppose that intellectuals would have

been chastened by their failures. But they make explanations of developments which leave themselves unindicted. They keep trying to improve the play by changing the scenery, refusing to see the connection between their programs and the consequences.

They have forgotten—forgotten that there is a God who is not mocked, that this is a firm premise upon which this country was founded. Forgotten that there is a moral order in the universe, that effect follows cause whether men recognize it or not. Forgotten that there is no way of regulating an economy without regulating men. Forgotten that all plans involve people, and that if governments attempt to put them into effect they must do so by force or the threat of force. Forgotten that morality proceeds from choice, and that choice depends upon liberty. Forgotten that there was an American tradition with profound sources and ultimate sanctions, that when institutions are cut loose from these foundations they will cease to work as they formerly did.

This is written, then, Lest We Forget.

Lest We Forget that these United States were founded upon governments of laws rather than the arbitrary rule by men:

> But where, says some, is the king of America? I'll tell you, friend, he reigns above, and does not make havoc of mankind like the royal brute of Britain. Yet that we may not appear to be defective even in earthly honors, let a day be solemnly set apart for proclaiming the charter; let it be brought forth placed on the divine law, the word of God; let a crown be placed thereon, by which the world may know that, so far as we approve of monarchy, that in America *the law is king.* For as in absolute governments the king is law, so in

free countries the law *ought* to be king; and there ought to be no other.

Thomas Paine, 1776

Lest We Forget that the foundation of our laws was natural, moral, and inherent right:

Let the bar proclaim "the laws, the rights, the generous plan of power" delivered from remote antiquity, inform the world of the mighty struggles and numberless sacrifices made by our ancestors in defense of freedom. Let it be known that British liberties are not the grants of princes or parliaments but original rights, conditions of original contracts, coequal with prerogative and coeval with government; that many of our rights are inherent and essential. . . . Let them search for the foundations of . . . laws and government in the frame of human nature, in the constitution of the intellectual and moral world. There let us see that truth, liberty, justice, and benevolence are its everlasting basis; and if these could be removed, the superstructure is overthrown of course.

John Adams, 1765

Lest We Forget that our liberty and order were based upon a strict adherence to constitutionalism:

Liberty and order will never be *perfectly* safe, until a trespass on the constitutional provisions for either, shall be felt with the same keenness that resents an invasion of the dearest rights, until every citizen shall be an Argus to espy, and Aegeon to avenge, the unhallowed deed.

James Madison, 1792

Lest We Forget that the United States government is a limited government:

Our peculiar security is in the possession of a written

Constitution. Let us not make it a blank paper by construction. I say the same as to the opinion of those who consider the grant of the treaty-making power as boundless. If it is, then we have no Constitution. If it has bounds, they can be no others than the definitions of the powers which that instrument gives.

Thomas Jefferson, 1803

Lest We Forget that the government was founded upon republican principles:

After all, Sir, we must submit to this idea, that the true principle of a republic is that the people should choose whom they please to govern them.

Alexander Hamilton, 1788

Lest We Forget that in America there is a federal system of government:

This balance between the National and State governments ought to be dwelt on with peculiar attention, as it is of the utmost importance. It forms a double security to the people. If one encroaches on their rights they will find a powerful protection in the other. Indeed, they will both be prevented from overpassing their constitutional limits by a certain rivalship, which will ever subsist between them.

Alexander Hamilton, 1788

Lest We Forget that in America the individual was believed to be of ultimate importance:

There will never be a really free and enlightened State until the State comes to recognize the individual as a higher and independent power, from which all its own power and authority are derived, and treats him accordingly.

Henry D. Thoreau, 1849

Lest We Forget that voluntarism was a central principle of American social order:

In all other respects, the *voluntary principle,* the principle of *freedom,* suggested to us by the analogy of the divine government of the Creator, and already recognized by us with perfect success in the great social interest of religion, affords the true "golden rule" which is alone abundantly competent to work out the best possible general result of order and happiness from that chaos of characters, ideas, motives, and interests: human society. . . .

This is then . . . the true theory of government, . . . to furnish a system of administration of justice, and then leave all the business and interests of society to themselves, to free competition and association; in a word, to the *voluntary principle.* . . .

The United States Magazine and Democratic Review, 1837

Lest We Forget that free economic intercourse was a pillar of the American system:

That is not a just government, nor is property secure under it, where arbitrary restrictions, exemptions, and monopolies deny to part of its citizens that free use of their faculties, and free choice of their occupations, which not only constitute their property in the general sense of the word; but are the means of acquiring property so called.

James Madison, 1792

Lest We Forget that private property is a cornerstone of the American way:

Government is instituted to protect property of every sort. . . . This being the end of government, that alone is a *just* government which *impartially* secures to every man, whatever is his *own.*

James Madison, 1792

Lest We Forget the principles of international harmony and national independence:

It is, unquestionably, our true interest to cultivate the most friendly understanding with every nation and to avoid by every honorable means the calamities of war; and we shall best attain this object by frankness and sincerity in our foreign intercourse, by the prompt and faithful execution of treaties, and by justice and impartiality in our conduct to all. But no nation, however desirous of peace, can hope to escape occasional collisions with other powers; and the soundest dictates of policy require that we should place ourselves in a condition to assert our rights if a resort to force should ever become necessary.

Andrew Jackson, 1837

Lest We Forget that all of this hinged upon an enduring belief in God:

And can the liberties of a nation be thought secure when we have removed their only firm basis, a conviction in the minds of the people that these liberties are of the gift of God—that they are not to be violated but with His wrath? Indeed I tremble for my country when I reflect that God is just; that His justice cannot sleep forever. . . .

Thomas Jefferson, 1785

Lest We Forget. . . .

2.

There Was an American Tradition

IN A RECENT conversation with the president of a small college in the South I pointed out that I supposed I was what is most commonly called a "conservative." Somewhat perturbed, he asked if I associated myself with a particular group—one which has been given a bad reputation by the press. I answered that I knew of this group only by hearsay, and that I belonged to no organizations engaged in promulgating such ideas. I went on to explain briefly some of my central beliefs. But, he said when I had finished, that is simply Americanism. I agreed that I thought so myself. And thereby hangs a tale.

How pleasant it would be if the matter could be handled so simply, if one could say that he believed in the individual, in individual liberty, in limited government, and in free enterprise—and let it go at that! How refreshing it is to pass, if just for a moment, from the clouded atmosphere of competing ideas and ideologies into the clear air of simple agreement! There was a time in American history when such general agreement existed that men seldom bothered to recur to principles. Such consensus no longer exists, though national leaders frequently try to make it appear that it does.

I suspect that it would have been easy, in the conversation alluded to in the beginning, to have found that we

were by no means of the same mind. It would only have
been necessary for me to point out a few practical applications of these American ideas to show that this has not
been the trend of recent years at all. I did not do so, pre-
ferring for the moment an illusion of harmony to the possibility of acrimonious debate. The point I would make is
this. The American tradition has left a residue of live coals
which still glow when breathed upon. Many Americans
still respond positively when these ideals and ideas are
called to their attention. There are, however, a great many
clinkers among the coals—these clinkers being mainly the
deposits from more recent accretions of ideas. It is not
possible at the moment to build a fire upon the live coals
of the tradition because of the interference of clinkers.
These latter must be separated and removed from among
the coals before a healthy fire can be built.

A Multiplicity of Traditions

This metaphor, however, assumes too much. It assumes
that there is or was an American tradition, that it can
be defined and delineated, and that it has continued value
and validity. If, as I have already said, there is no general
consensus upon these things, then they must be demonstrated, not assumed.

Would it not be more correct to refer to a multiplicity
of traditions in America? One theory has it that America
was a vast melting pot, combining elements from many
countries, cultures, and traditions. The result of this, according to some accounts, is a profound antitraditional
bias in America. In this view, Americans became a race
devoted to the sloughing off of tradition, to perpetual

change, to ever new movements in a framework of social mobility. Along with this, they developed a pragmatic temper consisting of experimental adjustment to changing circumstances. Following this line of description, America is an open society; Americans are casters-off of tradition, a people in constant rebellion against the fetters of established ways and patterns.

Of course, one can focus upon America in such a way that no tradition will come into view. That has been done in the above account. Suppose, instead, that one begins in the belief that there is a tradition and searches for it. He may then be struck by the number of traditions which have been lodged here at one time or another. Depending upon the locale (and the point of approach), there has been an English tradition, a Southern tradition, a New England tradition, a Puritan tradition, a Spanish tradition, and so on through all the cultural variants that have had an existence in America. Or, to look at the matter from the widest possible angle, there has been only the Western (or Christian) tradition.

But, one may observe correctly, none of these is an American tradition; they are either too narrow, too broad, or clearly non-American. The difficulty in locating the tradition is twofold: in not being clear about what we are looking for, and in not having our sight correctly focused.

Tradition Defined

The first difficulty can be surmounted by a definition. A tradition is a body of beliefs, customs, habits, ways of doing things which are handed down from generation to generation. The manner of its being taught would not seem to be essential, whether by schools, by parents, by associates, or by churches. It is not so much a matter of law as of the manner by which laws are enacted, what is an appropriate matter for legislation, and wherein the authority resides for enacting it. Anyone who doubts that there is an American tradition should observe a group of Americans organizing for some new undertaking. They will, predictably, adopt a constitution and by-laws, establish certain offices of which one will almost certainly be that of a president, elect certain of their members to fill these offices, and so on. That they will almost certainly do just this speaks eloquently of the existence of a tradition. The above, too, gives us a hint of the American tradition, for it is certainly of that.

The matter of correct focus is more difficult. If a tradition is understood as being prescriptive, there are many aspects of life and human activity which lie outside the American tradition. One may doubt that there is an artistic tradition, or a religious tradition (though there is a tradition of having a religion), or an aristocratic or class tradition, or, in many ways, a social tradition. The tradition, in America, may define attitudes toward these things but it does not prescribe them. It is, or was, the very essence of this tradition that it was limited. The very existence of these United States has depended upon limited prescription. In fact, there have been, and still are to some extent, many traditions in America, but they are local and regional in character. The American tradition must generally be, then, one which lies above these and does not ordinarily intrude upon them. It is in this restricted area that we should look for the American tradition.

If we focus our attention upon the restricted public

arena in which there has been an American tradition, this
is what we should discover. Historically, in that period
since the English began to come in numbers to America,
the outlines of not one but three traditions can be described in the course of our history. They are—to give
them names—the authoritarian, the American, and the
collectivist. I call the second the American because thus
far it has been the central tradition to emerge here. Other
names have been applied to it, but they have been subjected to such distortions that I prefer a more neutral
terminology until I have delineated it more fully.

There was an attempt to transplant the authoritarian
tradition from Europe to America in the seventeenth century. By authoritarian I mean the tradition of authority
being vested in a man or men. It carries overtones, too,
of reference to some external coercive authority. Those
who prefer semantic arguments to clarity of thought may
argue that men have always lived under some external
authority, and that it only changes its name from time to
time. The distinction, however, is that implied between
subject and *citizen*. The *subject* clearly recognizes the existence of the authority of a man over him; *citizen* implies an equality of condition in regard to the exercise of
authority.

At any rate, America was initially settled by men accustomed by law and tradition to hierarchical authority.
Authority over various colonies was vested in joint-stock
companies, proprietors, or in some body by charter. In
turn, these were grants stemming from the monarch.
Everyman's rights and privileges were either confirmed or
tacitly granted by the king. But the whole tradition was
permeated by authoritarianism. Puritans, who doubted

the king's authority in matters of religion, did not doubt that authority over men had been vested in the leaders of church and state. The emerging economy of the time—mercantilism—was authoritarian. Individuals engaging in economic activity frequently procured charters, grants, and monopolies from the crown. The state exercised extensive authority over commerce by way of tariffs, bounties, and regulations of quality and quantity. In the home, authority was vested by law and usage in the father, who exercised it not only over minors in the home but also over women of whatever age.

But this transplanted authority withered in the American soil. Rebellions against it were numerous, even in the seventeenth century. Virginians took unkindly to the derivative authority over them, and soon they established a legislative assembly. The Puritan oligarchy was soon under pressure to extend the franchise and to yield up its exclusive control. The economic controls established by the early companies soon gave way to a great deal of private and relatively free trade. Roger Williams and Anne Hutchinson would not bow to the Puritan orthodoxy. The Old World class structure hardly took root in America at all. Religious toleration and representative assemblies were increasingly used as lures to draw settlers to the newer colonies. Those who would hold settlers found it advantageous to offer land which could be acquired as private property. The vestiges of Old World authority were maintained well into the eighteenth century, but another order was clearly emerging. One might almost say that the American colonists tolerated the theoretical claims of the older authority until George III and his ministers attempted to effectuate it.

Animated by Liberty

We can discern almost from the beginnings of American settlement the making of an American tradition. This emerging tradition was one of individualism, voluntarism, constitutionalism, representative government, government by law, equality before the law, the recognition of a moral order in the universe, natural rights, and personal independence. It was, in essence, a liberal tradition, despite the semantic difficulties which the use of the phrase introduces. It was liberal in that it was animated by liberty as an ideal, embraced means consonant with liberty, and limited that authority over men which might intrude upon their liberty.

There are at least two difficulties in the way of calling the central American tradition liberal. One is that the term has been taken over in the twentieth century by those who are trying to graft collectivism onto the American tradition. The other is that "liberal" gained a partisan connotation in English-speaking countries in the nineteenth century. It was used to refer to the followers of Jefferson, Jackson, Mill, and Gladstone. It became associated with the opposition to established traditions.

When I refer to the American tradition as liberal, I intend to convey neither the collectivistic nor partisan meaning. By liberal tradition, then, I refer to the institutions by which liberty was established, the beliefs which supported liberty, and the customs, habits, and folkways that promoted liberty. So conceived, the liberal tradition was not the possession of a party but of a people, not a political program but a way of life, not simply a thrust for change but a means of maintaining order and continuity. It was the American tradition. It began to emerge around 1650, gained sway and was instituted between 1760 and 1800, and was maintained virtually unchallenged until around 1900.

A Non-Revolutionary Growth

In view of certain historical controversies, the point needs to be emphasized that the American tradition was *not* revolutionary. There are in American history no parallels to the revolutionary happenings of the French and Russian revolutions, no abolition of calendars and starting anew, no wholesale changing of street names, no reconstruing of the whole social system nor attempts to remake man in the image of some ideology. On the contrary, Americans took gladly from their own past experience and practices, and from those of other people as well. The posture of the Founding Fathers is not that of men who know better than anyone ever has how to do things; it is rather one of attempting to build upon *both* the successes and failures of the past a little better edifice for protecting liberty within a framework of order. This made it more of a tradition because it rested on other traditions.

By calling it the American tradition, then, I have not meant to imply that it took its whole shape and substance from America, or that Americans broke entirely from their European past. Far from it! There is a sense, of course, in which Americans have consciously sloughed off a part of the European heritage. But much more evident is the fact that they built upon it.

The concept of natural law upon which American liberty was based goes back at least to the time of Cicero. The debt of Americans to John Locke, Montesquieu, and Edmund Burke, to Athens and Rome, to Medieval France and Renaissance Italy, and to the whole Old World Heritage is beyond measure. Regarding the classical influence upon the founding of the American republic, a scholar recently has said:

> In no field were Greek and Roman sources more often invoked; and at no time were they more frequently cited than during the preliminary discussions, the debates on the Constitution, the ratifying conventions, the *Federalist* papers and such publications as John Dickinson's *Fabius Letters*. The framers of the Constitution did not merely echo or imitate this ancient material: they applied it to the task in hand and transmuted it into workable form.[1]

The imprint of the English heritage is writ large in the forms of American institutions. Moreover, there has been continual interaction between Europe and America from the outset.

Yet for all that, the tradition is peculiarly American. Even when the form is derivative, the articulation is American. Thus, the form for the office of President may have been derived on the one hand from monarchy and on the other from colonial governors, but the President is neither the one nor the other. The concept of right was fostered in America by a knowledge of privileges which monarchs granted, but the rights which Americans came to prize had no basis any longer in monarchical grants. Such a strictly limited government as they conceived had no precise model

---

[1] Richard M. Gummere, "The Classical Ancestry of the United States Constitution," *American Quarterly*, XIV (Spring, 1962), 4.

anywhere. How aptly it was designed for the American condition, not to bring unity out of diversity but to achieve sufficient unity for protective purposes while permitting the greatest diversity and liberty! Beliefs and practices on this continent acquired their own peculiar turn.

The Past Is Prologue

That the tradition which I have been describing is by right called the American tradition should be apparent. It was neither liberal nor conservative in partisan senses of those words. Rather, it was conservative in that it preserved from and was builded upon the past; liberal in that it was designed to protect liberty. It was in this frame that the state governments were constituted and the United States government instituted. It is American in that it grew out of the American situation and took shape in American conditions. There is, in fact, not even now any other tradition which can be called American.

That the central American tradition was erected around the goal of liberty is manifest in the great documents of our history. It was explicitly stated in the Declaration of Independence and implied in the structure of government provided for in the Constitution of 1787. Liberty was declared to be the object of the Massachusetts Body of Liberties of 1641, and was undoubtedly the purpose of the first ten amendments to the Constitution. The writings of Americans for two centuries are filled with declarations of devotion to liberty. This is true of Roger Williams, John Wise, Patrick Henry, Samuel Adams, Alexander Hamilton, George Washington, James Madison, Andrew Jackson, and Henry David Thoreau.

Of the "Colonial Mind" just before the American Revolution, one historian has said:

> Rarely if ever in the history of free government has
> there been so unanimous a "party line" as that to which
> the colonists pledged their uncritical allegiance. And
> rarely if ever has the party line been so easily reduced
> to one comprehensible concept, even to one wonderful
> word: *Liberty*. . . . One of the authors of the *Independ-
> ent Reflector* spoke for almost all colonial thinkers when
> he adopted as his "principal Design . . . opposing Op-
> pression, and vindicating the *Liberty of Man*"[2]

Massive Departures During the Twentieth Century

There have, however, been massive departures from this
tradition in the twentieth century. Around 1880 thinkers
began to lay the intellectual foundations for a new direction—that of collectivism. From the late nineteenth century on, elements of this new way were inserted piece by
piece into the American frame. The most dramatic movement in that direction was made in 1933, but it has been
gaining ground for most of the century.

Collectivists have not yet established a tradition in keeping with their ideas in America. Indeed, they have displayed a tendency to draw back in horror before actual
examples of a more thorough carrying-out of their ideas,
as in the Soviet Union. Collectivism begins with a conception of social unity which when carried through to conclusion leaves no room for diversity of practice or custom.
Collectivists conceive of the purpose of society in such a
way that common action must pervade every area of life.

---

[2] Clinton Rossiter, *The First American Revolution* (New
York: Harcourt, Brace, 1956), pp. 225-26.

The society must be homogenized, as it were, in order that it have only common needs which can be met.

The accomplishment of this tremendous purpose requires a coordinated central authority which is greatly hampered by the separation of federally distributed powers. Congress is a continual affront to collectivists because it will not act with that unanimity which all-pervasive collective action requires. The natural institutions of collectivism are totalitarianism and dictatorship. The natural (or unnatural) tradition of collectivism is the homogenized society, the centralized authority, the collective (i.e., government) ownership or control of the means of production and distribution of goods, and the merging of all individual, local, and regional autonomy with a vast social whole, in which it will be submerged and lost.

Changing the Meaning

American collectivists (at least those called "liberals") shrink from many of these implications. Rather, they have attempted to achieve collectivism within the American tradition, however much they might stretch it in doing so. Their collectivism they call by the generic name of democracy, and their programs they advance in the name of the general welfare of the people. They have, of course, wrenched these words out of the context of the earlier American tradition and distorted their meaning. But this has been a usual tactic, whether wittingly or not, to distort the American tradition and to make it appear to fit the collectivists' ideas.

A frequent tactic of historians has been to describe the making of the American tradition within a purely temporal and environmental framework. Thus, earlier practices were in keeping with the American environment and conditions. But these conditions, they say, have changed. Thus the American tradition must be reconstrued to fit changing needs and conditions. Individualism, they tell us, was appropriate to an earlier day, but its day is past. The state divisions were all very well in a more primitive America, but the growth of "urban complexes" has made of them silly anachronisms. The real American tradition, they add, has been one of pragmatic adjustment to new and changing conditions. Thus is collectivism advanced.

By these methods the real American tradition has been obscured, much of its meaning lost, and its vitality drained off into collectivism. My purpose in this and the ensuing chapters is to try to recapture some of the central features of that tradition, to describe how they emerged and were instituted, and to call attention to their rapid submergence in the twentieth century.

It is not my contention that back there somewhere was a perfect tradition, pure and undefiled, waiting to be discovered. Our ancestors were fallible men, even as we are. Let it not be forgotten that the justly revered Founding Fathers recognized and accepted human slavery in the Constitution. They fell short of their ideals in practice even as we do. All too often they compromised and bartered away liberty. Yet they conceived the noblest experiment in individual liberty that has yet appeared on this continent, or perhaps anywhere else, and if those live coals which are the memories of the tradition they bequeathed to us can be made to glow in such a way as to kindle a new flame, we shall have been repaid for recurring to that earlier tradition.

3.

Of Constitutionalism and Higher Law

ONE OF THE MOST difficult tasks in teaching history is to convey the uniqueness at its inception of some institution that has long since become familiar and accepted. I asked a class on an examination to "explain historically why Americans would have done so unusual a thing as to have a written constitution." The most common reaction was to assert that there was nothing "unusual" about it. Indeed, some of the answers had that quality of dutiful resignation displayed by a harried parent explaining the self-evident to an inquiring child. "What else would you expect them to do under the circumstances?"—they seemed to be asking. Obviously, if a people do not have a constitution—or, at any rate, a satisfactory one—they supply the need by drawing one up.

To have or not to have a written constitution was hardly an open question to my class. It had long since been settled, and indeed they could not readily imagine a time when it had been open. My students, of course, are informed by a well-established tradition. What is astonishing, however, is that it does not appear to have been an open question among Americans in 1787 or 1788 either. One seeks in vain in *The Federalist* for any lengthy justification of a written constitution. All sorts of objections were raised to the Constitution which had been recently

33

drawn at Philadelphia, but no one appears to h
tioned seriously the propriety of having such a d o

One might suppose from this that it was an es
custom for a country to have a written constitut
this was not at all the case. No major country at t
had any such instrument. Men did, of course, ref
British constitution, but in the later American sen
not a constitution at all. It was rather a combination of
established procedures, forms of organizations, customary usages, habitual relationships, plus some written ac-
knowledgments of rights and privileges. So far as other
great countries such as Spain, France, Russia, Prussia,
and Austria were concerned, most of these intangible procedures, customs, and forms had fallen into disuse or
been abolished. The seventeenth and eighteenth centuries
were periods of the rise of strong monarchs who ruled
more or less despotically. If Americans had followed prevailing practice, they would have sought a prince with
some hereditary claim to rule and proclaimed themselves
his subjects.

Apparently, here is a contradiction. On the one hand,
Americans in the 1780's acted as if the adoption of a
written constitution were an established tradition. On
the other, the usual practice in the world ran counter to
this. There is, as I have implied, a historical explanation
which disposes of the apparent contradiction.

Form and Substance

But before attempting to make it, it may be helpful to
draw a distinction between two aspects of a constitution:
the *formal* and the *substantive*. In the formal sense, a con-

stitution refers to the organization of a government, the procedures and offices through which it operates, and the relationships among the organs of government. It follows, then, that all peoples living under a government have a constitution of sorts, whether written or not, whether imposing severe limits or not, and whether recognized as such or not. In the substantive sense, a constitution confers powers, recognizes rights and privileges, imposes limits, contains prohibitions, and constitutes a higher law. It is true that the formal and substantive may be intertwined in an actual constitution. Thus, in the United States Constitution the formal division into three branches carries with it a substantive limitation upon the powers of each by check and balance.

Nonetheless, it is on the substantive side that the uniqueness of our constitution appears. The forms it prescribes were somewhat original, but having them written out was more so. By having a strict enumeration of powers, it had no antecedents to my knowledge, if the American states be excepted. That since 1787 many countries have produced and adopted such instruments should not obscure the fact that the American one was frequently the model. In its thoroughness and completeness, it stood alone in its day. By limiting and checking the powers in order to protect the liberty of the citizen against government, it made a signal breakthrough in human endeavor. Governments have usually been formed either by conquest or by a slow growth over long periods of time. It was an audacious thing for men to meet in convention and draw up a *new* instrument of government.

Why, then, if it was so original and unique, did Americans not debate and challenge the action? Why were they of one accord in desiring a constitution? The answer is to be found primarily in American history, not in world history. There was, of course, already an American tradition of constitutionalism in 1787. The Founding Fathers had been convened to propose changes in an existing instrument of government—the Articles of Confederation, itself the first American constitution. The thirteen states already had constitutions of their own.

And back of these lay profound traditions and beliefs which gave impetus to the forming of constitutions. The sources of constitutionalism can be reduced to three heads: (1) historical precedents, (2) belief in Higher Law, and (3) belief in limited government and individual liberty.

Historical Precedents

The historical precedents for constitutionalism do indeed antedate the American experience. There were the laws promulgated by Solon and Lycurgus in Classical Greece. One may read the Funeral Oration of Pericles to discover the consciousness of a constitution by which order and liberty are promoted. Above all, the Founding Fathers had in mind the example and constitution of Rome. Here were to be found the separation of power into branches of government. There were the Twelve Tables of the Law, and the deep sense of government by law in the Roman Republic. There were the great English precedents also: the Magna Carta, the Petition of Right, and the Bill of Rights. None of these had the completeness of the written constitution of 1787 in America, but they were precedents of which our ancestors were aware.

Yet these were precedents known to men of learning

throughout Western civilization, and they had not produced written constitutions elsewhere. Of course, the break from England had offered the Americans the opportunity to start afresh. But it was their American experience of the past 180 years that had prepared them for the undertaking, and that made the drawing of constitutions second nature to them.

Colonial Charters

Colonies were usually founded in America on the basis of contracts, compacts, or charters. Even the joint-stock company, the usual means of financing the early colonial ventures, was a contractual relationship among investors secured by a charter from the Crown. As it has been described, a "typical joint-stock charter of this time gave the company a name and a formally recognized legal position. . . . The charter usually vested control in a council, the original members of which were usually named in the document. . . . Sometimes the charter provided for a governor as the head of the company, in which case he was chosen by the council, usually from its own membership."[1] All stockholders met periodically in a general court for the purposes of elections and deciding questions which may have arisen. This is precisely how the Massachusetts Bay Colony was governed in its early years, and it provides a part of the basic pattern of colonial government. This was, it should be noted, government based upon written charters (i. e., constitutions).

---

[1] Alfred H. Kelly and Winfred A. Harbison, *The American Constitution: Its Origins and Development* (New York: Norton, 1955), p. 9.

Another ingredient in the formation of the constitution idea was the Puritan covenant. The covenant was an agreement voluntarily entered into among a group of people before God to live according to his commandments. Among the colonies founded upon this basis were Plymouth, Providence, and New Haven. The character of these is made clear in the introductory words of the most famous, the Mayflower Compact: "We whose names are underwritten . . . Do by these Presents, solemnly and mutually in the Presence of God and one another, covenant and combine ourselves together into a civil Body Politick. . . ."[2]

An even more striking example of constitution making is the Fundamental Orders of Connecticut, joined into by the inhabitants of three towns in 1639. They declared that in keeping with the requirement of the word of God "[we] do therefore associate and conjoin ourselves to be as one Public State or commonwealth; and do . . . enter into combination and confederation together, to maintain and preserve the liberty and purity of the gospel . . . ," and for the making of civil laws.[3]

These contracts, charters, and compacts were sometimes subject to revocation or change over the years. Yet most of the colonies had some such document, and it served as basic evidence of their rights and privileges, to which they turned from time to time when these were threatened. Thus, Americans became habituated to written constitutions.

---

[2] *Ibid.*, p. 17.

[3] Verna M. Hall, ed., *Christian History of the Constitution of the United States* (San Francisco: American Christian Constitution Press, 1960), p. 253.

Belief in Higher Law

But constitutionalism was much more than a habit. It was more, too, than a formal tradition that had taken shape over the centuries. It was a substantive tradition. Undergirding it, buttressing it, giving it impetus and meaning was the belief in a Higher Law. This belief, at its deepest, holds that man does not make law; rather, he articulates pre-existing law and gives it particular applications. There have been differing views as to how this law is discovered, as to what it consists of, but it is of the essence of substantive constitutions that such law exists. If a constitution does not embrace this Higher Law, and is not builded upon it, it has no reason for existing.

It should be clear that the Founders considered the United States Constitution in this light. Alexander Hamilton, in *The Federalist,* number 78, says: "A constitution is, in fact, and must be regarded by the judges, as a fundamental law." Again, "in regard to the interfering acts of a superior and subordinate authority, of an original and derivative power, the nature and reason of the thing . . . teach us that the prior act of a superior ought to be preferred to the subsequent act of an inferior and subordinate authority; and that accordingly, whenever a particular statute contravenes the Constitution, it will be the duty of the judicial tribunals to adhere to the latter and disregard the former."

This is precisely what the Supreme Court did in *Marbury* vs. *Madison* in 1803. The crux of that decision is the recognition of the Constitution as the Higher Law. The case and decision are worth recalling. William Marbury had received a last minute appointment as justice of the

peace by President John Adams, but his commission was
not delivered. The incoming Secretary of State, James
Madison, would not deliver it. Marbury went directly to
the Supreme Court for relief, as the Judiciary Act of 1789
prescribed. John Marshall, in the decision for the Court,
denied the petition. The grounds: the Constitution names
specifically the instances of the original jurisdiction of the
Supreme Court, and this was not one of them. This, as he
saw it, brought an act of the legislature into conflict with
the Constitution. In such a case, he maintained, the
Court is bound by the superior rather than the inferior
authority. Thus was legal standing given to the view that
the Constitution embodies Higher Law.

The English Tradition

There were three main sources of this tradition of a
belief in Higher Law in America. The first of these was
the conception of the laws of England as constituting a
higher law. Thus, the proprietary charter of Maryland
specified that "laws be made with the consent of the freemen and agreeable to the laws of England." Laws passed
in the colonies were, from time to time, subjected to review in England, and some of them were nullified. English
law, too, was thought to stand upon a foundation of
Higher Law. Kings and parliaments did not *make* law,
according to the medieval tradition; they *discovered* what
was the law and promulgated it. This was the customary
law which became, by recognition of the monarch, the
common law for all England.

Undoubtedly, deep and subtle justifications could be
made for considering that which had come down by us-

age as Higher Law. But it must have drawn much of its force at the time from the general veneration of the old and long established. Coming into the Modern Era, the Higher Law was thought to be derived from God, either directly through revelation (and the promulgation of those in authority, if one accepted the Divine Right of Kings) or indirectly by way of natural law.

William Blackstone, in 1765, stated this view of the Higher Law succinctly: "Upon these two foundations, the law of nature and the law of revelation, depend all human laws; that is to say, no human laws should be suffered to contradict these. . . . And herein it is that human laws have their greatest force and efficacy: for, with regard to such points as are not indifferent, human laws are only declaratory of, and act in subordination to the former." He gives as an example the matter of murder. "Nay, if any human law should allow or enjoin us to commit it, we are bound to transgress that human law, or else we must offend both the natural and divine."[4] There was, then, in the English tradition a fully developed belief in the Higher Law.

Higher Law in America

Americans continued, developed, and gave their particular articulation to this tradition. The second source for a belief in Higher Law has already been indicated from Blackstone; that is, that we have it from God by revelation. It is needful only to show that it was a belief congenial to Americans also. Nathaniel Ward, writing in the early seventeenth century, declared: "Moral laws, royal

---

[4] *Ibid.*, p. 143.

prerogatives, popular liberties are not of man's making
or giving, but God's. Man is but to measure them out by
God's rule: which if man's wisdom cannot reach, man's
experience must mend."[5] Elsewhere he says, "The truths of
God are the pillars of the world whereon states and
churches may stand. . . . "[6]

In the middle of the eighteenth century, Jonathan May-
hew said: "We may safely assert . . . that no civil rulers
are to be obeyed when they enjoin things that are incon-
sistent with the commands of God. . . . All commands
running counter to the declared will of the supreme leg-
islator of heaven and earth, are null and void: and therefore disobedience to them is a duty, not a crime. . . . "[7]
James Madison, in *The Federalist,* number 37, remarking
upon the fact that so many difficulties had been surmounted in the Constitutional Convention with such unanimity, was moved to this pronouncement: "It is impossible for the man of pious reflection not to perceive in it
a finger of that Almighty hand which has been so frequently and signally extended to our relief in the critical
stages of the revolution."

On the matter of the right of expatriation, Jefferson
exclaimed: "We do not claim these under the charters of
kings or legislators, but under the King of kings."[8] Alexander Hamilton, writing in 1775, said: "Good and wise
men, in all ages, have embraced . . . [this] theory. They

[5] Perry Miller, ed., *The American Puritans* (New York:
Doubleday Anchor, 1956), p. 107.

[6] *Ibid.,* p. 95.

[7] *Ibid.,* p. 140.

[8] Edward Dumbauld, ed., *The Political Writings of Thomas
Jefferson* (New York: Liberal Arts Press, 1955), p. 190.

have supposed that the Deity . . . has constituted an eternal and immutable law, which is indispensably obligatory upon all mankind, prior to any human institution whatever."[9]

Americans might have differed over how man can come to know the laws of God and to some extent what those laws are, but they were in agreement that there was such a Higher Law. In order to demonstrate this, I have passed over for a moment a great shift in emphasis which had taken place. In the early seventeenth century, most Americans who thought about it would have agreed that they knew God's laws through the revelations contained in the Bible. More and more men were coming to believe in the eighteenth century that we know God's laws through a study of nature in which they have been implanted—that is, that natural law is the Higher Law. The belief in natural law as Higher Law is the third source of the American tradition.

In this latter view, we come to know it through a study of the universe and by the use of reason. John Wise, writing in 1721, made this statement of it: "For that all law, properly considered, supposes a capable subject and a superior power; and the law of God which is binding is published by the dictates of right reason as other ways. 'Therefore,' says Plutarch, 'to follow God and obey reason is the same thing.' But moreover, that God has established the law of nature as the general rule of government is further illustrable from the many sanctions in providence. . . . "[10]

---

[9] Richard B. Morris, ed., *Alexander Hamilton and the Founding of the Nation* (New York: Dial, 1957), p. 9.

[10] Miller, *op. cit.*, p. 126.

Thomas Paine, with his usual facility and absolute reliance upon rationality, carries this position to a logical extreme. *"The word of God is the creation we behold;* and it is in *this word,* which no human invention can counterfeit or alter, that God speaketh universally to man. . . . It is only in the *Creation* that all our ideas and conceptions of a *word of God* can unite."[11] But Paine's extreme view should not be permitted to obscure the more usual position. It was that there is a Higher Law, stemming from God, and known to man by revelation, by experience, and by science.

Individual Liberty

The other major source and foundation of American constitutionalism was the belief in limited government and individual liberty. The substantive purpose of a constitution is to secure the rights of men under it. The formal purpose is to provide order and stability within which these rights may be enjoyed. Implicit in the business of making constitutions is the belief that governments are a major threat to human liberty, however necessary they are to order and stability.

The great documents which served as precedents for the United States Constitution contain eloquent proof that they have as their purpose limiting government and recognizing liberty. Thus, the Magna Carta says, "We have also granted to all the freemen of our Kingdom, for us and our heirs, forever, all the underwritten Liberties, to be enjoyed and held by them and by their heirs, from us and

---

[11] Thomas Paine, *The Age of Reason* (New York: Liberal Arts Press, 1957), pp. 24-25.

from our heirs."[12] The English Petition of Right of 1628 "demanded that 'no man hereafter be compelled to make or yield any gift, loan, benevolence, tax or such like charge, without common consent by Act of Parliament,' and that there should be no imprisonment without cause shown, no enforced billeting of soldiers, and no martial law in time of peace."[13] In like manner, the charter by which Virginia was founded declared that those who should betake themselves to the New World were granted "all Liberties, Franchises, and Immunities . . . as if they had been abiding and born within this our Realm of England, or any other of our said Dominions."

This same character of limits and recognition of liberties can be seen in the Massachusetts Body of Liberties, promulgated in 1641. "No mans life shall be taken away, no mans honour or good name shall be stayned, no mans person shall be arested, restrayned . . . , nor any wayes punished . . . , unlesse it be by vertue or equitie of some expresse law of the Country. . . . "[14] Regarding the state constitutions adopted after the Declaration of Independence, one history says: "All the constitutions continued the office of governor, though most of them denied the holder of this position the bulk of the executive powers he had enjoyed in colonial days. All of the new documents . . . included a bill of rights. . . . "[15] The Articles of Con-

---

[12] Reprinted in Eugen Weber, ed., *The Western Tradition* (Boston: Heath, 1959), p. 194.

[13] W. E. Lunt, *History of England* (New York: Harper, 1956, 4th ed.), p. 412.

[14] Hall, *op. cit.*, p. 258.

[15] T. Harry Williams, *et. al.*, *A History of the United States*, I (New York: Knopf, 1959), 142.

federation, the first constitution of the United States, severely limited the government it established, providing that "nine states must agree before Congress can take any important action," and that no changes should be made in the Articles unless agreed to by Congress and ratified by every state.

The Constitution of 1787 incorporated the essence of limited government in its features, and with the addition of the first ten amendments gave broad protections to the individual against government. The government was limited formally by separating it into three branches and making an enumeration of the powers of each of these, by reserving certain of the powers to the states and to the people, and by entwining the branches in action so that they must work together in order to act. Substantively, it was limited by denying certain powers to it. For example, the unamended Constitution contains such provisions as these: "No Bill of Attainder or ex post facto Law shall be passed." "No Money shall be drawn from the Treasury, but in Consequence of Appropriations made by Law . . . ," and so forth. The Bill of Rights more specifically prohibits governmental intrusion upon the liberties of individuals.

The above, in the main, is an outline recapitulation of the traditions which, when united, form the American constitutional tradition. In view of this, it was not unusual that Americans should have met to draw up a constitution. With such traditions and beliefs—historical precedents, Higher Law, compacts and contracts among the people for civil action, individual liberty and limited government—it would have been surprising had they done otherwise. Constitutionalism is itself the centerpiece of the American tradition.

But, as I pointed out in the preceding chapter (page 24), there have been not one but three traditions in this country: the authoritarian, the American (or liberal), and the makings of a collectivist. Constitutionalism in America emerged from resistance to or limitation upon the authoritarian and is being altered and diminished currently by collectivism.

Government by Law, Not by Men

Constitutionalism itself was always liberal in tendency, but many of the great precedents for it in the Anglo-American tradition come from an authoritarian setting. The Magna Carta was an attempt to limit the arbitrary authority of the king, as was the Petition of Right. Colonial charters were grants of the monarch, arbitrarily given to companies and individuals, conferring monopolies and special privileges, and presumably revocable at his pleasure. Yet the rights of Englishmen had deeper roots than the arbitrary authority of a man—or, for that matter, of a parliament—and when the English government ignored them, the colonists revolted. They based their revolt on a Higher Law. As Jefferson put it, they were the "laws of nature and of nature's God." On the basis of these laws, men "are endowed by their Creator with certain unalienable rights; that among these, are life, liberty, and the pursuit of happiness."

Thus had Americans gone beyond the rights of Englishmen to the rights of man. The Declaration of Independence is literally and symbolically the rejection of the last vestiges of a government of men. It explicitly prepares the way for a government of law. Arbitrary authority had be-

come ever more hateful to Americans. For decades they
had been devising ways of circumventing the powers of
royal governors sent upon them. Attempts to regulate their
trade had met with subtle and large-scale evasion. They
protested restrictions placed upon them. It was a noble
dream of theirs that they should establish governments
of law.

Constitutionalism was fully consonant with individual
liberty. Indeed, as I have suggested, substantively it had
as its aim the protection of individual liberty. The period
from 1780 to about 1914 in America was one of the great
ages of mankind for human liberty. Indentured servitude
vanished, and Negro slavery was abolished; most, if not
all, of the legal restraints upon liberty were abolished.
American constitutionalism was profoundly a part of the
American liberal tradition. But I oppose it not to conser-
vatism, for constitutionalism was equally and as profoundly conservative. It was based on an age-old tradition; the
American constitutions were based upon experience broad-
ened by the study of history and upon reason chastened by
piety. It is arbitrary authority vested in men, not lawful
authority derived from Higher Law, to which the American
liberal tradition was opposed.

Liberalism Perverted

But "liberalism" in the twentieth century has been largely transmuted into collectivism. Those who style themselves liberals now work to remove limitations upon governmental action, applaud concentrations of power, favor
"government by men" as it evinces itself in boards and
commissions, and propose solutions to problems by col-

lective (i. e., governmental) action. In short, limited government and individual liberty are deterrents to these new liberals. Collectivism is profoundly anticonstitutional, in a much more complex and profound way than the older authoritarianism was. Kings could continue to occupy their thrones after their authority had been limited. But collectivists cannot "succeed" until they can bring the whole weight of government to bear upon problems.

This is so because they favor a planned economy and society. They must concentrate power in order to effect their economic order. States' rights, separation of powers, enumerated powers, and constitutional prohibitions prevent this power concentration. Individual liberty must eventually be sacrificed also. For, as F. A. Hayek has said,

> The authority directing all economic activity would control not merely the part of our lives which is concerned with inferior things; it would control the allocation of the limited means for all our ends. And whoever controls all economic activity controls the means for all our ends and must therefore decide which are to be satisfied and which not.[16]

The thrust to collectivism in the twentieth century, then, has been accompanied by an assault upon constitutionalism. The belief in historical precedent and tradition was undermined by a progressivism informed by a Darwinism to which the past was substantially dead. The belief in a Higher Law was undermined by a humanism which admitted of nothing above the man-made and by a pragmatism which admitted of no hierarchical distinctions.

---

[16] F. A. Hayek, *The Road to Serfdom* (Chicago: University of Chicago Press, 1944), p. 91.

The belief in limited government was undermined by proponents of a democracy in which the general will is always to prevail. Historians such as Charles A. Beard, J. Allen Smith, and Vernon L. Parrington, denigrated the United States Constitution by describing it as a reactionary document produced by vested class interests. At the more popular level, the Constitution was said to be outmoded. It had been created for an agrarian society and was hardly adequate to the exigencies of an industrial one. Limits on government were all very well when colonists wrestled with monarchs or when the franchise was severely limited. But when the people rule, why should their powers be limited?

Change by Amendment

There have been some amendments to the Constitution—notably the fourteenth and sixteenth—which have altered the character and limitations of constitutionalism. But the amazing thing is how few amendments there have been in a time when vast substantive changes in governmental action have taken place. Since 1920 there have been only three amendments to the Constitution, two of these adopted in 1933. Except for the twenty-first, which repealed the eighteenth, these have dealt strictly with the formal side of the Constitution. The twentieth changes the dates of presidential inaugurations and the meeting of Congress, among other things. The twenty-second limits Presidents to two terms. The Constitution is still there, very much as it was, yet these United States move nearer and nearer to unlimited government.

How has this happened? To describe it in detail would

require volumes. They should be written. In the mean-
time, however, the outlines of it can be suggested. The
Constitution is reinterpreted by the courts. It is conceived
of as granting power to provide for the general welfare,
not as limiting the use of power. Increasingly, courts and
elected officials ask the pragmatic question of what the
effect of an action will be rather than whether it is au-
thorized by the Constitution or not. Indeed, the notion of
referring an act to or placing it beside the Constitution to
determine its constitutionality has been laughed out of
court as the "slot machine theory" of interpretation.
"The Constitution is what the Supreme Court says it is,"
we are told. And if the court ignores the Constitution's substantive limitations, it ceases to impose limits.

The Foundation Stands

There is still a tradition of constitutionalism alive among
the American people. It still promotes the acceptance of
the decision of courts. How much longer it can survive
this assault is anyone's guess.

But is the United States Constitution not outmoded?
What excuse is there for imposing limits upon popularly
elected officials? Have conditions not changed so drastically that what was formerly proper is no longer needed?
Should the hands of the President be "tied" by onerous
restrictions? What our government needs, we are told, is
flexibility to deal with the multiple problems which con-
front us. Perhaps these questions can be answered with
others. Is liberty less desirable today than it was in 1787?
Have men been perfected to the degree that they can be
trusted with unlimited power? Are governments no longer

apt to oppress the citizenry? If the answers to these questions are negative, then constitutionalism is as viable as it ever was.

Indeed, times have changed, and the Constitution is no longer adequate to the twentieth century. Governments have devised means of oppression unknown to our ancestors. New restrictions need to be conceived to protect the citizen in his life, liberty, and property. But for this the original Constitution can be built upon. This would be profoundly in keeping with the American tradition of constitutionalism.

4.

Of Republican Government

THERE IS NO SINGLE word which adequately describes the American system of government. Nor need there be. Lately, there has been debate as to whether the United States is a republic or a democracy. Some conservatives have taken an adamant position that it is a republic; many liberals would be deprived of their philosopher's stone if they could not refer to it as a democracy. Others have rushed into the breach to proclaim that it is both a republic and a democracy. Actually, neither term should be called upon to perform such a broad and comprehensive service.

The United States was conceived and elaborated as a *constitutional federated republic.* All three terms are essential to convey the barest outline of our form of government; none of them sufficiently implies the others to be omitted. And these do little more than describe the outward form. They leave unevoked most of the inner essence of the American political tradition—i.e., separation of powers, government by law, private rights, and so forth. But is there any need to reduce the political tradition to a single word? Is space so limited, vocabulary so impoverished, or memory so short that our central political ideas must be reduced to a single word?

Our penchant for reductionism, for oversimplification,

53

for overloading words so that they block the channels of communication has a more serious explanation. It stems from the bent to have an ideology which can be conveyed and propagated by a single word. With such a device, one may say—as if meaningfully—that a war is "to make the world safe for democracy," or refer to the world conflict between democracy and communism. No one has yet suggested, to my knowledge, that the conflict is between republicanism and communism, for the meaning of republicanism is still sufficiently clear to expose such nonsense. Still, given time and enough sloganizing, even republic might be used to signify an ideology.

Not an Ideology

Ideologues first reduce all of reality to the limited dimensions of their own minds. Then, they reduce these conceptions to catch-words, slogans, and shibboleths. These phrases are imputed to contain an implicit summation of reality, an analysis of what ails society, a prognosis for its future, and the solutions for its problems. Thus, Karl Marx reduced reality to matter, made technology the moving force, explained historical developments in terms of class conflict, attributed the ills of society to capitalism, predicted a generally worsening situation, and held out communism as the solution. The tendency to do this sort of thing can be detected even before Marx's works, but it spreads so rapidly in our day that it threatens to envelop and choke off all thought and discourse.

The point is this. The American political tradition should not be conceived of as an ideology. To do so would be to distort both the tradition and the historical setting in which it arose. An ideology is monolithic, reductionist, comprehensive (in its claims), starts with a uniform conception of man, and ends with uniformity in the society it prescribes. By contrast, the American tradition was born out of and tended to facilitate diversity, expansiveness, and variety of belief and practice, none of which were presumed to be complete or finished. One may detect the bent of some Americans toward ideology at the time of the articulation of our tradition into institutions— in Jefferson's thought, for instance—but little of this found its way into documents from which our institutions were framed.

Republic or Democracy?

To come to the matter at hand, "republic" is not an equivalent term to "democracy," as these words are now used. "Democracy" has been loaded with that complex of interrelated ideas which we associate with an ideology; whereas, "republic" retains mainly its descriptive usage. This was not always so. In the debates about the adoption of the Constitution, "republic" and "democracy" were used interchangeably by some speakers. Even where this is not the case, it appears that neither word is anything more than descriptive. In considering the American political tradition, then, it is necessary to divest ourselves of the tendency to reduce things to ideologies. Men, in those days, sometimes had philisophies, ideas, beliefs, and principles, but rarely, if ever, ideologies.

Of course, the United States government was conceived of, created as, and referred to by its founders as republican in *form*. In like manner, this government was to see

to it that the states had a republican form of government.
These are matters of record, not subjects for debate. But
what they meant by this does have to be deciphered.

Representative Government

Republican government refers primarily to two things:
the origin of the powers of a government, and the manner in which these powers are exercised. That is, they
come from the *public* (or people), and they are exercised
by representatives. Most commentators are in agreement
on these two characteristics. Thus, the *American College
Dictionary* defines a republic as "a state in which the supreme power rests in the body of citizens entitled to vote
and is exercised by representatives chosen directly or indirectly by them." James Madison said that "we may define a republic to be . . . a government which derives all
its powers directly or indirectly from the great body of
the people, and is administered by persons holding their
offices during pleasure, for a limited period, or during good
behavior."[1] Patrick Henry, who was apt to agree with Madison about little else at the time of the constitutional debates, said: "The delegation of power to an adequate number of representatives, and an unimpeded reversion of it
back to the people, at short periods, form the principal
traits of a republican government."[2] In short, republican
government is popular representative government.

At the time of the founding of these United States,
Americans disagreed about many things, but not about

---

[1] Benjamin F. Wright, ed., *The Federalist* (Cambridge: Harvard University Press, 1961), pp. 280-81.

[2] *Elliot's Debates*, Bk. I, vol. 3, p. 396.

the desirability of republican government. Few, if any, could have been found to debate the following propositions with Madison in 1788. "The first question that offers itself is, whether the general form and aspect of the government be strictly republican? It is evident that no other form would be reconcilable with the genius of the people of America; with the fundamental principles of the Revolution; or with that honorable determination which animates every votary of freedom, to rest all our political experiments on the capacity of mankind for self-government."[3]

All of this can be so easily misunderstood, taken out of context as it is. Those who have gone far toward deifying majority rule and popular government as ends in themselves may think they have found allies in the Founders. Those who view representation as a purely practical expedient standing in lieu of a more desirable direct democracy may conclude that they hold common ground with the constitution-makers. Both would be wrong.

A Means to an End

Republican government was conceived as a means to an end, not an end itself. Americans of the late eighteenth century used many words and phrases to describe the object of government: for example, "happiness," "domestic tranquility," "common defense," "general welfare," and so forth. These somewhat vague words have been informed with quite different meanings in our day from what they meant in the earlier usage. As a matter of fact, their earlier meanings can be conveniently reduced to three heads:

---

[3] Wright, *op. cit.*, p. 280.

order, security, and liberty. The object of governments as then conceived was to institute regular and lawful (orderly) means for conducting relationships among men, to secure the possessions and lives of men from predators and aggressors, and to insure to men the free use of their faculties, so long as they did no harm to others.

Edmund Pendleton pins down most of these meanings in the following excerpt from his speech before the Virginia Convention held to consider the adoption of the Constitution. (Incidentally, this is an argument for adoption.)

> I wish, sir, for a regular government, in order to secure and protect those honest citizens who have been distinguished—I mean the *industrious* farmer and planter. I wish them to be protected in the enjoyment of their honestly and industriously acquired property. I wish commerce to be fully protected and encouraged, that the people may have an opportunity of disposing of their crops at market, and of procuring such supplies as they may be in want of. I presume that there can be no political happiness, unless industry be cherished and protected, and property secured. Suppose a poor man becomes rich by honest labor, and increases the public stock of wealth: shall his reward be the loss of that liberty he set out with? Will you take away every stimulus to industry, by declaring that he shall not retain the fruits of it? . . . In my mind the true principle of republicanism, and the greatest security of liberty, is regular government.[4]

Republican government, then, was linked in his mind, as it was in the minds of many others, with order, security, and liberty—the objects of government.

------

[4] *Elliot's Debates*, Bk. I, vol. 3, pp. 295-96. Italics mine.

Consent of the People

By definition, republican government is government by the consent of the people (or public). But it is not obvious why popular government should be thought likely to produce the ends that these men desired. Conceivably, they might have believed that the people are naturally good and virtuous, that they are by nature bent to justice and order, that a majority will always make the right decision, and that the voice of the people is the voice of God. Had they started with these assumptions, it would be clear why they favored popular government (though we might still question their sanity).

But these emphatically were not the assumptions of most men who produced and favored the adoption of the United States Constitution. On the contrary, Alexander Hamilton said, "The voice of the people has been said to be the voice of God; and, however generally this maxim has been quoted and believed, it is not true to fact. The people are turbulent and changing; they seldom judge or determine right."[5] John Adams apparently acquiesced in the view that "whoever would found a state, and make proper laws for the government of it, must presume that all men are bad by nature; that they will not fail to show that natural depravity of heart whenever they have a fair opportunity."[6] Moses Ames, speaking in the Massachusetts Convention on the matter of direct popular government, said: "It has been said that a pure democracy is the best government for a small people who assemble in person. . . . It may

[5] *Ibid.*, Bk. I, vol. 1, p. 422.

[6] Vernon L. Parrington, *The Colonial Mind* (New York: A Harvest Book, 1954), p. 317.

be of some use in this argument . . . to consider, that it
would be very burdensome, subject to faction and violence; decisions would often be made by surprise, in the
precipitancy of passion, by men who either understand
nothing or care nothing about the subject; or by interested
men, or those who vote for their own indemnity. It would
be a government not by laws, but by men."[7] James Madison said that "on a candid examination of history, we
shall find that turbulence, violence, and abuse of power,
by the majority trampling on the rights of the minority,
have produced factions and commotions, which, in repub-
lics, have more frequently than any other cause, produced
despotism."[8] John C. Calhoun, writing considerably later,
said that the "truth is,—the Government of the uncontrolled numerical majority, is but the *absolute and despotic
form of popular governments. . . .*"[9]

Yet these same men, and others of similar views, were
devoted advocates of popularly based government. Alexander Hamilton declared: "The fabric of American Empire ought to rest on the solid basis of THE CONSENT OF
THE PEOPLE. The streams of national power ought to flow
immediately from that pure, original fountain of all legitimate authority."[10] Elbridge Gerry maintained that "it
must be admitted that a free people are the proper guard-
ians of their rights and liberties. . . .[11] Moses Ames said:
"The people must govern by a majority with whom all

---

[7] *Elliot's Debates,* Bk. I, vol. 2, p. 8.

[8] *Ibid.,* vol. 3, p. 87.

[9] Quoted in Russell Kirk, *The Conservative Mind* (Chicago:
Regnery, 1960, the rev. Gateway edition), p. 199.

[10] Wright, *op. cit.,* p. 277.

[11] *Elliot's Debates,* Bk. I, vol. 1, p. 493.

ɔwer resides."[12] A Mr. Lee of Westmoreland in Virginia ɔok a similar position: "I say that this new system shows, ι stronger terms than words could declare, that the lib- ʻties of the people are secure. It goes on the principle ιat all power is in the people, and that rulers have no ɔwers but what are enumerated in that paper [the Con- suitution]."[13] John Marshall "conceived that, as the gov- ernment was drawn from the people, the feelings and in- terests of the people would be attended to. . . . [14] James Madison asked, "Who but the people have a right to form government [sic]? The expression [We the People] is a common one, and a favorite one with me."[15]

A Paradox Explained

Apparently, here is a paradox; or worse, outright con- tradiction. On the one hand, we are told that the people are passionate, turbulent, changing, partial, and self-in- terested. The direct rule of the majority can lead to al- most certain despotism. On the other, some of the same men argue for the adoption of the Constitution on the grounds that it provides for popular government. The people are "that pure, original fountain of all legitimate authority." Can such differences be resolved?

They can, at the least, be explained, and the explana- tion will lead us to the heart of the American tradition of republican government. It must be remembered that we

---

[12] *Ibid.,* vol. 2, p. 8.

[13] *Ibid.,* vol. 3, p. 186.

[14] *Ibid.,* p. 420.

[15] *Ibid.,* p. 37.

are not dealing with an ideology. An ideologue would almost certainly turn to some other basis of government if he did not trust the people. Moreover, these men are not discussing plans for a perfect society; they are discussing prudent means to very limited ends. They do not have in view final ends, total means, or absolute positions. The very limited character of the undertaking made moderation appropriate. As Governor Edmund Randolph put it during the Virginia Convention:

> The gentleman expresses a necessity of being suspicious of those who govern. I will agree with him in the necessity of political jealousy to a certain extent; but we ought to examine how far this political jealousy ought to be carried. I confess that a certain degree of it is highly necessary to the preservation of liberty; but it ought not to be extended to a degree which is degrading and humiliating to human nature; to a degree of restlessness, and active disquietude, sufficient to disturb a community, or preclude the possibility of political happiness and contentment. Confidence ought also to be equally limited. Wisdom shrinks from extremes, and fixes on a medium as her choice.[16]

These may not be eternal truths, but they are practical possibilities when men are dealing not with ideologies but with limited means to limited ends.

Man's Natural Rights

Moderate attitudes do not, however, remove the apparent contradictions alluded to earlier; they merely provide favorable conditions for the removal. The problem can be resolved only by reverting to the ideas which informed

---

[16] *Ibid.,* p. 70.

the belief in popular government. These were ideas of the nature of *man,* not of the behavior of men. The Founders believed that man, by nature, possessed certain rights. These rights were variously described, but it captures the thought behind a common belief to say that they were the right of a man to *life, liberty,* and the *fruits of his labor.* These rights were believed to be inalienable; that is, they were his by virtue of existence and not subject to being contracted away. Governments exist, legitimately, to protect man in these rights. It is in the common interest and for the general welfare of all men that these rights be protected. Order, security, and liberty are the conditions within which these rights can be assured.

Thus, a popularly based government is, from one point of view, a government based on the nature of man. In this sense, the voice of the people might truly be said to be the voice of God. For God had implanted this nature in man, and He gave final support to these natural rights.

Broadly Based Control

But this does not touch the practical problems of constitution-makers. Theoretically, all men have rights and an interest in governments which will secure them. Why not rest all government directly upon popular action? Will this not be the best of all means for securing men in their rights? Here and there a man might be found—Patrick Henry, a budding ideologue, for instance—who thought so at the time of the founding of these United States. But most men were hardly of this persuasion. In founding and operating governments, men as they actually are, not simply what they have by nature, must be reckoned with.

In their actual behavior, men frequently seek their selfish interests, try to gain power over others, yield to their passions, and become intolerant.

Had they angels to govern them, the problem might be readily solved. But alas, they have only fallible men to govern them and fallible men to be governed. Some men, it is true, are more nearly dispassionate than others, better learned, more given to appeal to reason, more conscious of the general welfare. Even they are but men, however, and given a free rein they may ride roughshod over their fellow men. History is replete with instances cf this consequence of entrusted power. No, the broad body of the people must retain control over the government. Even though men at large are capable of great mischief, particularly when gathered in groups, the government must have an actual popular base.

Limitations Sought

The task, as conceived by the Founders, was a difficult one. They believed that men's rights would be secure only if they kept watch over them. But if all power were conceded to men in the aggregate, they might abuse it and become tyrannical. At any rate, they might group into factions and use government for partisan ends. Also, they wanted a government with sufficient energy to provide that order and security within which men might enjoy their liberty. To do this, they would have to concentrate power to some extent. This would be dangerous, of course. How could the general welfare of all be discovered but by the best of men?

A significant part of the means to these ends was the

representation principle. According to the mode of the United States Constitution, the people are the source of authority. The Constitution was referred to delegates for adoption. The Preamble opens with "We the people." All authority can be traced backward to its popular source. Thus, the members of the House of Representatives were to be chosen directly by popular vote. The Senate was to be chosen by state legislatures, some portion, or all, of which, was to be chosen by the electorate. But there were definite checks on the exercise of power by the electorate. The Senate was elected indirectly, so far as the populace was concerned. The President was to be elected by special electors, chosen for that purpose as the states might designate. The members of the federal courts are appointed by the President by and with the consent of the Senate.

No law can be passed without the concurrence of a majority of Representatives, chosen directly by the populace. But it was equally true that no law could be passed without the concurrence of a majority of Senators, not at that time directly elected by the populace. In this manner, the people are the source of authority. But by making most of their voice indirect, there was an attempt to prevent either factional use of the government or a too ready response to the turbulence of the crowd. By having authority exercised by representatives, and most of them chosen by a winnowing process, the hope was to obtain reasonable government rather than one based upon passion. These representatives serve for different terms and are balanced against one another in separate branches of the government.

The conception which many of the Founders had of the

role of reason needs to be made clear also. Reason was thought to be the means by which man discovered his natural rights. In like manner, he discovered by reason the nature of good government and of the kind of society appropriate to man. Thus, reason was thought to be particularly important to the security of men in their lives and property. Representation was also conceived as the best means, or the best hope, for getting reason to prevail in political affairs. By selection, a considerable number of the most reasonable men might be chosen; by making it cumbersome to take action the delays would give men time to "come to their senses"; by counterpoising branch against branch men might have to recur to persuasion.

In debates in representative assemblies, men are drawn toward a reasonable position, for by aligning himself with reason a man stands higher in his opinion of himself. It should be noted, too, that the great ages of belief in reason have more often than not been the great ages of representative governments. The debates of parliaments make little sense if men are not subject to yield to the better reason. When belief in reason declines, as in our day, parliaments and congresses become increasingly anachronistic. Thus, attacks on Congress mount, and more and more ways are devised to evade the necessity for congressional action.

A Traditional Concept

Americans did not, of course, invent republican government at the time of the writing and adoption of the Constitution. They were working within a centuries-old tradition. Both popular and representative government can be traced backward to the late Middle Ages in England. In the authoritarian and feudal surroundings of that time, representatives started out as advisers to the king, served sometimes to counterbalance the power of the monarch, and represented before the king the various orders of men in the realm. The House of Lords represented the nobles and the clergy; the House of Commons represented the gentry and the townsmen. Thus, the earliest English settlers in America were familiar with representative government when they came. As soon as they were able, they established representative assemblies in the New World, beginning with the House of Burgesses in Virginia in 1619. These developed apace in most colonies, and Americans usually governed themselves in most respects long before they broke from England.

The idea of government deriving from the people had yet another source. It is found in the various compacts and covenants by which communities constituted themselves bodies politic, i.e., the Mayflower Compact, the Fundamental Orders of Connecticut, and so forth. These not only served as forerunners of our constitutions but also as prototypes for the belief that governments derive their powers from the people.

The Form Remains

Apparently, some people are shocked to learn it, but the United States still has a republican form of government. There have been some alterations, of course. The Senate is now elected by direct popular vote. Electors who vote for the President are now regularly chosen by popular

vote, whereas, at the beginning some of them were chosen
by state legislatures. The elective franchise has been
much extended, but that in itself does not alter the republican character of the government.

This would not be in the least amazing had not the
United States been known for more than a century as a
democracy. This designation began to catch on around the
middle of the nineteenth century, and by World War I
there were few, if any, to deny its descriptive accuracy.
Children in the schools were taught that they lived in a
democracy; preachers verified it in their prayers; and politicians proclaimed it to their constituents. Meanwhile,
democracy was coming to stand for an ideology. Shaped
by John Dewey and others, it picked up collectivist ideas
and comprehensive and unlimited ends for the government
it was supposed to describe.

In the early twentieth century when these latter developments were getting under way, there was a great deal
of dissatisfaction with the government. The notion was
spread that America was supposed to be a democracy—
that was its aim and end—but this had not yet been
achieved. Reforms were pushed in the name of making
the country more democratic. For a time, there were efforts to make the government more responsive to direct
popular pressure through such devices as the initiative
and referendum. Actually, these devices made some headway at the state level, but the impetus toward this sort of
thing faded during World War I, and there has not been
a great deal of interest in reviving it since the reformers
got control of the executive branch of the government in
1933. They have turned their efforts since that time to
the positive use of government to accomplish substantive

"democratic"—i.e., largely collectivistic—reforms rather than formal ones. Democracy became an end in the midst of this rather than a means. Voting—the most obvious "democratic" activity—became an end also.

These changes do represent major departures from the American tradition, though not so much by changes of institutions as by changes in belief. The republican form is still there to be understood and used. It still acts to inhibit precipitate action and to slow down the pace of change. But it will serve its full and rewarding purpose again only when we view it as a limited means to limited ends, namely, order, security, and liberty, *not* as a poor substitute for democracy, which it was not intended to be.

5.

Of Federalism

UNDOUBTEDLY, I MUST have picked up a good bit more, but I can remember only one point from the introductory course I took in political science. It was this: Sovereignty is indivisible. The professor was a recent arrival from southeastern Europe, Rumania, I think. He must have made this point about sovereignty many times, for it stuck in my mind. Quite likely, his basic principles were affronted by the notion that sovereignty was divided in America. It was obvious to him that it could not be done, and to have thought that they had done so must have signified to him the political illiteracy of Americans.

All those who attended that course should have been forever unfitted for understanding the American tradition of federalism, assuming, of course, that we accepted what was taught. The concept of sovereignty is an utterly useless analytical tool for understanding the American system. Worse, it carries with it implications which lead to pernicious interpretations and wrong positions about American government. Sovereignty refers to the supreme or ultimate authority in a country. The modern conception of it was developed by Jean Bodin, a sixteenth century Frenchman. It was used to buttress monarchy, absolutism, and the nation-state. In short, kings were thought of and referred to thereafter as sovereigns—as possessing supreme and absolute authority.

Sovereignty, then, was an absolutist conception in origin and development. It became a central conception for analyzing governments and for discussing political economy. But it has never been divested of its absolutist trappings. In consequence, the moment one tries to locate sovereignty he is searching for the supreme authority. This has resulted already in a great deal of mischief in America. Since if there is a supreme authority, it must be located somewhere and not divided, many thinkers have taken positions as to where it is located.

Not a Question of Sovereignty

Three positions have been most commonly stated: (1) that the states are sovereign, (2) that the people are sovereign, and (3) that the federal government is sovereign. For example, a recent writer takes the position that the states are sovereign. He starts with the premise that sovereignty is indivisible. "Finality knows no degrees. In law, as in mountain climbing, there comes a point at which the pinnacle is reached. . . . The argument here is that the states, in forming a new perpetual union to replace their old perpetual union, remained in essence what they had been before: separate, free, and independent states. They *surrendered* nothing to the federal government they created. *Some of their powers they delegated; all of their sovereignty they retained.*"[1]

On the contrary, another writer states, though he does

[1] James J. Kilpatrick, *The Sovereign States* (Chicago: Regnery, 1957), p. 14.

not explicitly subscribe to it, the position "that the people are sovereign; that the people created both state and national governments and that therefore both levels of government are merely the agencies of the people."[2] C. M. Wiltse, however, maintains that the federal government emerged supreme in the Civil War. Referring to Lincoln, he writes: "The sovereign power of the nation rested in his hands, and he exercised it. The rebellious South was beaten back into the Union, and the great debate was finally over. . . . A century after the Stamp Act had been rejected . . . the United States of America itself emerged as a true national state, whose sovereignty was undisputed and whose will was uncontrolled within the limits of its power."[3]

None of these positions is even close to describing the American tradition of federalism. Supreme power was not vested anywhere in these United States. Of course, as regards the exercise of foreign powers over American citizens, these United States *are* sovereign, but within the country there is no seat of sovereignty. But surely, it may be argued, ultimate power is exercised in America. So it is. No greater power can be imagined than the power to take a life, and this power is frequently exercised. But where is the power to do this vested? Some will imagine that it is vested in some arm of the government(s). It is not. For the life of a man to be taken by due process of law he must be tried for the violation of pre-existing law by a jury before

[2] William Anderson, *The Nation and the States, Rivals or Partners* (Minneapolis: University of Minnesota Press, 1955), p. 14.

[3] Quoted in M. J. C. Vile, *The Structure of American Federalism* (London: Oxford University Press, 1961), p. 27.

a judge. His guilt must be determined by a jury drawn from the people; his sentence must be passed by a judge trained in the law, chosen directly or indirectly by the citizenry, and paid by government funds. All of this must take place by procedures that are rigorously prescribed for all such cases, not arbitrarily adopted for the occasion.

Limited and Dispersed Powers

In these United States, the tradition is of *limited* and *dispersed* powers, limited in part by their very dispersion. Neither the people, nor the states, nor the federal government were made sovereign, for all of these were limited finally by due process of law. Many commentators, including some of the Founders, have spoken of divided or dual sovereignty. This too is inaccurate, for it implies that between them the states and the central government are supreme. In fact, however, they are limited by constitutions and traditions. Let us discard the conception of sovereignty in the further discussion of federalism. It distorts the American tradition of liberty, rather than shedding light upon it. Happily, the American governments— and the relationships among them and to the citizenry— were not born out of abstractions rendered into absolutes.

Instead, American federalism was builded upon an historical tradition, was conceived to deal with a concrete situation, and was advanced to serve rather definite ends. To understand it aright we should begin not with abstractions but with the history which made it appropriate to the American condition.

The American colonies were settled for varying purposes, at different times, in diverging locales, with people

having dissimilar views and aims. The founders of Massachusetts Bay Colony hoped to set up a Bible Commonwealth; the settlers of Virginia hoped to find gold and a
Northwest Passage; the British government sought to create a buffer between South Carolina and Spanish Florida
by authorizing the settlement of Georgia; Lord Baltimore
wanted Maryland to be a place where Roman Catholics
might be secure from persecution. Men made their living
by quite different pursuits on the rocky coasts of New
England from those in the Tidewater of Virginia. The
colonies differed greatly in the religious practices which
they permitted or encouraged. In some, all Christians were
tolerated; in others, only those of a particular sect could
openly practice their religion. Negro slavery thrived in
South Carolina, but Pennsylvania Quakers began to have
compunctions about it in the eighteenth century. Some
colonial governments were virtually independent of England, while others were bound rather more closely to the
Crown.

Local Loyalties

These differences gave rise to regional and local cultures, each with its own particular flavor and ways. Men
grew attached to particular colonies and took pride in
those things which differentiated them from the inhabitants of other colonies. A Virginian writing in 1728 gave
voice to this sentiment which, with appropriate variations,
was shared to greater or lesser extent by colonists elsewhere. "If *New England* be called a Receptacle of Dis-
senters . . . , *Pensylvania* [sic] the Nursery of Quakers,
Maryland the Retirement of *Roman Catholicks, North*

Carolina the Refuge of Runaways, *South Carolina* the Delight of Buccaneers . . ., *Virginia* may be justly esteemed the happy Retreat of *true Britons* and true Churchmen."[4]

Local Government

Within the rather loose framework of the British empire, each colony developed its own government. The major handicap to local self-government was that in Royal and Proprietary colonies the governor was frequently appointed from England. These appointees were sometimes viewed as interlopers. Robert Beverley, a Virginia gentleman who published a book in 1705, indirectly accused one governor of behaving like an "Otteman . . . Bashaw," that is, in an "Arbitrary" and "Despotick" manner. He accused Governor Nicholson of violating individual rights by instituting censorship to keep unfavorable mail from getting to England. Not only was mail intercepted, said Beverley, but spies were set upon people and the governor "condescended to act the low Part of an Evesdropper [sic] himself, and to stand under a Window to listen for Secrets, that would certainly displease him."[5]

My point is that colonists were not only attached to their colonies but also that they began to identify local government with liberty and representatives from elsewhere as sources of tyranny. The colonies were seedbeds of the development of self-government and shields against outside interference.

---

[4] Hugh Jones, *The Present State of Virginia* (New York: Reprinted for Joseph Sabin, 1856), p. 48.

[5] Robert Beverley, *The History and Present State of Virginia*, Louis B. Wright, ed. (Chapel Hill: University of North Carolina Press, 1947), pp. 90-91.

A Bias for Home Rule

Americans inherited a British tradition of local government and administration and built upon it. Counties and towns were the basic units of government which performed most of the functions of government in New England. In South Carolina and Virginia this was done by county and parish. One historian has concluded: "In general, the central governments of the colonies exercised even less control over local institutions than did the mother country over the colonies. Self-government was doubly the rule in colonial America."[6] Colonists prized their local prerogatives, were eager to extend their number and scope, and resisted any attempt to reduce them, resorting finally to arms to preserve local government.

Many of us have never become aware of what they knew well, living as they did in a sparsely settled land. Tyranny upon one's neighbor is seldom practiced. Not only is this so because one may see immediately the effects of his actions but also he must live among those whom he has wronged. Thus, a sheriff must act circumspectly if he expects to live in peace among those over whom he has exercised authority. Jurors will wish to be very definite about a decision if they are to live out their lives in contact with the relatives of a man whom they have sentenced to death. At any rate, Americans were accustomed and devoted to governments as near to hand as practicable.

American federalism, then, was conceived to deal with a concrete historical situation. No man of good sense in the 1780's would have proposed seriously that a unitary

---

[6] Clinton Rossiter, *The First American Revolution* (New York: A Harvest Book, 1956), p. 119.

state be erected to embrace all English Americans. Almost
every man's hand would have been against him. Thus, to
have created a single sovereign power in America would
have been to do so at the expense not only of popular
favor but of liberty as well. Some states had established
churches, while others had none. A single sovereign must
have one established church or none, but either course
would alienate some large part of the population. Only a
tyrant beyond the capacities of most of the "enlightened
despots" of the eighteenth century could have imposed
such uniformity upon America.

A More Perfect Union

Yet some sort of union was reckoned to be essential by
most of those who attempted to assay the American condition. The Americans were in the midst of a war with
England when they declared their independence. Their
only hope for success lay in making common cause against
the enemy. In these circumstances they sought the requisite unity by way of confederation, a union formalized in
1781 by the adoption of the Articles of Confederation. By
this plan they hoped to preserve the virtual independence
of the states while presenting a united front to the rest
of the world.

Those who favored a new constitution in 1787 maintained that this government had failed, that it was not
respected by foreign countries, that it could not pay its
debts, that some states would not respect its levies, that
property and life were insecure in America. America
needed a more energetic government, they declared, one
with some direct powers over the citizenry. Defenders of

the Confederation accused these advocates of change of being alarmists, and there are still differences of opinion as to which side was right in the contest.

Be that as it may, those favoring a stronger government of the union went ahead and drew up plans for a federal government, and it was this plan which became the Constitution of which we speak. The Constitution not only became the basis for an American tradition of federalism but it embraced and recognized a much older tradition of local government, colonial and state divisions, and diversity in the habits of individuals and groups. It recognized an existing system of governments and provided for a government of the Union.

Defense, Peace, Trade, Justice

The central (or federal) government was created to realize certain *limited* objects. These were felicitously enumerated in the Preamble to the Constitution, which reads:

> We the people of the United States, in Order to form a more perfect Union, establish Justice, insure domestic Tranquility, provide for the common defence, promote the general Welfare, and secure the blessings of Liberty to ourselves and our Posterity. . . .

It should be noted that this is not a grant of power but a statement of the ends for which the government is erected. Moreover, some of these phrases have been reinterpreted since, as we shall see. Thus, it will be well to examine what those who participated in the adoption of the Constitution thought the objects of the general government were.

John Jay, arguing for adoption before the convention

held in New York state, said that the general government was very limited in its scope, and had but few objects. "They comprehend the interests of the states in relation to each other, and in relation to foreign powers."[7] In defending the need for a federal judiciary, Edmund Randolph gave his understanding of the general purpose of the central government: "That it shall be auxiliary to the federal government, support and maintain harmony between the United States and foreign powers, and between different states, and prevent a failure of justice in cases to which particular state courts are incompetent. . . . Self-defence is its first object. . . . Its next object is to perpetuate harmony between us and foreign powers."[8] James Madison observed that the "powers of the general government relate to external objects and are but few."[9] Edmund Pendleton declared that the "general government" was to act "in great national concerns, in which we are interested in common with other members of the Union. . . . "[10] More heatedly, at another point, he emphasized the limited extent of the government:

I should understand a consolidated government to be that which should have the sole and exclusive power, legislative, executive, and judicial, without any limitation. Is this such a government? Or can it be changed to such a one? It only extends to the general purposes of the Union. It does not intermeddle with the local, particular affairs of the states.[11]

---

[7] *Elliot's Debates*, Bk. I, vol. 2, p. 283.

[8] *Ibid.*, vol. 3, p. 570.

[9] *Ibid.*, p. 259.

[10] *Ibid.*, p. 301.

[11] *Ibid.*, p. 40.

From these quotations it appears that the objects of the general government were largely (1) protection from foreign invasion, (2) maintenance of peace among the members of the union, (3) facilitating of commerce among the states, and (4) establishing justice and liberty.

Enumerated Powers

Under the federal system as provided by the Constitution the United States government was limited in several ways in powers held and to be exercised. First, it was limited by an enumeration of powers actually granted. For example, Article I, Section 8, of the Constitution reads, in part:

> The Congress shall have Power to lay and collect taxes. . . .
> To borrow money on the credit of the United States;
> To regulate Commerce with foreign Nations, and among the several States, and with the Indian Tribes. . . .

Second, the powers of the government were limited by specific prohibitions in the original Constitution:

> The privilege of the Writ of Habeas Corpus shall not be suspended, unless when in Cases of Rebellion or Invasion the public Safety may require it.
> No Bill of Attainder or ex post facto Law shall be passed.
> No Title of Nobility shall be granted by the United States. . . .

In addition to other restrictions not mentioned here but contained in the Constitution of 1787, other limitations were placed on the general government by the first ten amendments to it, commonly called the Bill of Rights. For example:

> Congress shall make no law respecting an establishment of religion, or prohibiting the free exercise thereof; or abridging the freedom of speech, or of the press; or the right of the people peaceably to assemble, and to petition the Government for a redress of grievances.

More pointedly, a blanket limitation on the government of the Union was imposed by Amendment X:

> The powers not delegated to the United States by the Constitution, nor prohibited by it to the States, are reserved to the States respectively, or to the people.

Third, it was limited by its formal dependence upon the states for its basis and operation. Before the Constitution could go into effect it had to have the approval of the electorate *by* states. To be amended, there must be favorable action on the amendment by three-fourths of the states. James Madison explains further the dependence of the general government upon the states:

> The State governments may be regarded as constituent and essential parts of the federal government; whilst the latter is nowise essential to the operation or organization of the former. Without the intervention of the State legislatures, the President of the United States cannot be elected at all. They must in all cases have a great share in his appointment, and will, perhaps, in most cases, of themselves determine it. The Senate will be elected absolutely and exclusively by the state legislature.[12] Even the House of Representatives, though drawn immediately from the people, will be chosen very much under the influence of that class of men, whose

---

[12] Changed to direct election by the Seventeenth Amendment.

influence over the people obtains for themselves an election into the State legislatures. Thus, each of the principal branches of the federal government will owe its existence more or less to the favor of the State governments, and must consequently feel a dependence. . . .[13]

This dependence, it was thought, would serve to restrain the central government and act effectively to limit its exercise of power.

Fourth, both the federal and state governments were limited by the balance of powers granted to each of them. This was intended to deter either of them from usurping the rights belonging to the people. Alexander Hamilton argued that the states would serve as a brake upon the powers of the general government:

> This great cement of society [the administration of criminal and civil justice by the states], which will diffuse itself almost wholly through the channels of the particular governments . . . would insure them so decided an empire over their respective citizens as to render them at all times a complete counterpoise, and, not unfrequently, dangerous rivals to the power of the Union.[14]

He explains further:

> The separate governments in a confederacy may aptly be compared with the feudal baronies; with this advantage in their favor, that from the reasons already explained, they will generally possess the confidence and good-will of the people, and with so important a support, will be able effectually to oppose all encroachments of the national government.[15]

---

[13] Benjamin F. Wright, ed., *The Federalist* (Cambridge: Harvard University Press, 1961), p. 327.

[14] *Ibid.*, p. 169.

[15] *Ibid.*, pp. 170-71.

In the New York convention Hamilton elaborated:

> This balance between the nation and state governments ought to be dwelt on with peculiar attention, as it is of the utmost importance. It forms a double security to the people. If one encroaches on their rights, they will find a powerful protection in the other. Indeed, they will both be prevented from overpassing their constitutional limits, by a certain rivalship, which will ever subsist between them. I am persuaded that a firm union is as necessary to perpetuate our liberties as it is to make us respectable. . . .[16]

Just as the federal government was limited in its powers, however, so were the states. Each of the states had and has a constitution which limits its power. The United States Constitution restricts state powers in two ways: (1) by giving exclusive jurisdiction in certain matters to the central government and (2) by specifically prohibiting the states to take certain kinds of action. For example of the latter, the Constitution says: "No state shall enter into any Treaty, Alliance, or Confederation; grant Letters of Marque and Reprisal; coin Money; emit Bills of Credit; make any Thing but gold and silver Coin a Tender in Payment of Debts; pass any Bill of Attainder, ex post facto Law, or Law impairing the Obligation of Contracts, or grant any Title of Nobility." Every state must have a republican form of government, and by custom and tradition, if not otherwise provided, all legal action must follow the forms of due process of law. All levels of government are limited by the fact that those who make law and policy—at least officially—must be subject to re-election or removal at regular intervals by the electorate.

---

[16] *Elliot's Debates,* Bk. I, vol. 2, pp. 257-58.

Authoritarian Moorings

The American tradition of federalism began to take shape in the authoritarian framework of the seventeenth century. The governmental powers which the colonists exercised stemmed from their "dread sovereign," the King of England. The exercise of these powers came in the course of time to be thought of as rights. At any rate, colonial legislatures, courts, and local governments became bulwarks against the exercise of power from England. In like manner, dispersed power became identified as a major buttress to liberty. This view was given depth by the feudal tradition which preceded it, and by the ideas of Montesquieu which had great currency at the time of the American Revolution.

When it was cut loose from its authoritarian moorings, federalism became a profound part of the American tradition. I have placed much emphasis upon the historical circumstances within which federalism was embraced. But this does not lead to the conclusion that it was all a matter of expediency. It is true that there was little hope of creating a consolidated government in 1787, but, it must be remembered, there was little desire either. Edmund Randolph thought it a blessing that there were great differences among the people in America, for it served to assure the liberty of all. In the matter of religious sects, he argued thusly:

> I am a friend to a variety of sects, because they keep one another in order. How many different sects are we composed of throughout the United States? How many different sects will be in Congress! We cannot enumerate the sects that may be in Congress! And there are now so many in the United States, that they will pre-

vent the establishment of any one sect, in prejudice to the rest, and will forever oppose all attempts to infringe religious liberty.[17]

My point is this: Federalism was conceived not only as a practical means of getting the requisite measures for the defense of the country but as a lasting means for preserving liberty—the highest end of all government. Hence, it was an essential ingredient to the liberal tradition because it provided for the dispersion and counterbalancing of powers.

There were contests over power between the federal and state governments almost from the beginning. This was intended. And many examples could be found where one or the other has been prevented from encroaching upon the rights of the people by the contest, whether it was conclusive or not. But what concerns us here is the tremendous shift in the balance of power. Surely no one today will deny that the federal government has vastly augmented its powers from what they were in the beginning and that there is mounting pressure for effectually reducing the states to administrative units of a consolidated central government. Federalism remains, of course, but it is much the worse for the wear.

Trend Toward Collectivism

How did these developments come about? Some claim to see a gradual extension of the powers of the federal government from the outset. True, Hamilton worked assiduously in the early years of the Republic to advance

---

[17] *Ibid.*, vol. 3, p. 204.

those powers, and John Marshall wrote decisions for the Supreme Court which frequently served to extend the sway of the central government. But the Jacksonians reversed this trend in the mid-nineteenth century, and the states re-asserted their vitality. During the Civil War and Reconstruction the federal government extended its sway once more, but in the late nineteenth century the courts nullified much of this. Thus, if my analysis is correct, the great and mounting shift has occurred in the twentieth century.

This shift has been impelled largely by the thrust toward collectivism. Theoretically, collectivism might be advanced and perhaps achieved at the local and state level. Indeed, much collectivization has gone on at these levels, viz., city owned electrical systems and state minimum wages and "fair" prices. But the federal system posed two major obstacles to collectivism. The federal courts, particularly in the latter part of the nineteenth century, disallowed much of the state action, basing their decisions on the Fourteenth Amendment. Second, collectivism did not appeal to some people, notably manufacturers and industrialists. Hence, it was noted that as the states entered upon regulation and control, industrialists sought more favorable sites for their new factories. When unions entrenched themselves by violence and coercion, undeterred by state authorities, industries migrated, for example, the textile industry from New England into the South.

The point was not missed by many collectivist reformers. In order to achieve collectivism, it would have to be done on a nationwide basis, and the courts would have to change the character of their decisions. How much of this was consciously realized I do not know, for reformers have advanced their programs under the protective cover of necessity, and they have rarely exposed their aims and ends to open discussion.

At any rate, the powers of the federal government have been greatly extended. Several means have usually been employed. The clauses in the Constitution referring to the promotion of the general welfare have been misinterpreted as grants of power, which they were not.[18] The interstate commerce clause has been stretched to extend the power of the government over almost every kind of economic activity.[19] There have also been constitutional amendments which have served to augment the power of the central government. Most noteworthy of these have been the Fourteenth and Sixteenth. The Fourteenth provided the basis by which the courts have become positive actors on the American scene, and the Sixteenth opened the way practically for the federal government to engage in the redistribution of the wealth.

"States' Rights" a Misnomer

Defenders of the American system of federalism have frequently fallen into a ready trap. They have usually become earnest defenders of what have come to be called "states' rights." By so doing, they misname what they should be defending and confuse means with ends. Anyone who would care to examine the quotations in this es-

---

[18] For such a misinterpretation, see, for example, Mr. Justice Cardozo's decision in *Helvering et. al.* v. *Davis*.

[19] Madison indicates in *Federalist* number 42 that the aim was to *facilitate* commerce among the states, thus, not to control it in the present sense.

say from Americans who established the tradition will discover that they did not refer to any governments as having *rights*. They referred regularly to the *powers* of government, and they did so consistently. *Rights*, at that time, were conceived of as something belonging to the people as individuals. Power was granted to governments for the purpose of maintaining justice and order so that liberty might be exercised by individuals. Dispersion of power was conceived as a means to the end of fostering liberty.

These distinctions we should revive, for they too are a part of the American tradition. Those concerned with the recovery of liberty in America may well work for a restoration of the balance of power among the governments, but they should keep in mind that it is not for the rights of states but for the rights of man for which they labor.

6.

Of Individualism

A TRADITION IS NOT primarily a complex of ideas. It may, of course, be described, explained, justified, or denounced by the use of ideas. Quite often, traditions have been buttressed by elaborate theories, which may lead the unwary to conclude that they are only dealing with theories. Those who did so in the case of the American tradition of individualism would certainly be wrong, for it can only be properly understood as a set of customs, habits, ways of doing things, and social arrangements which, when it came under attack, got full verbal articulation long after it had become a part of the way of life of a people.

In treating individualism as a tradition, it is my intent to deal with it primarily as practices regarding relationships among people. I shall approach it as a way in which people live their lives and maintain and carry on social relations. In this sense, I understand by individualism those social arrangements in which the individual is largely freed from compulsory social relations at some point in life, in which his childhood training is aimed at preparing him for this freedom, in which he is primarily responsible for his own well-being, in which he may contract or enter into a variety of relationships of his own will, in which there is a discernible and extensive private realm protected

by law and custom, and in which compulsory relationships
are kept at a minimum. This condition, in turn, would be
buttressed by a system of morality within which it had
meaning, a code of laws, and definable rights and privileges.

But the American tradition of individualism did not
exist in the abstract; it was a concrete way of life with its
own particular features. Thus, to understand it we should
turn to the history of its formation and development. This
approach is advantageous also because it will become more
clearly defined by seeing it against the background of that
to which it is opposed. The American tradition of individualism lies historically between the corporatism of Medieval
and Renaissance societies and contemporary collectivism.
Let us, then, examine its emergence from the earlier framework and pursue it to the threatened submergence by
present-day collectivism.

Differing Approaches

To trace the history of anything so dependent upon definition as individualism is exceedingly difficult. Almost any
statement about it may raise controversy. For example,
Jakob Burckhardt declared that in the Middle Ages "man
was conscious of himself only as a member of a race,
people, family, or corporation—only through some general
category." According to him, the great change came with
the Renaissance: "In Italy this veil first melted into air;
. . . man became a spiritual *individual,* and recognized himself as such."[1] On the contrary, Maurice de Wulf maintains

---

[1] Jakob Burckhardt, *The Civilization of the Renaissance in
Italy* (New York: Modern Library, 1954), p. 100.

that Medieval scholastics gave primacy to the individual over any group. Regarding their thought on the relation of the state to the individual, he says that "every human being has a certain sacred value, an inviolable individuality, and as such he has a personal destiny, a happiness which the state must aid him to realize."[2] "Thus, scholastic philosophy justifies from an ethical point of view the conception of the worth of the individual as against the central power."[3]

But the Medieval way to the realization of the individual was not individualistic; it was what may be called corporate. Medieval man found his identity in some class, order, or grouping of men. This identity was symbolized by distinctive garb and insignia: the robes of the priest, the *pallium* of the archbishop, the seal of the family or corporation. This corporate identity was signalized by referring to a man as a cleric, a knight, a craftsman, a serf, and so forth. Such rights and prerogatives as Medieval man could exercise were usually derived from his membership in some corporate body: guild, university, monastic or clerical order, and town, to mention a few. More comprehensive but less corporate groupings were the Roman Catholic Church and Medieval monarchies.

The movement of an individual from one order or class to another was frequently very difficult. Excepting for church vocations, membership in most orders and classes was inherited. Even particular jobs were handed down from father to son. Land was hardly a personal possession; the rights to it belonged to the family.

---

[2] Maurice de Wulf, *Philosophy and Civilization in the Middle Ages* (New York: Dover, 1953), p. 223.

[3] *Ibid.*, p. 228.

Membership in classes, orders, and families carried with it prescribed ideals, beliefs, duties, obligations, and tasks for the individual. The monk might be bound to poverty, chastity, and obedience; the merchant might have to accept an established just price; the vassal owed military service, hospitality, and ransom, when needed, to his lord; the serf owed week work, boon work, tolls, and fees to his master. Church membership and marriage partner were likely to be decided by the family and the society. These may have been ways for the realization of the individual, but major matters were hardly left to individual choice.

Medieval Institutions Fall

Modern individualism, then, arose in the wake of the breakdown of Medieval customs and institutions. As Medieval civilization disintegrated the groups lost control over many activities, and the area for individual endeavor and choice grew larger. Many historians place the onset of this disintegration in the fourteenth century, and its culmination anywhere from the sixteenth to the early nineteenth centuries, since feudalism was not officially abolished in France until 1789, and the relics of the Holy Roman Empire survived until 1806. However, in the main the breakdown of Medieval civilization is associated with such developments as the residence of the popes at Avignon, the Hundred Years' War, the obsolescence of feudal warfare, and the break-up of the guilds. The rise of individualism, on the other hand, is associated with such developments as the rise of capitalism, the Protestant Reformation, and the spread of humanism.

As older ties were loosened, as corporations lost control

of many activities, as institutions crumbled, individuals were freed from the circumscription of the group. The fifteenth and sixteenth centuries were a great age of prominent individuals, of men of great wealth, of master artists, of revolutionary innovators, of such men as John Huss, Martin Luther, Jakob Fugger, Leonardo da Vinci, Francis Drake, Lorenzo de Medici, Johann Gutenberg, Nicolaus Copernicus, Charles V, and Henry VIII. The confiscation of church lands made much new landed property available to individuals who had formerly been controlled by groups. As the cash nexus replaced older means of commanding service, property became attached to the individual and could be more readily transferred from one to another. With the proliferation of sects, the individual sometimes had a choice of religious denomination, though dire consequences might befall him for exercising it.

No Climate for Cowards

Individualism was not for the timid or cowardly in those times, if it ever is. Indeed, the individual was unusually exposed; older protections had been lost, but few new ones had been instituted. A bold individual like Columbus might venture forth to shores unseen before by the white man and claim the New World for Spain, but his achievement only exposed him the more to his enemies, and he died in disgrace. Savonarola might rise in his wrath to denounce the decadence of Rome, but the flames devoured him for his trouble. Thomas More courageously took his stand for what he believed was right; it cost him his head. Martin Luther escaped, but not because of any instituted protection to freedom of conscience.

The central problems, which have plagued individualism since, emerged in these conditions. They are: (1) the temptation of the individual to seek refuge from his exposure in some new all-embracing collective; (2) the opportunity for those in power to totalize it since there are little more than lone individuals to counter such a development. Modern European history is replete with instances of both of these developments carried to their logical extremes—virulent and all-embracing nationalisms, on the one hand; absolute rulers, on the other.

Tendencies in these directions appear in the fifteenth through the seventeenth centuries. Much of the power formerly exercised by the church, the nobles, and the corporations was absorbed by monarchs. The nation-state began to emerge in western Europe to claim the loyalty of subjects. The personal loyalty once owed to the nobility, to the hierarchy in the church, to the master craftsman was shifted to the monarch, who served as a symbol of the state. These monarchs sometimes provided protection, but it was frequently personal and arbitrary, subject to removal without notice. Authoritarianism tended to replace corporatism. These monarchs were soon styling themselves absolute, in the manner of Louis XIV and James I, and claiming to rule by divine right. The restraints upon the power of the king—those posed by the nobility, clergy, burghers—were weak and ineffectual. Individuals were freed from older restraints only to be threatened by the emerging comprehensive power of the monarch and the nation-state.

Modern individualism might have died aborning had developments continued the way they appeared to be going in the seventeenth century. But developments were not following the simple line of the growth of monarchical power. There were men of land and money seeking favorable conditions within which to operate and rights to their possessions which should be inviolate. Privileges granted by monarchs were soon claimed as rights. Contending religious sects vied for liberty to practice their religions and served as a counterbalance against the authority of the king. There were those still willing to defend ancient rights and privileges. Ideas were being promulgated which when embodied in institutions would protect the individual. The difficulties of transportation and communication limited the power of monarchs; technology had not yet provided the means for a totalization of power.

Favorable Conditions in America

Several circumstances contributed greatly to the development of a tradition of individualism in English America. The discovery, exploration, and settlement of America was coincident with the widespread disintegration of Medieval civilization. Moreover, this development took place more thoroughly in England than on the continent. It can even be argued that feudalism had never been as firmly fixed in England as it had in France, for instance. For another thing, the claims of the monarchs were stubbornly resisted by Parliament and the courts. The Stuart kings who reigned for most of the seventeenth century were under constant harassment by Commons, Puritans, merchants, and judges who insisted that the king was limited by law. Out of this struggle came monarchical recognition of many individual rights of the citizenry, recognitions acknowledged in the Petition of Right and the Bill of Rights.

Some of the protections from government, then, which are a part of individualism were already a part of the tradition of Englishmen when they came to America. Americans built upon these and added to them in their new surroundings. They transplanted and developed representative government which was frequently used as a means of protecting the individual from the arbitrary exercise of power by agents of the king. A court system was continued, and due process of law was accepted as one of their inherent rights. In the New World, colonists had few of the residues of feudalism to wrestle with: no class system of any rigidity ever gained hold, and the mercantilistic corporations soon lost their powers or had them greatly modified.

Limited Government

The great documents associated with the founding of the Republic carry the imprint of their basis in individualism. The Declaration of Independence declared that all men are "endowed by their Creator with certain unalienable rights; that among these are life, liberty, and the pursuit of happiness." It maintained further that the reason for establishing governments was to assure these natural rights. The constitutional period was rife with theorists pondering the limits of the common authority to be vested in governments and the extent of individual liberty. The constitutional prohibitions against bills of attainder and ex post facto laws were important protections of the individual in his rights. Prior to this, governments often seized the property of individuals by attainting it. If there was to be government by law, the laws must exist and be known prior to the offense. The Bill of Rights placed enumerated limitations upon the United States government, carving out an area for the individual beyond the reach, at least, of the central government.

For the first two-thirds of the nineteenth century the main tendency in the United States was to develop individualistic customs, folkways, and institutions. American life abounded with such developments. In law, the abolition of entail removed one of the last restraints upon individual control of property. The abolition of primogeniture, however, was more equalitarian than individualistic, but it did permit greater latitude in bequeathing and inheriting property. The individual was increasingly on his own: in joining and supporting a church (with the disestablishment of churches), in making a living, in gaining position in a community. Americans usually lived in separate houses both in town and country, and the houses in rural areas were usually some distance from one another. Social relations were frequently more dependent upon proximity than upon class or caste.

American thinkers, too, presented ideas and theories to explain, justify, and uphold individualism. I have been trying to deal with individualism as a tradition, not as an ideology, and it is my intention to deal with the ideas within this framework. Ideas become a part of the tradition as they become beliefs by which people justify their practices and inform the institutions which are created in consequence of holding them. This is not to imply that they necessarily precede the tradition or that any particular articulation of ideas is essential to the tradition. There is no opportunity in so brief a survey to do justice to the breadth and richness of thought by Americans on individualism, but I can touch upon that of a few men to exemplify it.

Thomas Paine and Thomas Jefferson

Two names stand out in the revolutionary period—
Thomas Paine and Thomas Jefferson. Thomas Paine, itinerant revolutionist whose nimble mind could turn profound doctrines into flaming shibboleths, declared that all
men had certain rights by nature. These rights are of two
kinds: first, the right of thinking and acting in matters
which concern only the individual; second, civil rights,
which are natural rights which man possesses as a member of society. All those rights which the individual could
exercise without society—thinking, owning and managing
property, etc.—he keeps for himself inviolate when he enters society. Civil rights are those which he would be fitted
to exercise but lacks the power to assure his right to do
so. But the fact that the individual is impotent to enforce
his rights against society does not mean that society has
the right to deprive him of them. It is rather for the purpose of protecting these rights that individuals join together to form a government.[4]

The rights which Paine enumerated were: the right to
equality with other men, to do what injures no one else,
to participate in government, to be tried according to pre-
established methods and rules, to free expression and
thought, and the right to property which should be sacred
and inviolate.[5] Each of these rights, Paine declared, carries
with it the duty of respecting the same rights for others.[6]

Thomas Jefferson, despite his active life and many
talents, thought deeply about the relation of the individual

---

[4] Thomas Paine, "Rights of Man" in *Basic Writings* (New
York: Willey Book Co., 1942), pp. 37-38.
[5] *Ibid.*, pp. 89-91.
[6] *Ibid.*, pp. 92-93.

to society. He did not deny that a man has social obligations, but he did maintain that however great the degree in which man was made for society, he was in an even greater degree made for himself.[7] Society, as Jefferson conceived it, was merely an aggregate of individuals, not a real entity with rights and prerogatives of its own.[8] Jefferson was an avid believer in individual rights. It has ever troubled some men that under liberty there will be abuses. But Jefferson said, "I would rather be exposed to the inconveniences attending too much liberty, than those attending too small a degree of it."[9]

Certain rights Jefferson thought were essential: the right of individual conscience, or the right of every man to care for his own soul;[10] freedom of expression; freedom of commerce (to have dealings with others unhampered); freedom of the person; and the right to ownership and management of property.[11] Concerning the latter, Jefferson said: "The true foundation of republican government is the equal right of every citizen, in his person and property, and in their management."[12]

Henry David Thoreau

Nineteenth century essayists added idealism and the subjective bent of Romanticism to the idea of individualism. Henry Thoreau will serve to exemplify this tendency.

---

[7] Thomas Jefferson, *Democracy*, Saul K. Padover, ed. (New York: D. Appleton-Century, 1939), pp. 22-23.

[8] *Ibid.,* pp. 55-56.

[9] *Ibid.,* p. 79.

[10] *Ibid.,* pp. 167-68.

[11] *Ibid.,* p. 23.

[12] *Ibid.,* p. 53.

He will serve well, for his faith in the individual way knew no limits, and was not cluttered by reservations and casuistry. He caught at the central tendency of the tradition and gave it forceful statement. Note this affirmation:

> I heartily accept the motto,—"That government is best which governs least"; and I should like to see it acted up to more rapidly and systematically. Carried out, it finally amounts to this, which also I believe,—"That government is best which governs not at all"; and when men are prepared for it, that will be the kind of government which they will have.[13]

If it can be said of Thoreau that he had too much faith in men, then it can be said with equal justice that most of us have too much faith in government. This latter was no fault of Thoreau. He said of government, "It has not the vitality and force of a single living man; for a single man can bend it to his will."[14] Moreover,

> this government never of itself furthered any enterprise, but by the alacrity with which it got out of its way. *It* does not keep the country free. *It* does not settle the West. *It* does not educate. The character inherent in the American people has done all that has been accomplished; and it would have done somewhat more, if the government had not sometimes got in its way. For government is an expedient by which men would fain succeed in letting one another alone; and, as has been said, when it is most expedient, the governed are most let alone by it. Trade and commerce, if they were not made of India-rubber, would never manage to bounce over the obstacles which legislators are continually putting in

---

[13] Henry D. Thoreau, "On the Duty of Civil Disobedience," pub. in *Walden*, Norman H. Pearson, intro. (New York: Rinehart, 1948), p. 281.
[14] *Ibid.*

their way; and, if one were to judge these men wholly by the effects of their actions and not partly by their intentions, they would deserve to be classed and punished with those mischievous persons who put obstructions on the railroads.[15]

Thoreau has caught here the heart of the American tradition—that it is individuals who actually do and accomplish things, not groups, organizations, collectives, nor governments. These latter are at most aids, at worst obstructions.

William Graham Sumner

In his earlier writings, William Graham Sumner was an articulate advocate of the individual way. Particularly, he advanced the belief in individual responsibility and denied the validity of the emerging idea that the state was responsible for the well-being of individuals. The state, he thought, is not an entity; it is merely all the people joined together for the common purpose of protection. Hence, the state has no obligations which an individual does not have. He conceived American society to have been composed of free and independent men joined by a contract of their making. This contract was made, he said, to give the "utmost room and chance for individual development, and for all the self-reliance and dignity of a free man." No man might claim the help of another as a right, whether the other be a single individual or a group of individuals joined by contract to form a state.[16] The purpose of government,

---

[15] *Ibid.*, p. 282.

[16] William G. Sumner, *What Social Classes Owe to Each Other*, Albert G. Keller, intro. (New York: Harper, 1920), pp. 26-27.

he thought, is to protect civil liberty. Civil liberty is *"a status created for the individual by laws and institutions, the effect of which is that each man is guaranteed the use of all his own powers exclusively for his own welfare."*[17]

Choices and Responsibilities

A tradition of individualism, then, had taken shape in America. The folkways and customs of Americans were built upon it; the political institutions had been designed to safeguard it; a way of life had been built around it; theories had been developed to bolster it.

The way of individual liberty is not always an easy one. A society organized in this way holds an individual responsible for his own well-being, places the blame directly upon him for any violation of the rights of others, makes charity a voluntary matter, places the opportunity (and burden) of choices directly upon him, denies him its force to do his will. Of course, it leaves open to individuals all sorts of voluntary arrangements by which they may work together with others for common ends. Still, there must always be the temptation to many to be rid of the onerous burden of choices and responsibilities, to weld groups into more permanent and powerful forces by law, to merge oneself finally with some collective. Too, there is the ever-present fact that when men are rewarded according to ability and effort, as they will tend to be under liberty, that some will have much more than others. Greed is ever a powerful motive for men to join together to divest others of their holdings. In well ordered lands, such groupings are re-

---

[17] *Ibid.,* p. 34.

ferred to as gangs or bands of robbers. In these disordered times, they are known by euphemisms which appear respectable when they use government to effect their ends.

Probably there was never a time in American history when the individualistic way completely triumphed over or pushed out the use of force for dubious common ends. Slaveholders used the state to maintain their sway over their slaves. State and local governments were often apt to use their borrowing powers to advance some private or group interest. The control which the United States government has over legal tender has often been used by certain interests to advance their cause at the expense of those individuals who suffered by inflation or deflation. Nor is it likely that we shall ever be entirely free of the abuse of power so long as it is necessary to concentrate some of it, and it is and probably will remain necessary to do so.

A Shift Toward Collectivism

Let us not, however, confuse the occasional abuse of power, which is hardly to be avoided, with a central shift of direction. Since the latter part of the nineteenth century Americans have turned more and more from the tradition of individualism toward at least one of the modern forms of collectivism. I think it would be true to say that collectivism has nowhere simply arisen as a tradition in the modern era, though some historians have struggled to demonstrate its evolutionary emergence. In fact, however, it has been advanced everywhere by ideologies and is imposed by force or the veiled threat of force.

The signs of the shift to collectivism began to appear in

America with the growth of labor unions, the activities of farmer organizations to promote legislation favorable to them, and the rise of large business combines. These developments were accompanied by efforts to arouse class consciousness and the development of nationalistic thought and sentiment. New conceptions of society, of democracy, and of the desirability of a "positive" role of government were advanced in America by populists, by socialists, by Progressives, and by assorted other reformers. All of them tended to conceive of man as a part of some social class or whole and pointed the way to his fulfillment by way of collective action. Collectivism virtually triumphed after 1933 with the empowerment of groups, the massive use of government to redistribute the wealth, the promotion and protection of groups by law, and the widespread adoption of a new social ethos.

Many thinkers of the nineteenth century had thought that the inspiring story to be discovered in history had been the gradual emergence of the individual from the mass, of the growth of protections around the individual to support him in his liberty, of the emergence of a clearer conception of morality, of natural law, and of the individual as the motive power in human affairs. We can be happy for them that they could not see a little into the future, when intellectuals would be proclaiming the growth of collectives to be progress, when politicians unabashedly took from some to give to others under the cover of morality, when individuals would be gladly yielding up the hard won liberty that their forefathers had vouchsafed to them in order to receive the comforts of submergence in the mass.

Yet we know that individual morality still lives in the

thoughts and actions of most, that if it did not, things would be worse than they are. We know that there are many who would repudiate the trend of this century toward collectivism if they could perceive it clearly. We believe that if the protective cover of rhetoric under which collectivism has been advanced could be removed, men would act gladly to restore a vital tradition.

7.

Of Equality

IT WOULD BE DIFFICULT today to discover a conception about which there is greater confusion than there is about the meaning of equality. Writers speak of legal equality, spiritual equality, social equality, political equality, and economic equality. The concern with the equality of individuals is complicated by talk of racial equality. For some, equality is virtually a dirty word; for others, it is the *summum bonum,* a highest good, which has been "thingified" into an ideal. American opinions differ (and have differed) widely as to how much and what kind of equality is desirable. At any time in American history there has been considerable leveling sentiment, countered, on the other hand, by a thrust to superior status and position by individuals and groups. With all of these differences in mind, one might well despair of discerning a tradition from among them.

It is not my intention, however, to try to discover the tradition of equality from among the various expressions of ideas about it. Nor would I hope to discover it by looking for a "true" definition by way of semantic exercises. Consensus there may well have been from time to time, but it is to be found mainly by analysis of institutions, constitutions, customs, and practices, not by the review of debates—however useful these may be for discovering justifications that may have been given for a practice. Indeed, traditions are more often to be found in matters that do not come up for debate than in controversial matters. It is unlikely that contemporary pollsters would discover any tradition by their methods; they would only discover opinions about one. A tradition is something that has become embedded in the texture of the lives of a people, and it is there that it must be uncovered.

"All Men Are Created Equal"

Let us look for the American tradition of equality first in the most familiar statement of it, the one found in the Declaration of Independence. The familiar phrase begins, "We hold these truths to be self-evident, that all men are created equal. . . . " But we are in trouble already. What do these words mean? They are little illuminated by the text from which they are drawn. Does this mean that all men have equal capacities at birth? Does it mean that there are no essential differences among those who are born? Does it mean that all our differences are a product of environment and nurture? Does it mean that heredity counts for nought? Is it a surreptitious promise of a redistribution of wealth, the militant rhetoric of revolutionaries trying to rally the have-nots to their cause? It is none of these things. Yet I do not draw my conclusion from semantic analysis nor from a poll of the men who affixed their signatures to the Declaration—though both methods are helpful in support of such a conclusion.

The meaning of the controversial phrase—"that all men are created equal"—is made clear in the first place by its historical context. The Declaration of Independence was addressed to the "Powers of the earth," which at that time meant the European powers. It was directed to people who were accustomed to hierarchical social arrangements, to hereditary classes and fixed orders. This pronouncement was set against a historical background of similar practices with which Americans had been familiar.

Medieval Inequalities

The American tradition of equality emerged, then, from the Medieval and authoritarian background of inequality. In the Middle Ages, there was not even a bent toward equality. On the contrary, the tendency was for each man to have a station within a hierarchy, and for this position to be passed on from father to son. This tendency was buttressed by the belief that such a social order reflected a divine order in the universe. As one historian describes it, "The world was a great allegory, whose essential secret was its meaning, not its operation or its causes; it was a hierarchical order, extending from lowest to highest, from stones and trees through man to the choirs upon choirs of angels. . . . "[1] Within this greater order, men had their orders and ranks. Thus, John of Salisbury, a twelfth century philosopher, describes a commonwealth and likens it to the body of a man. He says:

> The place of the head in the body of the commonwealth is filled by the prince, who is subject only to God and to those who exercise His office and represent Him on earth, even as in the human body the head is quickened and governed by the soul. . . . Officials and soldiers

---

[1] John H. Randall, Jr., *The Making of the Modern Mind* (Boston: Houghton Mifflin, 1940, rev. ed.), p. 36.

correspond to the hands. . . . The husbandmen correspond to the feet, which always cleave to the soil. . . .[2]

According to feudal theory, there were three orders of men: clergy, nobility, and peasants and burghers. Each of these orders had rights, privileges, and responsibilities. Within any given order, men were ranked in hierarchies. Thus, within the clergy there were ranks ranging from archbishop and bishop at the top to deacons and sub-deacons at the bottom. The nobility ranged from archdukes to lowly knights. Within the guilds the range was from master craftsman to apprentice. Even crafts were apt to be ranked in hierarchies; there were lesser guilds and greater guilds. Each order tended to have courts of its own to enforce its rights. Hence, benefit of clergy once meant the privilege of a clergyman to be tried in a clerical court. The right to a trial by a jury of his peers meant the right of a man to be tried by others of his rank. Even ranks were apt to have special privileges, spelled out in great detail. Note these provisions in the Magna Carta:

> Earls and Barons shall not be amerced but by their Peers, and that only according to the degree of their delinquency.
> No Clerk shall be amerced for his lay holding, but according to the manner of the others as aforesaid, and not according to the quantity of his ecclesiastical benefice.
> All Barons who have founded Abbeys, which they hold by Charters from the Kings of England, or by ancient tenure, shall have the custody of them when they become vacant, as they ought to have.[3]

---

[2] James B. Ross and Mary M. McLaughlin, eds., *The Portable Medieval Reader* (New York: Viking, 1949), pp. 47-48.

[3] Eugen Weber, ed., *The Western Tradition* (Boston: Heath, 1959), pp. 196-97.

It is doubtful that this system was ever absolutely rigidly established anywhere. Certain it is, too, that in many places feudalism was breaking down in the fourteenth, fifteenth, and sixteenth centuries. Yet as late as the seventeenth century in England, at the time of the beginning of American colonization, rank and order were still very important. One historian says:

> When Lord Berkeley returning from London came down over the terraces of the Cotswolds to the hundred of Berkeley in the Severn valley, he was met by troops of tenants and retainers. His progress toward his castle was indicated by the peals of bells from the church tower of each village as he reached it. . . .
>
> The prestige of peers of whatever rank was still great. The general public looked upon them as men whose duty it was to stand round the King and be his advisors.[4]

They were still likely to be first in line for lands which the Crown had at its disposal, for patents to be awarded, and they still possessed numerous prerogatives denied to other men.

Class Traditions in Colonial America

The early settlers who came to America were usually conscious of rank and its prerogatives. As Notestein observes, "Few of those English who came to the New World were of gentle stock, but they brought traditions of class with them. When a lawyer grew rich and important in a New England Village, he was often dubbed 'the squire,' as many gentlemen in England were called. In Virginia

---

[4] Wallace Notestein, *The English People on the Eve of Colonization* (New York: Harper, 1954), pp. 36-37.

. . . they set up plantations modeled on the manors they had known in England, and tried to live, as best they could, like country gentlemen."[5] One may still read such nice distinctions as "mister" and "goodman" attached to the signatures of those who signed the Mayflower Compact. But hereditary position was never firmly fixed on American soil. There was no monarch residing in America to build a following by appointing nobles. Nonetheless, class distinctions were perpetuated, or, more accurately, efforts were made to perpetuate them. Massachusetts passed an act in 1650 which said in part: "We declare our utter detestation and dislike that men and women of mean condition should take upon themselves the garb of gentlemen, by wearing gold or silver lace or buttons, or points at their knees, or to walk in boots, or women of the same rank to wear silk or tiffany. . . . "[6] Indentured servants occupied an inferior legal position. Landed estates were transmitted whole from father to eldest son by the rule of primogeniture. Even so, younger sons could advance by their own efforts, and "it was relatively easy for a servant to become a small landowner or independent artisan. . . . Excepting the fixed status of slaves, the flexibility of colonial society was its distinguishing feature."[7]

The above, then, is the historical background for understanding the meaning of Jefferson's phrase—"that all men are created equal." He was disavowing hereditary rank

---

[5] *Ibid.*, p. 45.

[6] Quoted in Curtis P. Nettels, *The Roots of American Civilization* (New York: Appleton-Century-Crofts, 1963, 2nd ed.), p. 327.

[7] *Ibid.*

and privilege. Within the context of the Declaration, he was saying that the Creator has not established a position for any person at the creation. That is not to say that all men are equal in capacity or that they will remain equal in ability or effort. Nor does it imply that there are to be no distinctions among men during the course of their lives. On the contrary, it implies that such distinctions as a man shall acquire shall be his without benefit of legal prescription based on heredity.

Two Kinds of Equality

Two kinds of equality, so far as individuals are concerned, are treated in the Declaration of Independence. First, there is *equality before the law*. This means that every man's case is tried by the same law governing any particular case. Practically, it means that there are no different laws for different classes and orders of men. The definition of premeditated murder is the same for the millionaire as for the tramp.[8] A corollary of this is that no classes are created or recognized by law. Second, the Declaration refers to an *equality of rights*. The second part of the sentence already alluded to read, "that they are endowed by their Creator with certain unalienable Rights, that among these, are Life, Liberty, and the pursuit of Happiness." Each man is equally entitled to his life with every other man; each man has an equal title

---

[8] It does not follow that the members of a jury will hold the same opinion of a millionaire as of a tramp. Nor does it mean that each of these men will have an equally good defense. Perhaps they should have (though that is a questionable proposition), but it was no part of the American tradition that they would have.

to God-given liberties along with every other. The probable meaning of "pursuit of Happiness" is that each man is entitled to the use of his faculties for his own well-being (pleasure).

It is not my intention, however, to found this interpretation of the tradition upon semantic renderings. The Constitution offers considerable institutional support for the above interpretation. For example, Article I, Section 9 contains this provision: "No title of Nobility shall be granted by the United States: And no Person holding any Office of Profit or Trust under them, shall, without the Consent of the Congress, accept of any present, Emolument, Office, or Title, of any kind whatever, from any King, Prince, or foreign State." This was designed to prevent the creation of an hereditary aristocracy. The same section prohibits Congress to pass bills of attainder by which some class of disabled persons might be created. It also contains this interesting provision:[9] "No capitation, or other direct, Tax shall be laid unless in Proportion to the Census or Enumeration herein before directed to be taken." In view of later developments, this provision deserves comment. It was an attempt to provide for an equality of taxation, if any direct taxes were levied. It must have meant that no greater proportion of taxes could be levied upon any one man than upon any other.

There are other indirect attempts to acknowledge an equality of rights within the Constitution. Powers denied to the Congress and to the states are an implicit protection of rights. The Bill of Rights, by prohibiting action of the Congress, tends toward the establishment of an equal-

---

[9] Since abridged by the Sixteenth Amendment.

ity of rights. If government cannot intervene, it cannot
confer rights on some and deny them to others. States
also established certain rights beyond the reach of their
governments.

A Major Exception

A major exception to equality before the law and equality of rights, however, existed and was recognized at the
time of the founding of the Republic. It was Negro slavery. Slavery was an inferior status, and it was inherited
in America. The Constitution tacitly recognized slavery
by referring to free persons and *others*. State laws, where
slavery was practiced, distinguished between slave and
free in numerous ways.

This large-scale departure from the principle of equality troubled many people at the time of the setting up of
the government. Northern leaders argued that slavery
must not be disturbed, else the Constitution would not
be accepted. Many Virginians, at least, inclined to blame
England with fastening slavery upon America, which
strikes us as somewhat disingenuous. The point is that
they saw the inconsistency, but saw no practical way of
coping with it. At that time, it was hoped by those who
were troubled that slavery would disappear and that perhaps the Negroes would assume a position of equality of
rights. There must have been a great variety of opinions
on this, however, and it was not generally much debated.

Reconstruction Amendments

Later constitutional amendments removed both slavery and the disabilities attached to it. The Thirteenth

Amendment, adopted in 1865, abolished slavery. The Fourteenth Amendment, proclaimed as ratified in 1868, provided, among many other things, that no state should "deprive any person of life, liberty, or property, without due process of law; nor deny to any person within its jurisdiction the equal protection of the laws." As regards equality, these amendments may be considered as an extension and establishment of the tradition of equality before the law and equality of rights.

It should be noted, however, that insofar as the Fourteenth Amendment provided for the extension of federal authority it interfered with an equally important tradition of federalism. The Fifteenth and Nineteenth Amendments may also be regarded as extensions of equality in that they prohibit the denial of the elective franchise on the basis of race or sex. Again, however, they extended the central government into matters theretofore reserved to the states. Moreover, they refer to the "right . . . to vote," which introduced a confusion into constitutional language from which we have not begun to recover.

Voting Is a Privilege

The rights of which the Founders spoke were natural rights. Voting could not be a natural right, for these were conceived as something existing prior to society or governments. Voting obviously is something which can only be exercised in a society with an organized government. Hence, voting could be described properly as a privilege, a privilege granted by government. But if it is called a right, and there is to be an equality of rights, then everyone should be entitled to it, including children, presum-

ably. This is only one example of the confusion in which
we are caught that has been occasioned by the loose use
of language.

The above, with exceptions noted, does indicate the
main lines of the development and delineation of an
American tradition of equality. Further evidence that it is
the tradition may be found in expressions of contemporary documents and statesmen. For example, the Virginia
Bill of Rights, adopted in 1776, has this to say on equality:

> That all men are by nature equally free and inde-
> pendent, and have certain inherent rights, of which,
> when they enter into a state of society, they cannot, by
> any compact, deprive or divest their posterity; namely,
> the enjoyment of life and liberty, with the means of
> acquiring and possessing property, and pursuing and
> obtaining happiness and safety.[10]

The Massachusetts constitution of 1780 stated that "all
men are born free and equal, and have certain natural,
essential, and unalienable rights."[11] It further declared
that governments were organized "for the protection, safety, prosperity, and happiness of the people, and not for
the profit, honor, or private interest of any one man."[12]
More, "each individual of the society has a right to be
protected by it in the enjoyment of his life, liberty, and
property according to standing laws."[13] The Virginia con-

---

[10] Quoted in Rousas J. Rushdoony, *This Independent Republic* (1963), no page numbers.

[11] Quoted in Robert J. Harris, *The Quest for Equality* (Baton
Rouge: Louisiana State University Press, 1960), p. 19.

[12] *Ibid.*

[13] *Ibid.*, p. 20.

stitution proclaimed that no one is entitled to "exclusive or separate emoluments or privileges from the community, but in consideration of public services."[14]

Other References to Rights

There are other important expressions of the meaning of equality that can be gleaned from the debates over the adoption of the Constitution of 1787. Edmund Pendleton delivered himself of this opinion regarding classes and equality, speaking to the Virginia Convention:

> I am unfortunate enough to differ from the worthy member in another circumstance. He professes himself an advocate for the middling and lower classes of men. I profess to be a friend to the equal liberty of all men, from the palace to the cottage without any other distinction than that between good and bad men. . . .
> Why bring into the debate the whims of writers—introducing the distinction of *well-born* from others? I consider every man *well-born* who comes into the world with an intelligent mind, and with all his parts perfect. I am an advocate for fixing our government on true republican principles, giving to the poor man free liberty in his person and property.[15]

There was much talk of aristocracies and of the fear that they would come to dominate the new government. R. R. Livingston answered this charge in the New York debates. "The truth is, in these republican governments, we know no such ideal distinctions. We are all equally aristocrats. Offices, emoluments, honors, are open to all."[16]

---

[14] *Ibid.*, p. 19.
[15] *Elliot's Debates*, Bk. I, vol. 3, pp. 294-95.
[16] *Ibid.*, vol. 2, p. 278.

Presidents over the years added their descriptions to the tradition of equality. Jefferson, in his First Inaugural Address, declared that an essential principle of our government was "equal and exact justice to all men, of whatever state or persuasion, religious or political. . . . " He said "that the minority possess their equal rights, which equal law must protect, and to violate would be oppression." The content of equality he spelled out in this phrase: "entertaining a due sense of our equal right to the use of our own faculties, to the acquistions of our own industry, to honor and confidence from our fellow-citizens, resulting not from birth, but from our actions and their sense of them. . . . " Andrew Jackson provided this memorable definition of equality:

> Distinctions in society will always exist under every just government. Equality of talents, of education, or of wealth can not be produced by human institutions. In the full enjoyment of the gifts of Heaven and the fruits of superior industry, economy, and virtue, every man is equally entitled to protection by law; but when the laws undertake to add to these natural and just advantages artificial distinctions, to grant titles, gratuities, and exclusive privileges, to make the rich richer, and the potent more powerful, the humble members of society . . . who have neither the time nor the means of securing like favors to themselves, have a right to complain of the injustice of their Government. There are no necessary evils in government. Its evils exist only in its abuses. If it would confine itself to equal protection, and, as Heaven does its rains, shower its favors alike on the high and the low, the rich and the poor, it would be an unqualified blessing.[17]

---

[17] Quoted in Harris, *op. cit.*, p. 17.

Andrew Johnson expressed this thought: "Here there is no room for favored classes or monopolies; the principle of our Government is that of equal laws and freedom of industry."[18]

A Limited, Negative Role

Certain salient features of the American tradition of equality emerge from the above discussion. First, it is a very *limited* kind of equality that is avowed. *Equality before the law* and an *equality of rights* subsume the various expressions of it. Second, it assumes a *negative* role for government. This theme occurs repeatedly: Congress shall make *no* law . . . ; *No* bill of attainder . . . shall be passed; *No* title of nobility . . . shall be granted; *No* room for favored classes . . . ; *No* capitation or other direct tax shall be laid. . . . The impact of this is positive, though the statements are negative. It means that men are freed from the restraints of fixed classes and orders, that they can use their energies to achieve their ends, so long as they do not violate the equal rights of others in doing so. Third, it in no way prescribes that men shall cease to make distinctions nor that differences will cease to exist. On the contrary, in the absence of legally prescribed positions, *there may be as many differences of degree as there are individuals*, to the despair of sociologists no doubt. Each man has the opportunity—so far as law is concerned—to rise as high as he can, to acquire as much as he can, to achieve whatever deference his neighbors will pay to him. Fourth, such a conception of *equality is consonant with liberty;* indeed, it is a concomitant of the greatest liberty.

---

[18] Rushdoony, *op. cit.*

I make this point because many thinkers have thought they perceived an inevitable tension between liberty and equality. But so long as equality is limited to the narrow sphere defined above, so long as the role of the government is negative, so long as men are free to move within informal social arrangements, there is no necessary antipathy between liberty and equality.

But equality can, and often has, become the basis for revolutionary action. It can be transformed easily into a social goal which when men adopt it can be the proclaimed end for laying waste to the social order and erecting tyrannies. This is why I have felt it necessary to treat it very gingerly thus far. I believe that equality was a viable part of the American tradition. I also believe, however, that it has been subtly transformed in the course of our history until today it is being used as a basis for oppression. This situation came about by subtle changes in the content of the word equality wrought by shifting the meaning of ideas which informed it.

Government Redistribution

Let us take an example to demonstrate how the shift occurred. Many would assent to the proposition that the American tradition of equality is one of equality of opportunity. This is true of the older tradition only in a very limited sense. If by equality of opportunity is meant that legally all men may undertake whatever pursuit they choose with no legal distinctions among them, this was at the heart of the tradition. But suppose we begin to think about it in an another way. Suppose we notice that in fact men are not on an equal footing when government remains neutral. Some men have the advantage of having had wealthy parents, of a better cultural environment, of more formal education, of better manners taught in the home, of greater native intellectual ability, and so on. We might conclude, as many Americans did, that without some positive governmental action men do not have an equality of opportunity.

One of the first widespread efforts to close this gap was by providing education for all at the expense of the taxpayers. Beyond this, the progressive educationists, following John Dewey's ideas, have attempted to equalize opportunities by lavishing attention upon the slower students and relatively neglecting the brighter ones, if not holding these latter up to scorn. This was but a beginning, of course. Some children do not get a good diet at home, and their lunches are inadequate. The situation might be further equalized by providing inexpensive lunches for the children. Some children do not get the maximum benefit from their meals because of dental defects. Free dental examinations, at the least, are then provided. I could go on, but surely everyone knows of the proliferating programs of the schools for providing an "equality of opportunity."

But these programs have only scratched the surface of the inequalities among children. Some children still come from homes on the "wrong" side of the tracks. Some still have minority religious, racial, and ethnic backgrounds which may call forth different treatment from their "peers." A start might be made on "equalizing" these things by removing all references to religion from the school and by mixing racial and ethnic groups with the general population.

Forced Equalization

Logically, however, much more must be done to provide "real" equality of opportunity. All environmental and
cultural differences will have to be obliterated. This would
probably mean that children would have to be taken from
their parents shortly after birth and brought up in a
uniform environment provided by the state. Even the
lustiest of American reformers have usually shrunk
from such a thorough program, though Jean Jac-
ques   Rousseau—their   spiritual   godfather—recommended it two hundred years ago. The most we can
say at the moment is that the American "pragmatic" experiment in equality has not yet reached the stage where
this final step appears "necessary." It is, however, a logical extension of steps currently being taken.

The major changes in ideas which altered so drastically the content of equality can be stated briefly. Equality
came to be interpreted positively, materialistically, and
realistically. This followed a general shift in thought in
America that began to be felt in the latter part of the nineteenth century. This was accompanied by the spread of
the idea that the government should act positively to effect an equality of condition. In short, equality was to be
advanced collectively by the use of the power of the state
which was now conceived by some as the arm of the people considered collectively. Equality became an unlimited
concept—an ideal (or goal) for the society—something
to be sought and accomplished by the society. Democracy,
conceived as political participation by the "people," was to
be the means to this end; but democracy, conceived as an
equality of condition, became an end of itself.

The New Deal

There is not space here to demonstrate all of these changes. The following example, quoted from Franklin D. Roosevelt's Second Inaugural Address, demonstrates a political expression which followed upon this transformation:

> I see a great nation, upon a great continent, blessed with a great wealth of natural resources. . . . I see a United States which can demonstrate that, under *democratic* methods of government, national wealth can be *translated* into a spreading volume of human comforts hitherto unknown, and the lowest standard of living can be raised far above the level of mere subsistence.
>
> But here is the challenge to our *democracy:* In this nation I see tens of millions of its citizens—a substantial part of its whole population—who at this very moment are denied the greater part of what the very lowest standards of today call the necessities of life. . . .
>
> It is not in despair that I paint you that picture. I paint it for you in hope—because the *Nation*, seeing and understanding the injustice in it, proposes to paint it out. We are determined to make every American citizen the *subject* of *his country's interest and concern.* . . . The test of our progress is not whether we add more to the abundance of those who have much; it is whether *we provide* enough *for those who have too little.*[19]

We are all familiar with many of the programs by which the efforts to effect equality have been made, with Social Security, with the Federal Housing Administration, with the various direct relief programs, with minimum wages and hours legislation, with special concessions made to unions to "equalize" their bargaining power, with the

---

[19] Italics mine.

graduated income tax, with excess profits taxes, with the Tennessee Valley Authority to "equalize" the price of electricity, with regulated freight rates, with the efforts of the Supreme Court to integrate the schools, and with numerous other programs, some less dramatic than those mentioned.

We are familiar, too, with complaints of conformity among the young, of the uniformity of housing financed with F. H. A. loans, of the unimaginative content of the school programs, of spreading crime and delinquency, of the tenacious blot of unemployment, of union violence and race riots. We have been troubled by inflation, by proliferating government regulations, by the ubiquitous tax collector, by the disintegration of the family.

"Equality" by Discrimination

Are there connections among these developments? I believe so. Once government acts positively to equalize the conditions of the citizenry, it must act *unequally* upon the individual members of the populace. The *government* must make distinctions among people. If it is to redistribute the wealth, it must take from those who produce and give to those who do not, thus making an invidious distinction between producers and nonproducers. If it is to prevent racial discrimination, it must acknowledge the race of litigants. If it is to balance the "power" between employers and employees, it must make a distinction between the two, granting to one and withholding from the other. In effect, our government has taken long strides toward creating special classes of people: i.e., union members, racial and ethnic minorities, farmers, government workers by way of civil service, and so on. In order to make men equal—or with that proclaimed objective—the government must perpetuate inequities, at least in the traditional sense. It should not surprise us if all sorts of unwanted social consequences follow upon such action.

If my analysis is correct, we have broken drastically with the American tradition of equality. Many practices have now been institutionalized which run almost directly counter to it. This idealized conception of equality threatens revolution in contemporary society, and could only be realized, if at all, by rooting out the last vestiges of liberty, removing choice, and obliterating differences from one man to another. Even then, I think it will fail of its objective. Those who work by government to effect these ends will erect new distinctions and classes more in keeping with their desires. It has already happened in other countries animated by the goal of equality.

8.

Of Rights and Responsibilities

IDEAS that have come unsprung from the context which gave them vitality, practices that have been cut loose from the tradition in which they subsisted, may be likened to cancerous cells which prey at will upon the physical body. Again, when such developments have occurred, the resulting growths may be compared to the parasitic suckers on a corn stalk which sap the life of the original plant but produce little or nothing of their own. Something analogous to the above has happened to the American tradition of rights and responsibilities. "Rights" proliferate like wild cancer cells: e.g., the "right" to an education, the "right" to a "decent" wage, the "right" to a comfortable home, the "right" to adequate medical care, the "right" to vote, the "right" to the use of public buildings, and so on. The "right" to strike is fastened like a "sucker" upon and saps the vitality of the right of a man to the use of his property. The thrust to the provision of "rights" for minorities threatens to crush the residue of individual rights in America.

It is no different in the matter of "responsibilities." They grow apace, in number and variety, while those matters which were formerly held to be the responsibility of individuals wither and die. President Kennedy has exhorted us: "Ask not what your country can do for you, but what you can do for it." If juvenile delinquency increases, we are all somehow to blame, according to the current mythos. If Negroes are mistreated, all Americans have a part of the guilt. If peoples in faraway lands are "underprivileged," it is somehow the fault of the well-fed American. On the other hand, less and less is left solely for the individual to do for himself.

Under Cover of Confusion

Undoubtedly, it is true that those whom the gods would destroy they first make mad. It may be said with equal validity that those whom the gods would destroy they first *confuse*. At any rate, there should be no doubt that the deterioration of the American tradition has taken place beneath a cover of widespread confusion. There are many sources of this confusion. The belief that people have certain rights is a part of the heritage of Americans. But when something has been long established, people tend to forget the sources of it. Once established, practices tend to continue to be followed, and people will forget the basis of them.

But the current confusion about rights and responsibilities has more direct causes also. There has been a general decline in the precision of the use of language and a neglect in the teaching of logical thinking. Thus, vague expressions of ideas and questionable practices may go unchallenged. Reformers in America have found it practical to advance their programs indirectly and to install them gradually. To accomplish this, they have employed the rhetoric of tradition—which includes such words as rights and responsibilities—to promote their programs which are profoundly antitraditional. Collectivist, statist, and egalitarian ideas have been subtly advanced to replace the traditional principles. This has been carried to the point where many Americans must feel that their rights come from the state, that their responsibilities are collective, and that everybody is entitled to a minimum of worldly goods, if not an equality with every other man.

There is confusion, too, about the relation of rights to responsibilities. Conservatives may have contributed more to this confusion than "liberals," for they are given to asserting that rights entail duties and responsibilities. Since people tend to interpret assertions in terms of the prevailing ethos, the assertion may be taken to mean something quite different from what the conservative intended. Many people would no doubt interpret it to mean something like this: We owe the state a great deal in return for the rights it has granted to us. Indeed, President Kennedy has only taken the thought a step further and concluded that we should focus our whole attention upon duties and responsibilities to the state. Such a development, I would interpret as a measure of our general confusion about rights and responsibilities today.

Some Vital Questions

It is a difficult undertaking to find the remains of the American tradition beneath the luxurious growth of rights and responsibilities which now obscure it. Rather than attempt to do that, it will be more profitable to go back in time and try to reconstruct the tradition historically. Some questions will serve to guide us in this task, namely: What was the American tradition of rights and responsibilities?

What was the source of rights? Of responsibilities? Within the tradition, what was the relationship between rights and responsibilities? What were the rights which men claimed? What were the responsibilities? What was the relationship of governments to these rights? Did they grant them, recognize them, protect them? By what practices were rights protected? With what sanctions were responsibilities promoted?

Most of these questions about rights, so far as they involve ideas, have been answered with the utmost brevity in the Declaration of Independence:

> We hold these truths to be self-evident, that all men are created equal, that they are endowed by their Creator with certain unalienable Rights, that among these are Life, Liberty and the pursuit of Happiness. That to secure these rights, Governments are instituted among Men, deriving their just powers from the consent of the governed. . . .

Of course, there is much more to a tradition than felicitous phrasing in an honored document. A tradition is a body of practices, habits, customs, and institutions which may be buttressed by beliefs and ideas. Yet we can only write about it in terms of ideas, so it may be well to approach the tradition of rights and responsibilities from the vantage point of ideas.

There have been many phrasings of the rights which Americans believed were theirs. Jefferson's "life, liberty and pursuit of happiness" is the best known but not necessarily the most apt. Not only are the words not defined but also some of the phraseology is exceedingly vague, laying it open to a great variety of interpretations. For example, what does it mean that one has a "right to life"?

It is possible to interpret the phrase in the following manner. In order to live, one has to have the means of livelihood, i.e., food, shelter, clothing, and so forth. The right to life could be interpreted as a claim upon someone to provide the means of livelihood. The "right to the pursuit of happiness" is so vague that it could be used to justify any licentious pursuit that the most debauched person might dream up.

Life, Liberty, and Property

We know, of course, that these were not the meanings intended by those who subscribed to the sentiments in the Declaration of Independence. The whole ethos of the time as it can be discovered in the writings and documents which remain indicates that something quite different was meant. The usual way of summing up the rights which men believed they possessed was the "right to life, liberty and property." The Massachusetts Declaration of Rights, drawn by John Adams, spells out the meaning which most men of the time would have attached to the words quoted from the Declaration of Independence:

> All men are born free and *independent*, and have certain natural, essential, and unalienable rights, among which may be reckoned the right of enjoying and defending their lives and liberties; that of acquiring, possessing, and protecting property; in fine, that of seeking and obtaining their safety and happiness.[1]

Jefferson defined liberty at one time in such a way that there should be no doubt as to his meaning:

---

[1] *The Political Writings of John Adams*, George A. Peek, Jr., ed. (New York: Liberal Arts Press, 1954), p. 96.

Of liberty then I would say that, in the whole plenitude of its extent, it is unobstructed action according to our will, but rightful liberty is unobstructed action according to our will within limits drawn around us by the equal rights of others. I do not add "within the limits of the law," because law is often but the tyrant's will, and always so when it violates the rights of an individual.[2]

In short, the right to liberty is the right to think, say, and do what we will so long as we do not trespass upon the right of others to do likewise. Happiness, to these men, was the state of enjoying their liberties and the fruits of their labor (for which "property" was a convenient shorthand expression). John Adams suggested additional content to the word "happiness," content which others of his contemporaries may or may not have concurred in. "All sober inquirers after truth, ancient and modern, pagan and Christian, have declared that the happiness of man, as well as his dignity, consists in virtue. . . . If there is a form of government, then, whose principle and foundation is virtue, will not every sober man acknowledge it better calculated to promote the general happiness than any other form?"[3]

No Claim Against Anyone Else

It should be clear from the foregoing that these rights did not establish a positive claim on anyone. On the contrary, they require only that other men respect them and that government protect the citizenry from trespass upon

---

[2] *The Political Writings of Thomas Jefferson,* Edward Dumbauld, ed. (New York: Liberal Arts Press, 1955), p. 55.

[3] Peek, *op. cit.,* p. 85.

their rights. The point can be made more emphatically by investigating the sources of these rights. They were, as the above quotations indicate, conceived of as natural rights, as God-given, as subsisting in the nature of the universe. They were in no sense grants of governments nor bequests of states.

When the Founding Fathers said that man had a right to life, they meant that no one else had a claim on his life, that he was born free and independent. His right to life was his right to do with it as he would, to cherish and nourish it, to dispose of his time and energies as he saw fit. In practice, as modified by tradition, it meant that a man came to the fullness of enjoyment of his rights when he reached an age of maturity. But before that, no one might take the life of another.

The corollary of this proposition is that no one has a natural claim upon the life of another. It follows, then, that the right to life cannot be the right to a livelihood, if it involves any claim upon someone to provide it. For such a claim would be at the expense of another man's right to the use of his life.

The natural rights theory has been the subject of much controversy over the years. Indeed, the theory has now been obscured by the confusion resulting from the controversies. Those who have opposed the validity of this theory have usually argued on the assumption that the belief in natural rights is based upon the historical existence of a "state of nature," and that in this state of nature men enjoyed certain natural rights.

Now there is no doubt that writers in the eighteenth century frequently referred to a state of nature. There should be considerable doubt that they were referring to

an actual historical condition. The historical mode of reasoning, which is most common nowadays, was rarely, if
ever, employed in the eighteenth century. This mode only
came into its own after the publication of the works of
Marx and Darwin, among others. The Founders were thinking in terms of an enduring condition, not one that is
basically changed by the passage of time. True, some
writers did attach the "state of nature" to primitive man,
but this is an accidental connection rather than an essential one, if one is employing a philosophical rather than
an historical mode of reasoning. The "Laws of Nature and
of Nature's God," to which Jefferson refers, are obviously
a permanent part of the universe. They do not await the
confirmation of anthropologists; they are something dis-
coverable in the here and now by the employment of reason. In short, natural rights, to these men, were those
rights which one has by nature.

Unalienable Rights

To demonstrate, let us reconstruct their mode of reasoning. Who has the right to the life of a man? Who could
have gained such a title? Surely *no other man* has it. Who
could have given him such a title? Can one man possess
the life of another? Societies can and have conferred such
titles, of course, but they are fraudulent, according to the
natural rights theory. A man's life is his *in trust;* not
even he may sell it in its entirety. His right to life is "unalienable." Would anyone really care to argue otherwise
today?

Or take a related question. Who has the right to the
fruits of the labor of a man? Would not any man possessed

of common sense conclude that that which he has produced with his own hands from his own materials is *his*? Whose else could it be? Property rights, properly worked out, are only social means for enforcing this individual right.

In the same manner, who can have a right to the use of the faculties of a man, to his liberty? Will it be argued that they really belong to someone else? Can such a right really be conferred by society or the state? The very nature of man proclaims otherwise: He alone can will the use of his faculties and bring them into constructive use. True, a man may be induced by coercion to use his faculties against his "will," but who could legitimately claim a prior right to do this? These rights bear no necessary connection to any real or imagined condition of savages. The introduction of anthropological findings into the discussion of natural rights has only served to confuse the issues. The source of the rights, as conceived within the American tradition, was concisely stated by John Adams:

> I say RIGHTS, for such they have, undoubtedly, antecedent to all earthly government—*Rights* that cannot be repealed or restrained by human laws—*Rights* derived frcm the great Legislator of the universe.[4]

Nonetheless, governments were believed by the Founders to be capable of serving useful functions regarding natural rights. Indeed, Jefferson tells us that governments are created for the express purpose of protecting and defending these rights. In this sense, it could well be said that governments are ordained of God. If there were no governments, the individual would frequently be unable

---

[4] *Ibid.*, pp. 4-5.

to defend his life, liberty, and property. He would be at the mercy of stronger individuals and of bands of men who might despoil him and his. Thus, it is in the true interest of every man that governments be instituted to maintain law and order, to protect life and property, to punish the trespass of some upon others.

Natural Responsibilities of Man

Elaborate theories of "natural responsibilities" did not usually accompany presentations of natural rights theories. One might conclude from this that Americans placed a great deal more emphasis upon rights than upon responsibilities. I think, however, that such conclusions are not warranted. As they conceived them, responsibilities are but the opposite side of the coin on which rights are inscribed, no more separable than is a single coin. It would even be possible to construct a theory of "natural responsibilities" which would be in keeping with what Americans believed and did. I propose to do so here.

What are the natural responsibilities of a man? First, he is responsible for his own acts. Even if coerced, he alone could have released the energy and directed the efforts which consummated a deed. Second, a man is naturally responsible for his own well-being, responsible for providing himself with the comforts of life. He is equipped, by nature, with sensations which inform him of his needs and with faculties which enable him to satisfy these needs. Third, a man is responsible for fulfilling the terms of any contract he enters into. Thus, if a man marries, he incurs knowingly and willingly an obligation to care for his wife in a manner befitting his position and abili-

ties. Fourth, he becomes responsible for any children he
and his wife have brought into the world, to nurture
them until they have reached an age when they can become independent. Nothing could be more natural than
that those who have been responsible for producing life
should care for it during the period when it cannot fend
for itself. Fifth, he has some responsibilities to the society which has provided a framework within which he
can use his faculties for his own ends and for the fulfillment of his obligations. John Adams put the matter
in this way:

> Each individual of the society has a right to be pro-
> tected by it in the enjoyment of his life, liberty, and
> property, according to standing laws. He is obliged,
> consequently, to contribute his share to the expense of
> this protection, and to give his personal service, or an
> equivalent, when necessary.[5]

These responsibilities, it may be noted, bear a demonstrable and complimentary relation to the rights set forth
above. If a man has the right to the use of his faculties,
he is responsible for the manner in which he uses them.
His right to his life embraces the responsibility for caring for himself and his own so that he exerts no claim on
another man's time. It might be added that since he has
unwittingly claimed the time of his parents he has in-
curred some obligation to them. Since by nature they will
probably live into their declining years, he should be
obliged to look after them during the period of their se-
nility. Since government exists to protect a man's rights,
he is responsible for maintaining it in its performance of

---

[5] *Ibid.*, pp. 98-99.

this function. Military service in defense against aggressors is an obvious obligation of a man. These responsibilities reinforce rather than diminish the rights claimed earlier. It is true that a tax for the support of governments and armies will take some portion of the fruits of the labor of a man. But if government contents itself with its protective function, the amount of the diminution should be small and the advantage of the protection would more than make up for the loss.

Moral Obligations

What of numerous other responsibilities which might be named? Are there not "neighborhood effects" of a man's action. Should not a man contribute to the education of other men's children? Are there not moral obligations to help the needy, to support churches, to contribute to those who have been victimized by some natural catastrophe, to care for widows and orphans, and so forth? Perhaps these are *moral* obligations. Many of us believe that they are. But by bringing them up for discussion, I have crossed the line from *natural* rights and responsibilities to *moral* obligations and duties. If there is to be a distinction between the *legal* and the *moral* realm, this line must not be transgressed by law. In the American tradition, natural rights were something to be protected by law. Natural responsibilities could also be enforced by law, though this was not always the case. In themselves, these rights and responsibilities were believed to be moral, but they did not begin to embrace the whole moral realm.

If pressed to deal with this distinction, many men at

the time of the making of the American tradition would
probably have said that beyond the realm of the natural
lies the supernatural, beyond the physical lies the metaphysical, beyond reason there is revelation. But this region
"beyond" is a matter for religion, a matter for the individual conscience, a matter for a man and his intimate
relationship to his God. It would be presumptuous for human beings to legislate about such matters. To protect a
man in his natural rights and to hold him to his natural
responsibilities is but to free men for the assumption of
their obligations and duties as they shall choose. But to
impose these moral obligations and duties by law would
be to strip them of their morality for the individual by removing the element of choice. It is one of the curious
anomalies of our time that the courts which have been
so assiduous of late in protecting children from hearing
the Bible read have been not at all concerned about governmental forcing of someone's ideas about our moral
duties to other people's children, to other people's parents,
to people in other countries, upon us. The Supreme Court
strains at gnats and swallows camels. Its piddling decisions
about separating church and state ignore the massive imposition of people's notions of morality upon us.

Governments Restricted

There were numerous American habits, customs, documents, and institutions which indicate that the above ideas
did inform the tradition of rights and responsibilities.
Since the rights claimed were natural rights, they needed
no positive enactments of law to confer them. There was
the danger, however, that the governments created to

protect these rights would usurp them. Thus, governments were prohibited by the various constitutions from invading the rights of Americans. The Bill of Rights is an example of this at the national level, and state constitutions usually contained similar features. Property was protected by requiring payment and due process of law for its alienation from an individual. Life and liberty were protected by numerous safeguards also. The enumeration of the powers of the various branches of government was an attempt to restrict the activities of government to those functions deemed desirable for the protection of life, liberty, and property. Negro slavery, which certainly ran counter to this whole philosophy, was in time abolished, and the rights of Everyman were secured in America. Such a statement ignores many violations and usurpations of the rights of individuals which undoubtedly occurred from time to time, but it would be true to say that these were exceptions to the rule.

Voluntarily Assumed Obligations

Responsibilities were quite often not imposed by law. In the nineteenth century, wars were usually fought with volunteers. The opinion of the community was quite often sufficient to impel men, who might otherwise have evaded them, to the living up to their responsibilities. It was expected that parents would feed and clothe their children, educate them formally or otherwise, prepare them for their lives as adults. It was expected that the children would look after aged, disabled, or destitute parents, that relatives would provide for widows and orphans, that the community would come to the aid of those who could not support themselves and were without relatives to help them. Houses were often large in an earlier America, and it was not unusual for a family to take in maiden aunts and disabled relatives. Charity was extended voluntarily to those in need on a large scale, as I have shown elsewhere.

Such was the American tradition of rights and responsibilities. But, as I indicated at the beginning of this chapter, the ideas have come unsprung from their context and practices have been cut loose from the tradition. Americans still speak of rights. Indeed, there seems to be no end to the rights which they claim. One does not hear much any more of the right to life, liberty, and property (especially, *not* property), but there is a great deal of talk about the right to work, to strike, to equal treatment from everyone, to a decent wage, to a comfortable home, to medical care, to an education, to security in old age, to protection from unemployment, and to all sorts of goods and services.

There are new responsibilities, too: to the state, to the world, to the community, to the school, to the tax collector, to labor, to farmers, to the "underprivileged," to the armed forces. By the same token, older responsibilities have been sloughed off. The Public Welfare Department will look after aged parents with tax moneys. The community will educate the children, if it can't get federal aid. A man need not take too seriously his responsibility to provide for himself and his own; if he fails, he will be buoyed up by unemployment compensation, social security, and prepared for other work by retraining programs. All of this is supported by taxation, of course.

It should be abundantly clear that these new "rights"

and "responsibilities" are not natural in their origin. Instead, they must be provided by the state. In order to provide them, the state must curtail property rights, diminish the right of a man to the fruits of his labor, and undercut the basis of independence upon which the exercise of rights depends. Moreover, the state can only provide these "rights" by increasing its powers greatly. Since there is no natural (or reasonable) basis for these new "rights," the result is the augmentation of power which is then used arbitrarily—in short, oppression.

Latter-Day Rights and Duties

Although these latter-day rights and responsibilities have no natural basis, they do have a foundation of sorts. They are founded upon an ideology. In effect, this means that they are the creations of intellectuals. They are based upon what some intellectuals think should be, rather than what is. These men are the only ones privy to their motives. For aught we know, they may have the best of intentions. Confusion is widespread, and there is little evidence that many intellectuals are not victims of it also. They may be fully convinced that their new creations are "rights." At any rate, they have used the traditional rhetoric to advance them. Most of them have accepted the notion that the theory of natural rights has been discredited, but they have relied upon the traditional belief in rights to advance their own. Modern intellectuals are not noted for their piety, but they have appealed to sentiment and morality to get public acceptance of their programs.

But let us not play with words longer. There is no right to strike, no right to an education, no right to employ-

ment, no right to medical care, no right to decent housing, and no other right which man can create at will. Insofar as these things are provided, they are governmentally granted privileges. They are privileges granted at the
expense of the rights of men. Natural rights could be a
part of the tradition of Americans because they stem from
the nature of human existence and most men would believe them, or act upon them, if they had never heard of a
theory of natural rights. A little child knows that if he has
made something with his hands, it is his. On the contrary, it takes great ingenuity by thinkers and widespread
confusion for people to be convinced that the fruit of
the labor of others is theirs. Undoubtedly the complexity
of modern economies may make such confusion easier.
But the strange conclusions are the work of intellectuals,
not simply the product of complexity.

Unreasoned Assumptions

In like manner, the new "responsibilities" have to be
dinned into our ears constantly, in the hope that we will
accept them. It is easy for a man to understand that he
is responsible for nurturing a child that he has fathered,
but he cannot readily see that he is responsible for suffering in Vietnam. There is a reason for this difficulty. Most
of us are *not* responsible for the suffering in Vietnam, or
anywhere else in the world. The bread that we eat did not
come from their fields. The clothes that we wear were
not made in their mills. If they are hungry, our fullness
did not create it. In short, each of us is *not* responsible for
all of us, and all of us are *not* responsible for each of us.
Such conceptions of responsibility cannot stand the light

of reason; they prosper only in the darkness produced by the heavy cloud of confusion.

The American tradition of rights and responsibilities could stand close examination. It was based upon realities that were and are close to everyone, realities that are either timeless or unlikely to change. Government-granted privileges and imposed duties and obligations are the figments of fertile imaginations, word covers for a thrust to power, whatever the intentions of those who have advanced them. They are temporary things, existing at the whim of legislators and administrators. On the other side of the cloud of confusion, if we persist in wandering through it, lies an age-old tyranny.

9.

Of Voluntarism

$\mathbf{M}$AN IS IN MANY ways a social be-
ing. Many undertakings are beyond the abilities, energies,
or powers of an individual to accomplish. Most men not
only need the help of others at many times but they also
take pleasure in the company of others while they work.
Voluntarism is the means of undertaking joint ventures
without the use of compulsion. It is the way of persuasion, not coercion; of choice, not dictation; of willed action, not forced participation; of variety, not uniformity;
of competition, not monopoly; of freedom, not subjection.
If the amount of liberty in a society could be measured,
it would probably be in terms of the number of joint undertakings that are left to voluntary effort. Voluntarism
is the complementary side of the coin to individualism;
it is the means of getting social tasks done that is consonant with liberty.

The distinction between the compulsory and the voluntary is between that which is prescribed and enforced by
public authority and that which is left to the initiative of
individuals and groups. There are some difficulties with
this distinction, at least in America. Where the matter at
issue has been decided upon by representatives chosen
by the people, they may be said to have given their assent
to it. Thus, governmentally undertaken action takes on

144

some of the color of voluntary action. It could be argued with the backing of much evidence, too, that the distinction between public and private was neither very clear nor very rigid until well into the nineteenth century. Moreover, there was probably never a time in American history when public undertakings were brought to an irreducible minimum and private raised to the maximum.

These difficulties, however, grow out of the confusion of the tradition with the web of the reality from which it is to be discerned. They are added to by the doctrines of latter day democrats who apparently believe that the onus of compulsion is removed from any prescribed action by voting on it. But the fact that a majority favors it does not remove compulsion from government action, certainly not for the minority. Majority approval does not make governmental action voluntary; rather, it intrudes elements of voluntarism into what would otherwise be unmitigated compulsion.

Man Has Flaws

Assuming that certain governmental functions are essential, the interpenetration of consent to support them helps to make them acceptable and may help to prevent oppression or tyranny. It could be voluntary only if everyone to whom it applied willingly consented to its action at all times. But this is so unlikely that if perpetual voluntary consent were made a condition of the existence of governments, none would exist. Viewed from this angle, majority rule does not justify the extension of public action, for it must still be done at the expense of voluntarism. It only serves to legitimate that minimum of action which

is essential to the protection and order within which individual liberty and voluntarism can operate. This conception lay at the heart of the American tradition.

In addition to being a social being, there is evidence
that man is a flawed being. He is given to enthusiasms
about what is good for other people. Under the sway of
these, he wishes to prescribe and enforce by law the particular sorts of undertakings that accord with his vision.
The particular flaw present in this conceit is a lack of
faith. He fears that if whatever he wants done is not
made compulsory, it will not be done. Persuasion may not
work; exhortation may fail; if the matter is left to choice,
some will neglect that which is so desirable. Some parents
will neglect to provide this good for their children; the innocent will suffer.

The notions about what must be provided (or denied)
by compulsion vary from time to time. Thus, at one time
compulsory church attendance was deemed essential to
the well-being of society; at the present time compulsory
school attendance is believed by many to be a good beyond
question. In discussing these matters with a colleague, I
pointed out that very similar arguments to those made for
compulsory public education could be made for compulsory public religion. Religion, it could be argued, is essential to morality, good citizenship, and the fulfillment of
the individual. If church attendance is not made compulsory, some people will not attend and, what is more to the
point, some parents will not require their children to go
to church, and the innocent will suffer. Moreover, unless
religion is tax supported, some people will have finer
churches and more articulate ministers than others. Some
communities could hardly support a church at all and

would be deprived of any but a part-time minister. Of course, my friend was unmoved. He had a sovereign reply. What I had said would be quite valid in a religious age, but this was a secular one.

His argument might be conveniently turned by replying that if this situation prevailed, it would be all the more reason for requiring public religion. Actually, however, I was not making an argument *for* compulsory religion but *against* compulsory enforcement of someone's views on others. Nor should his conclusion be accepted so readily. By what criteria do we judge that this is a secular age? Not by externals, certainly. Expensively appointed churches dot the land, their ministers probably better paid than ever, their programs better supported, membership at all-time highs, and attendance good by comparison with other ages. If many rural churches have fallen into decay, many suburban churches have been erected in their stead. All of this has been accomplished, too, without compulsion. All things considered, it should be reckoned to be a modern miracle.

A Sign of Vitality

Anything that could survive on such a scale in our day without the support of public authority and tax money must have great vitality. It may be true, as many say, that much of American religion lacks an inner vitality. Having taught in the schools, however, I can report that a similar lack of vitality characterizes much of education. Rather than saying that this is a secular age, it might be more accurate to say that a secular tone has been imparted to the age by way of the unnatural separation of religion and education resulting from public support of education. The consequent tendency to state monopoly of education has polarized two functions which have ordinarily been complementary and has served to drain some of the inner vitality from both. Such a result might be expected from an attempt to intermingle contrary principles in a society.

Why, then, is religion voluntary and education compulsory in America today? No simple answer will suffice. There was a time in colonial America when religion was generally compulsory and education was voluntary. There was a time when both were voluntary in most places. As everyone knows, the earlier situation has been reversed today: religion is voluntary and education is compulsory. If the voluntary be conceived as an area, then it was a growing and extending area in America in the colonial period and in the early period of the United States. It expanded until it embraced even religion.

Established religion was still a very live issue at the time of the drawing of our constitutions. For various reasons—including the love of liberty—the Congress was forbidden to establish a church, and either before or in a few decades, states made similar prohibitions and disestablished the churches. Education was not at this time "established" by law, and its future "establishment" would hardly have appeared as a threat at the time. Hence, constitutional safeguards against compulsory education were not incorporated into fundamental law. The door was left open, as it were, for a departure from voluntarism which was not envisioned at the time.

The central American tradition is one of voluntarism. The evidence for this is so immense that it has never been assembled, nor is it likely that it ever will be in its entirety. But a mountain will tend to dominate an extensive plain, even if the mountain be little more than a hill. Thus, the doings of governments have captured and held the attention of historians over the years, though at an earlier time in our history governments were expected to do and did very little. Every rock on the little mountain which represents government has been overturned while the fertile plain of voluntarism has been largely untended. This bias in our historians has kept hidden from us the great achievements of voluntarism and has greatly exaggerated the importance of government. If we knew better the accomplishments of voluntarism, it might take less faith than we had imagined to rely upon it once again.

The Proper Setting

The story of the American tradition of voluntarism is best told against the background of authoritarianism and the foreground of the current compulsory welfare state. Between these two poles of compulsion lies the bulk of American history. The colonists arriving in America brought with them a considerable heritage of compulsion. They were used to established churches, to mercantilistic restrictions, to monopolistic charters, to initiative for many things stemming from kings or their agents. Early governments were apt to exercise broad and extensive powers.

Religion was prescribed for early colonists in nearly as much detail as is now given to the income tax. For example, Governor Dale of Virginia proclaimed, in 1611, that those persons "who failed to attend daily prayers were to be deprived of their rations for a first offense, whipped for a second, and sent to the galleys for a third. Those who indulged in gaming on the Sabbath or failed to attend Sunday worship were to be even more severely dealt with—the penalty for a third offense being death."[1]

Another writer points out that on the same day of 1636 in which the Massachusetts General Court passed an act authorizing what was to become Harvard College "it granted £5 for loss of an eye to a certain George Munnings; it ordered the towns of the colony to fix wages; and it ceded an island to the town of Charlestown on condition that it be used for fishing."[2] The ubiquitous state is not entirely new to the twentieth century.

Examples of Voluntarism

The relics of transplanted compulsory authority tended to wither like an alien plant in the new soil. More precisely, authority lacked many of the means for maintaining its sway. Not only were conditions different in the New World but also there was no central administrative authority in America, no land monopoly which could be maintained, no hereditary class to wield the authority, and no established bureaucracy to administer the rules. Unoccupied lands were available for the disaffected; colonies competed with one another for immigrants; men showed a "distressing" preference for freedom over authority.

---

[1] Nelson M. Blake, *A History of American Life and Thought* (New York: McGraw-Hill, 1963), p. 45.

[2] Frederick Rudolph, *The American College and University* (New York: Knopf, 1962), pp. 4-5.

By and large, Americans did not become hermits, prizing their independence to the disparagement of all social undertakings, though some Americans did, of course. Instead, they tended to favor voluntary activities. A great deal of voluntarism characterized their undertakings from the first. The earliest colonies were settled by joint-stock companies which were voluntary economic associations chartered by the monarch. The governments in some of the colonies were voluntarily comprised by compact. Communities were apt to be founded by voluntary associations of heads of families. Indeed, "public" and "private" were hardly absolute distinctions. Harvard College was initially started with a grant from the Massachusetts General Court, but an endowment from the estate of the Reverend John Harvard was the source of its name, and it was to become a great private institution. When government has come into being during the lives of and by the agency of living men, it will not appear much different from other voluntary associations.

Early Education

Nevertheless, the trend was away from the compulsory to the voluntary. This appears rather clearly in the matter of education. Massachusetts did enact a law in 1647 requiring towns with a certain number of inhabitants to provide teachers or schools. This did not become the pattern elsewhere, however. The Dutch established some public schools in New York. But when the English took over the colony, these schools "became parochial schools, managed and supported by the Dutch Reformed Church. . . . The English and other non-Dutch groups had to se-

cure education for their children through private schools
maintained by itinerant schoolmasters. . . . "[3]

Pennsylvania attempted a public school at first, but
it was discontinued in 1689. Thereafter, education was
left to private and group initiative. The Quakers, according to one historian, "maintained some of the best ele-
mentary and secondary schools in America. The support
of such schools by subscription and endowment was a
favorite Quaker philanthropy. A large majority of the
pupils paid tuition, but the poor, both Quaker and non-
Quaker, were allowed to attend without paying fees."[4] Thus,
voluntarism developed apace in education. In Virginia,
"old-field schools" demonstrated the classic method of
voluntarism. "Several families on neighboring properties
would cooperate in erecting a rude building, often in an
abandoned tobacco field. Here a master hired by the parents
would teach during the months from April to Septem-
ber."[5] The tendency in the founding of colleges over the
years was from government support initially to private or
denominational schools.

Relief of Poverty a Private Responsibility

In caring for the destitute, the impoverished, and the
disabled, colonists apparently favored private charity to
governmental effort. Loosely, the Elizabethan Poor Laws
applied in America from the beginning. They put the
burden for support initially upon the individual, then
upon the family, and, failing that, the local community.

---

[3] Blake, *op. cit.*, p. 59.
[4] *Ibid.*
[5] *Ibid.*, p. 55.

This, too, became a part of the American tradition. But voluntary charity was more favored by Americans than a tax upon the members of the community.

Cotton Mather, one of the great Puritan divines, was an ardent advocate of private charity. He taught that helping others was a Christian duty, an honor, and a privilege. Significantly, though, he was not only "a one-man relief and aid society," as one writer describes him, but also an advocate of joint voluntary efforts. "He was a tireless promoter of associations for distributing tracts supporting missions, relieving needy clergymen, and building churches in poor communities."[6]

William Bradford told the story of an early charitable action at Plymouth, with his obvious approval of the behavior.

> In ye time of most distress, there wus but 6. or 7. sound persons who to their great commendations be it spoken, spared no pains night nor day, but with abundance of toyle and hazard of their owne health, fetched them woode, made them fires, drest them meat, made their beads, washed their lothsome cloaths, cloathed and uncloathed them; in a word, did all ye homly & necessarie office for them . . . all this willingly and cherfully, without any grudging in ye least, shewing herein true love unto their friends & bretheren.[7]

Another and perhaps better example of voluntary charity in the formation of the American tradition can be seen in the organization of the Scot's Charitable Society in Bos-

---

[6] Robert H. Bremner, *American Philanthropy* (Chicago: University of Chicago Press, 1960), p. 14.

[7] Quoted in *The Heritage of American Social Work*, Ralph E. and Muriel W. Pumphrey, eds. (New York: Columbia University Press, 1961), pp. 12-13.

ton in 1657. They agreed to assemble a treasure "for the releefe of our selves and any other for the which wee may see cause (to make a box) and every one of us to give as god shall moue our harts. . . . "[8]

Many Voluntary Groups

By the time of the War for Independence Americans had become habituated to doing many things voluntarily. The great age of voluntarism, however, was from the time of the revolt from England until World War I. Mercantilistic restrictions were cast off along with the political ties with England, though some of them were perpetuated for a time by some states. A great "common market" was opened by the adoption of the Constitution of 1787. Churches were disestablished in the ensuing years, and religious observance became a voluntary matter so far as governments were concerned. States voluntarily entered the Union. Government offices were filled by those who sought them willingly, without prescription or compulsion. The variety of activities that were performed at one time or another by voluntary associations of people is truly amazing. Wars were usually fought with voluntary armies. Volunteers formed fire departments, brought law and order along the frontiers, made up the posses which sheriffs used on occasions, organized churches, built schools, orphanages, libraries, hospitals, and joined political parties to effect their aims. Men pooled their resources in partnerships, joint-stock companies, and corporations for undertaking large economic endeavors.

----

[8] *Ibid.*, pp. 30-31.

European visitors to America in the nineteenth century usually remarked the great number and variety of associations and organizations. For example, Captain Frederick Marryat, an Englishman who visited America in the 1830's, declared that "the Americans are society mad." He listed 22 of the most prominent benevolent societies in 1834—e.g., American Education Society, American Bible Society, American Sunday School Union, Prison Discipline Society, American Temperance Society, and so on—, but found it necessary to add that there "are many others. . . ."[9]

Voluntary associations ranged from those formed for some temporary task to those which expected to be perpetual. Thus, people gathered in rural America for corn huskings, and women held quilting bees. On the other hand, there were fraternal organizations, associations of veterans of wars, clubs, societies, professional groups, foundations, labor unions, business associations, charitable organizations, and groups for the maintenance of standards. Almost any task that might conceivably warrant joint action was likely to become the basis for some organization and, what was most common, competing groups.

The Happy Consequences

What were the consequences to the society of leaving so much for voluntary groups to do? Economically, America entered the nineteenth century an "underdeveloped nation" and entered the twentieth century a great indus-

---

[9] Frederick Marryat, *A Diary in America,* Sydney Jackman, ed. (New York: Knopf, 1962), p. 309.

trial nation. Most of this was certainly accomplished voluntarily, with a minimum of compulsion. In charity, there is some evidence that there was more giving to the poor than was thought at the time to be good for them. At any rate, associations proliferated. One writer says, "The principle of voluntary association accorded so well with American political and economic theories that as early as 1820 the larger cities had an embarrassment of benevolent organizations."[10]

During the Civil War there was apparently an overabundance of relief to dependents, expended both by voluntary associations and governments. "Measured by money expended, the largest charitable efforts, North and South, were devoted to relieving families of service men. Oft-repeated warnings of the dangers of unwise giving were forgotten for the moment as community and statewide relief organizations solicited contributions. . . . "[11] It might not be accurate to say that no one suffered deprivation undeservedly, though such suffering must have been rare in America. It should be pointed out, too, that governments never entirely abandoned giving some form of relief, but this was usually small during the century.

There can be little doubt that religion flourished after it assumed a voluntary status. New denominations were born; revivals swept whole areas; religion took on a vitality it had not had in America for a long time, if ever. Even a critic of disestablishment had this to say: "I believe that in no other country is there more zeal shown by its various ministers, zeal even to the sacrifice of life; that

---

[10] Bremner, *op. cit.*, p. 47.
[11] *Ibid.*, p. 79.

no country sends out more zealous missionaries; that no country has more societies for the diffusion of the gospel; and that in no other country in the world are larger sums subscribed for the furtherance of those praiseworthy objects as in the eastern states of America."[12]

Educational Opportunity

Education flourished under voluntary auspices also. Sunday schools were begun initially to instruct those in the rudiments of learning who could not get it elsewhere. But the Sunday school soon restricted itself to religious teaching. Private, voluntary, and philanthropic schools were numerous, however. Parochial schools provided education for many. "Provision of schools for poor children without religious affiliations became a favorite charity for public-spirited citizens."[13] The Lancasterian method was imported from England and used to provide the rudiments of learning to many very inexpensively. Of colleges, there was a veritable glut. Over seven hundred passed out of existence before 1860. Why? The reasons are no doubt numerous and complex, but they apparently had little to do with unavailability or inexpensiveness. Francis Wayland of Brown observed, in 1850: "We have produced an article for which the demand is diminishing. We sell it at less than cost, and the deficiency is made up by charity. We give it away, and still the demand diminishes."[14]

There was foreign aid in the nineteenth century, too, though in a somewhat different form than that to which

---

[12] Marryat, *op. cit.*, p. 292.
[13] Blake, *op. cit.*, p. 225.
[14] Quoted in Rudolph, *op. cit.*, p. 220.

we have become accustomed. The Greeks received aid in the 1820's, relief garnered by the activities of voluntary committees. In the same period, many Greek war orphans were brought here for adoption. "In the autumn of 1832, when the starving people of Cape Verde Islands rowed out to a ship hoping to buy food, they were astonished to learn that the vessel had been sent from the United States for the express purpose of relieving their necessities. Individuals and churches in New England, Philadelphia, and New York had heard of their need and had raised thousands of dollars for their assistance."[15] It should be pointed out that Americans were beneficiaries of "foreign aid" from Europe. But it was not from governments. It came from private investors who put money in many American undertakings in the hope of profit. It might be well to point out that they were justified in doing so, for property was secure, and contracts were generally respected in nineteenth century America.

Much is missing from my account of American achievements by voluntary arrangements. No mention has been made of the bountiful sums given by philanthropists such as John D. Rockefeller and Andrew Carnegie, of the support of research, of colleges, of libraries, of medical work, of musical programs, and of churches. No record exists of many humbler but nonetheless important stories of voluntary activities, of farmers spared some deprivation by a collection made up by their neighbors, of the tending of the sick by thoughtful members of the community, of the adoption of children by relatives, and, above all, of those many honest individuals who suffered somewhat on occasion

---

[15] Bremner, *op. cit.*, p. 56.

rather than to yield up their self-respect which they valued more than ease of circumstance.

Defenders of Voluntarism

But enough has been told, surely, to indicate that the voluntary way was very much a part of the American tradition. It was a tradition that fitted into a way of life, a way of life which embodied individual independence, responsibility, morality, as well as social concern, activity, and family and community respect. This way of life approved both generosity and gratitude. There were those who knew how to defend it in the nineteenth century. For example, President Pierce vetoed a bill in 1854 which would have provided federal aid for the care of the insane. He had this, among other things, to say:

> I readily, and I trust feelingly, acknowledge the duty incumbent on us all, as men and citizens, and as among the highest and holiest of our duties, to provide for those who, in the mysterious order of Providence, are subject to want and to disease of body or mind, but I cannot find any authority in the Constitution for making the Federal Government the great almoner of public charity throughout the United States. . . . It would, in the end, be prejudicial rather than beneficial to the noble offices of charity. . . .[16]

Or note the horror with which Daniel Webster described a proposal to draft an army in 1814. "That measures of this nature should be debated at all, in the councils of a free government is cause of dismay. The question is nothing less than whether the most essential rights of per-

---

[16] Pumphrey and Pumphrey, *op. cit.*, p. 133.

sonal liberty shall be surrendered and despotism embraced in its worst form."[17]

Opposing the creation of a national university supported by the taxpayers, President Eliot of Harvard, speaking in 1873, declared that "our ancestors well understood the principle that to make a people free and self-reliant, it is necessary to let them take care of themselves, even if they do not take quite as good care of themselves as some superior power might."[18]

Much of the heritage of voluntarism has come down to the present day. Many colleges and universities are still aided by individual bequests, foundations, alumni, and friends. Community Chests are still assembled from private giving. Voluntary associations, fraternal organizations, and groups for various purposes still abound. But this should not disguise from us the massive departures from the tradition of voluntarism that have occurred in this century. More and more activities which were formerly left to voluntary effort are prescribed, compelled, and done by governments. It has reached the point that President Kennedy may circle a "disaster area" in a helicopter before the Red Cross arrives. I do not exaggerate. In the midst of a recent natural catastrophe, the newscaster announced that the President was in touch with developments and stood ready to offer aid.

There is not space here to detail the story of the decline of voluntarism and the growth of compulsion in America. Its outlines can only be suggested. Reformers

---

[17] Merle Curti, *et. al.*, eds., *American Issues* (New York: Lippincott, 1960, 4th edition), p. 151.
[18] Quoted in Rudolph, *op. cit.*, p. 185.

abounded in the 1830's and 1840's, some of whom wanted to use government to effect for everyone what they desired for society. Such efforts resulted in the beginning of public (tax) supported education in several states in the 1820's and 1830's, and in the adoption of the first compulsory attendance law in 1852. Some reform ideas were advanced at first on a voluntary basis, such as temperance (or total abstinence), but were turned into lobby organizations to get government action. Labor unions tended to use coercion and violence from the outset, but courts in the nineteenth century usually denied them this as a "right." However, in the twentieth century, they received government protection and exemptions.

The Decline of Freedom

By the late nineteenth century, more than reformers and their enthusiasms was involved in the shift from voluntary to compulsory methods. Various collectivist ideologies were gaining adherents, and many intellectuals fell under the sway of these new ideas. Hence, as conditions changed in America, thinkers and publicists were precommitted to government rather than voluntary solutions, leaving the tradition unsupported and undeveloped. State governments assumed more and more responsibilities: providing "free" schools, public sanitariums, building roads and highways, providing relief, and regulating and controlling economic endeavors.

The thrust was for ever larger governmental units to take over the responsibility of providing services and the task of regulating the endeavors of the citizenry. Thus, we have federal aid to education (already, though to a

limited extent), federal aid to highways, federal aid to
housing, and the federal government engaged in various
economic undertakings. Indeed, more and more "voluntary" undertakings are interpenetrated by government aid
and exemptions. The federal government is well installed
in many universities today by way of the support of various research projects and the provision of scholarships. In
a negative way, government interpenetrates most charitable and religious gifts by allowing them to be tax exempt.

The full extent of the compulsion that follows upon this
expanded governmental activity emerges only gradually.
By executive decrees, by legislation, and by court decisions, it begins to appear that if government has so much
as granted a license for an undertaking this may be used
to justify regulations. This is the principle (or lack of
principle) which is emerging from the current racial dis-
turbance. How long it will take the courts to decide that
any undertaking has a "public" character which has bene-
fited from tax exempt funds is anybody's guess. The hand-
writing is on the wall, however.

There are activities appropriate to government and to
which it is essential. There are other endeavors which
could be left to individuals and voluntary groups. The
historical record of those who settled in English America
and formed these United States suggests that voluntarism
could be utilized to take care of most matters. Records,
old and new, point up the fact that if liberty is to prevail, voluntarism *must* be used to do so. We may know that
it is a part of the American tradition that Americans
should rely upon voluntarism as the method for accomplishing most of their common tasks.

10.

Of the Civilizing of Groups

NEWSPAPER HEADLINES call attention to the events. They tell of demonstrations, of threatened nation-wide strikes, of freedom marches, of crowds turning ugly in their behavior and becoming mobs, of union violence, of sit-downs and sit-ins, of panty raids, of protest meetings, and of giant rallies. Pictures which accompany these stories frequently show police employing night sticks, cattle prods, bloodhounds, and fire hoses, or the National Guard advancing with fixed bayonets behind the cover of tear gas. The particular actors and causes change from time to time. In the 1930's, union violence was the most prominent national phenomenon. In the 1950's, rebels without a cause formed gangs of teenagers to prey upon one another, as well as the innocent. In the 1960's, Negroes and their sympathizers are the actors.

Taken together, however, these events constitute major trends of our times. On the one hand, the developments can be described as massed action by some group, which frequently is transformed by its fervor, or by some unfortunate event, into mob action. On the other, there are the harsh methods of the law enforcers, which appear to become harsher with each new device employed.

The chances are good, of course, that the headline writers will have found new topics before this is published. Shifting from ephemera to ephemera as they do, they are not likely to convey any sustained sense of crisis, even when one exists. It is possible, but unlikely, that Congress will have dealt satisfactorily with the railroad issue and with civil rights. It is much more probable, however, that if they pass any labor legislation it will be but another expedient patch to stave off the inevitable consequences of the crazy-quilt of protective legislation passed earlier.

Be that as it may, it is most unlikely that the trends of this century will be reversed in the immediate future. Massed action by groups, and terror and violence to contain it, are not exclusively, or even particularly, American phenomena. They are world-wide in scope. Violence by groups has been epidemic in this century. It may be reviewed in its most instructive manifestation in Germany during and before the rise to power of the Nazis. Hitler's followers terrorized the opposition and capitalized on the crucial failure to restrain them. Once in power, Hitler used brutal coercion to subdue his own forces and to remove competitors among them. But this was only a more dramatic example of patterns of behavior among communists, fascists, Moslems, newly created African countries, and older European and American countries.

It is tempting to draw the conclusion that civilization has broken down. Those who use the blunderbuss approach to social analysis have pre-empted the position already. But such a conclusion is too all-inclusive to be useful, and it is of doubtful validity. By any criteria that we would be likely to devise, civilization still prevails in many countries and may, for aught we know, be spreading to the remainder. Nevertheless, if my surmise is correct, civilization is gravely endangered by massed group action and political terror and violence.

The phenomena to which I call attention have not gone unobserved, nor is there a lack of popular explanations. Current explanations usually follow one of two lines. If the explainer approves of the group action, he usually accounts for it in terms of intolerable social conditions which have provoked it. For example, it is now a cliché that labor strikes arise from deprivations of the laborer. (Anyone who thinks that this view has been much modified by sociological studies should read some books on economic history.) Already, Negro demonstrations are being explained environmentally. On the other hand, if the writer disapproves the objectives of the action, he will incline to make psychological explanations, e.g., of Nazi behavior or of current American "rightist" movements (which, despite the fact that they have not resorted to violence, are treated by many writers and speakers as if they were underground movements to overthrow the government). Such explanations reveal the ideological predispositions of those who make them. The explanations are chosen to fit the explainer's program.

Mob Action Is a Product

It is not my intention, however, to join the psychologizers and environmentalists in their methods of accounting for group action. Most of what they have to say is either guesswork or irrelevant. History is replete with sufferings which could have provided occasions for mass eruptions. In most cases, no such action occurred. Nor is there any consistently demonstrable connection between the degree of deprivation and the occurrence of resistance. Even if they were right in their causal explanations, however, they offer little by way of solution for the problems raised by mass violence. A man being chased by a mob would receive small comfort from the notion that it was "all in their minds." A Kulak would still be unprotected when he had been told that his fate had been occasioned by economic deprivation. Mobs must still be subdued if anarchy is to be forestalled, whatever the explanation for their existence, subdued by whatever means are necessary.

My point is this: *we are forgetting and have to a considerable extent discarded the methods for civilizing groups. Techniques* for *subduing* mobs are substituted for *methods* of *civilizing* groups. Learned treatises on mob psychology vie for attention with psychological and environmental explanations of group behavior. The police and armies get special training in dealing with groups, and modern technology provides the instruments. Terror and violence used by modern dictators to hold the masses in check are but an extension of methods employed almost everywhere to a more moderate degree. Both the mob action and the techniques by which it is quelled are eloquent testimony to our failure to civilize groups. The current alternatives favored by "liberals" amount to admonitions to submit to the pressure and coercion of the group.

As implied above, there is another possibility of dealing with groups. It is to civilize them. And there *was* an American tradition of the civilizing of groups. But it has rarely, if ever, been articulated, and it has now fallen into such obscurity that it must now be exhumed, as it were. I may be pardoned then for taking a circuitous path to view the remains. The tradition can best be understood after we have reviewed the steps we have taken away from it.

Our failure to civilize groups stems from three directions: (1) not keeping clearly before us the important distinctions between individuals and groups; (2) falling prey to certain delusions about group behavior; (3) discarding the principles men have learned for civilizing groups. The corrective of these was once a part of the American tradition.

Group Action Is Different

Groups are not simply collections of individuals. This fact is well enough known, yet it needs to be spelled out in order to demonstrate that we have fallen into some delusions. Any reflective person should be able to provide examples from his own experience of differences between individuals and groups. For example, everyone must have had this happen to him. In a conversation with one other person, you have discovered that person to be sympathetic, polite, and thoughtful. You may go away from such an experience concluding that you have met and are coming to know a genuine human being. Your next meeting, however, may take place in a group. Here the person who was congenial when alone with you may make cutting remarks and align himself with the others of the group against you on matters upon which you were sure you would agree. A little reflection should convince us, if we are not entirely unusual, that we have done the same thing ourselves.

An explanation for this transformation is not far to

seek. Most of us are to some extent insecure when we enter a group, however casual and temporary the grouping. To allay this uneasiness, most men will attempt to identify with the crowd. In so doing, they take on the coloration and mood of the group, tend to suppress their differences, subordinate their reason to the common passion, and make common cause against whoever or whatever would upset the mood. Little boys will give chase to the one whose differences are too apparent; grown men will turn upon the intruder and subject him to ridicule.

If the grouping is temporary and the occasion social, men will soon go their separate ways and reassume their individual identities. However, if the grouping is more nearly permanent, if it articulates a cause or has been brought together for a cause, the identity of the individual may be more nearly merged with it. In that case, the sense of power which comes from identification with and of righteousness in a shared cause will replace the insecurity. At this point, a group can easily become a mob; at the least, it poses a potential threat to all outside of it. Not all groups, of course, become mobs. But that is my point. There are useful groups, and there are dangerous groups. The difference between them is the degree to which they have been civilized.

Anyone who has worked with aggregates of people should have noted some differences between groups and individuals. Groups do not think or reason; that is solely a function of the individual. On the other hand, individuals, feeling the strength of numbers, are emboldened to do things which they would be afraid to do alone. Children in a classroom will become defiant if they sense the class is with them, and one may observe them darting their eyes about over the room to assure themselves that the others are behind them. At a more serious level, anyone who has endured the abuse of massed pickets when he crossed the line can testify to the loss of inhibition which accompanies the merging with a group. People tend to lose their sense of individual responsibility as they become a part of a crowd. Moreover, it is very doubtful that groups can create, whereas, they are very adept at destruction. No mob could erect a building, for such an undertaking requires an ordering of activity which would remove the mob character of a collection of people, but a mob can readily wreck a building.

Delusions About Group Behavior

With these differences in mind, some contemporary ideas about groups take on the appearance of delusions. The most general of these notions is that direct action by groups (or the *people*) is desirable. In American history, this idea was advanced most forcefully by those whom we call Progressives. They were particularly prominent in the early twentieth century, but most of the political reforms enacted since were promoted during this time. Progressives had in mind the more or less direct political action involved in the direct election of Senators, the recall of judges, and the initiative and referendum. This, as it turns out, was the program of reformers out of power, for once in the power they have preferred to use the established machinery of government for their ends.

Other kinds of direct action by groups, however, were fostered by reformers over the years, under such rubrics as "industrial democracy" and "agricultural democracy."

Under the former, union members voted to bind individuals to their decisions; under the latter, farmers voted themselves a cut of the tax take. Such direct action, of course, advances the interest of the in-group both at the expense of the individual and of the general welfare.

Another delusion is that causes and ideologies can provide a sufficient basis for controlling groups in their common endeavors. This is a delusion which appears to pervade intellectual circles around the world. Ideologies *can,* at least in theory, unite people; causes can provide a focus for collective action. But they do not usually contain limits which would control the people. For example, democracy is considered by many in the West to be a sufficient cause for social unity and common action in the world today. By contrast, many in the East have succumbed to the notion that communism can provide an ideology which will accomplish these ends. Both are wrong. Democracy, cut loose from its mooring in an older tradition, serves, as do all ideologies in our day, as a shibboleth by would-be dictators in their thrust to power.

This is not accidental; it is central. We appear to be regularly astonished that governments which were announced as democratic, by our press as well as the propaganda outlets within the country involved, shortly become despotic and quite often turn into military dictatorships. I cite Castro's regime as an example, but the number of them around the world today is legion. The people cannot create; they can only destroy when they act collectively and directly. Ideologies cannot change this. They can serve as a basis of unity for destroying whatever exists, but this only raises the problem of order rather than settling it. Most modern revolutions have foundered as the leaders attempted to come to grips with this problem. If a predetermined ideology is to be realized, if tradition is discarded, that order must be centrally directed and imposed from above. For this, dictators, terror, and violence are the usual means.

The third delusion is the belief that the end justifies the means. So baldly stated, I suppose that most Americans would deny that they believe it. Yet many Americans speak and act as if they believed it. Direct group action is supposed to be justified if the circumstances are bad enough to warrant it, or if the cause is sufficiently just in the eyes of the person making the judgment. Thus, direct action violence and sabotage by labor unions would be supposed by many to have been justified by the deprivation of the workers. Or, to take a current example, many people apparently believe that direct action by Negro groups is justified by wrongs that have been perpetrated upon Negroes. But the righteousness of the cause does not alter the character of groups. For aught I know, the violence of groups during the reformations of the sixteenth century was activated by the purest of human visions, the protection of the immortal souls of men, but this did not prevent the rape and pillage which were widespread. In like manner, "nonviolent" Negro groups are readily transformed into violent groups, and even mobs.

There are various other delusions about groups which I can only suggest here. There is the belief that some are made "good" by the make-up of their membership, i.e., laborers, farmers, minority groups, and so forth. This is sheer nonsense, and it would need to be disproved only to those who are victims of ideologically induced blindness. There is the notion that the individual's interest is permanently merged with that of some group. Yet this is only so if his belonging is prescribed by law. Otherwise, men will shift from group to group depending upon inclination and circumstances. One of the prime delusions is that freedom can be advanced by direct action. Having loosed the potential mob, however, nothing is more likely than that dictatorship and oppression will be used to contain it. The French Revolution is the classic example of the working out of the eventualities of the arousal of the crowd while destroying the traditional checks upon it.

Forgotten Principles of Law and Order

In large, my point is that the ideologies to which many intellectuals have fallen prey, along with those who have simply been attracted by the glowing phrases informed by ideology, have tended to rely upon some kind of group action and solidarity. But they have not taken into account the nature of groups, and thus the thrust toward the realization of these ideologies has been accompanied by terror, violence, dictatorship, and totalitarianism. In America, of course, the violence has been somewhat restrained thus far, the repression less pronounced. This was true because Americans had a long tradition of law-abidingness, and American institutions provided a framework for civilizing groups. Ideologues have been shielded from the consequences of their ideas by the very tradition they have deplored.

With this background in mind, the American tradition of the civilizing of groups can be profitably examined. More than one way has been devised for civilizing groups, however. Medieval Europe developed quite different means from those we associate with America, and the American tradition was made both in opposition to this older way and with the remains of it. Thus, something should be said on this head. It will be useful also in providing a standard of comparison.

In the Middle Ages, groups were civilized, to the extent that they were, by giving legal recognition to them, chartering them, giving them status, and regulating them. Workmen were organized in guilds, landholders and fighters into a nobility, students in colleges, people with a religious vocation into clerical orders, and so forth. Orders were granted privileges presumed to be suited to their tasks, or their members claimed rights by ancient usage and by virtue of their role in society. Charters served as a basis for regulating the activities of townsmen. Guilds minutely regulated the quantity and quality of goods produced, the prices for which they could be sold, and the methods of tradesmen. The nobility was regulated by a hierarchy of nobles in which the members were bound together by oaths of allegiance and fidelity.

Conflicts between groups occurred, of course, and were even ritualized into tournaments. Men were supposed to be held to their oaths by fear of the dread consequences which were expected to follow if they should be broken. The church could punish offenders in a variety of ways, such as denying absolution, excommunication, and refusal to bury the dead in consecrated ground. As kings grew in power, they were able to subdue unruly groups by force.

One of the most potent means for the civilizing of groups is the use of rules, forms, and rituals. These are to groups what good manners are to the individual—habitual and customary means for order and discipline. Ideals may also be most useful in restraining and directing the behavior of groups. All of these were dramatically exemplified in the Middle Ages. Almost every activity was preceded by ceremony and done according to prescribed forms. Elaborate rituals were developed for initiation into certain groups. For example, here is a description of the ceremony by which some became knights:

> The candidate was first given a ritual bath . . ., a sort of baptism purifying him from sin. He was then clothed in a white linen tunic symbolic of his purity, a scarlet robe to remind him of his duty if need be to shed his blood for the Church, and black hose to symbolize death. He must fast for the twenty-four hours preceding his initiation, and spend the night watching upon his arms before the high altar of the church. . . . The following morning he must confess his sins, attend Mass, and make his communion.[1]

After which, the formal ceremony of knighting took place. In addition, knights were supposed to conform to a code of behavior and strive to realize certain ideals. John of Salisbury described these duties as follows:

> To defend the Church, to assail infidelity, to venerate the priesthood, to protect the poor from injuries, to pacify the province, to pour out their blood for their brothers (as the formula of their oath instructs them), and, if need be, to lay down their lives. . . . But to what end? . . . Rather to the end that they may execute the judgment that is committed to them to execute; wherein

---

[1] James W. Thompson and Edgar N. Johnson, *An Introduction to Medieval Europe* (New York: W. W. Norton, 1937), p. 324.

each follows not his own will but the deliberate decision of God, the angels, and men, in accordance with equity and the public utility. . . .[2]

The relationships between lord and vassal were spelled out in great detail in contracts. If a man had more than one lord, these contracts became quite complex, as in the following example: "I, John of Toul, make known that I am the Liege man of the Lady Beatrice, Countess of Troyes, and of her son Theobald, Count of Champagne, against every creature, living or dead, saving my allegiance to Lord Enjorand of Coucy, Lord John of Arcis, and the Count of Grandpré."[3]

Other orders lived according to rules as well. Here is a description of some of the rules under which the Cistercian Order lived:

They have two tunics with cowls, but no additional garment in winter, though, if they think fit, in summer they may lighten their garb. They sleep clad and girded, and never after matins return to their beds. . . . Directly after [singing] . . . hymns they sing the prime, after which they go out to work for stated hours. They complete whatever labour or service they have to perform by day without any other light.[4]

The following are prescriptions for those who occupied certain papal lands:

These are the things which the people of Nimfa should do. They should do fealty to St. Peter and Lord Pope Paschal and his successors whom the higher cardinals and the Romans may elect. Service of army

[2] Quoted in James B. Ross and Mary M. McLaughlin, *The Portable Medieval Reader* (New York: Viking, 1949), p. 90.
[3] Quoted in Thompson and Johnson, *op. cit.*, p. 302.
[4] Ross and McLaughlin, *op. cit.*, p. 57.

and court when the court may command. The service which they have been accustomed to do . . ., they should do to St. Peter and the pope. The fourth which they ought to render henceforth, they should render at the measure of the Roman modius. . . .[5]

It would be difficult, if not impossible, to determine how well the medieval system succeeded in civilizing groups. It is probably an irrelevant question, in any case. Most of the system has long since disappeared, preserved only in records and some practices of the Roman Catholic Church, hardly enough to offer a viable alternative in contemporary circumstances. Suffice it to say, the medieval system was designed to establish order and stability, that it provided little room for liberty and was entirely antithetical to equality.

As the medieval order broke down, groups were either crushed by monarchs or made subservient to them. The long range tendency was for the powers once vested in groups to be subsumed by kings, who ruled more or less absolutely. These powers, in turn, came to be vested in the state, according to the doctrine of sovereignty and modern practice. Both individuals and groups were often at the mercy of capricious monarchs. It is too gross a judgment to say that the countries of continental Europe never managed to develop a tradition that would provide for individual liberty and the civilizing of groups. Yet much of modern history is filled with the anarchy of contending groups and the oppressions by which they were brought to heel.

England and America followed a different course, and

---

[5] Norton Downs, ed., *Basic Documents in Medieval History* (Princeton: D. Van Nostrand, 1959), p. 54.

it looked for a time in the nineteenth and early twentieth century as if Europe might follow their example. Currently, the direction of emulation has been to a considerable extent reversed, of course. I would speak, however, of the emergence of the American tradition of the civilizing of groups.

The American tradition can be reduced to several principles.

(1) *Americans used forms and rituals for the civilizing of groups.* These were largely from the inheritance from the Old World. They consisted of parliamentary rules for debates, prayers at the beginning and end of meetings, inaugurations, and installations of officers, the taking of oaths of office, and similar practices of great number and variety. To the thoughtless, these practices may seem of little moment. They are not. Every gathering of people is potentially disorderly, and as numbers increase, the threat to the peace and to individuals mounts. Following rules and forms diminishes this danger. The meeting that begins with prayer is less likely than otherwise to end riotously. The observance of parliamentary rules protects individuals who would speak out and helps to maintain order. Following predetermined orders of business helps to prevent precipitous action.

(2) *The American tradition is one of limited action by groups or the populace as a whole.* Constitutionalism was the device adopted to serve this end. The Constitution set limits upon what governments could do, and, by implication, denied the force of government to groups who might use it for unlimited ends. True, the Constitution could be amended, but it takes so long and is so cumbersome that

groups are not likely to maintain solidarity long enough to amend it. If they do, the more dangerous aspects of group behavior are likely to have been stilled.

(3) *The republican form of government prescribes indirect political action.* Laws were supposed to be passed by *representatives* of the people. When the crowd cannot act directly, much of its force is lost, and its danger is apt to be dissipated. Representatives, even when they represent groups, are likely to be confronted by representatives of other groups in a large country, or so James Madison argued in *The Federalist,* number 10. In that case, they will probably have to resort to reason and persuasion to win their case. The group is civilized not only by having had a voice in decisions but also by participating indirectly and by having to submit to the discipline of parliamentary rules.

(4) *The United States Constitution did not give legal recognition to groups.*[6] At law, there were no classes, orders, or groupings of men possessing privileges, duties, immunities, or exemptions. A New York judge was speaking out of this tradition when he delivered his opinion on the actions of a tailor's union in 1836:

> The law leaves every individual master of his own individual acts. But it will not suffer him to encroach upon the rights of others. He may work or not, as suits his pleasure, but he shall not enter into a confederacy with a view of controlling others, and take measures to carry it into effect. The reason for the distinction is

[6] The one exception was Negro slavery, and that was abolished, of course, by the Thirteenth Amendment. However, states sometimes recognized the existence of groups by privileges and exemptions.

manifest. So long as individual members of the community do not resort to any acts of violence, their hostility can be guarded against. But who can withstand an extensive combination to injure him in his calling? When such cases, therefore, occur, the law extends its protecting shield.[7]

When groups are prohibited by law from committing depredations, long strides have been made toward civilizing them.

(5) *Groups were dependent upon the recruiting of volunteers for their membership and upon their appeal for their continuation.* Individuals were free to join or not to join, to continue their membership or to resign. Far from bringing about the end of all organizations, however, groups of all sorts proliferated in America. Visitors from other shores were astounded at their number and variety. Note, too, that this system made possible the greatest amount of liberty both for individuals and for groups. In this tradition, there was no need to prescribe rules for groups by law. The members of a group could do nothing legally that they could not do as individuals. The group is deactivated as a mob, actual or potential, when it is broken up into individuals. This, the American tradition provided for doing.

Departure from Tradition

To say that there was an American tradition of the civilizing of groups is not to say that groups always be-

[7] *New York* v. *Faulkner,* reprinted in Henry S. Commager, ed., *The Era of Reform,* 1830-1860. (Princeton: D. Van Nostrand, 1960), p. 106. It does not speak well for his objectivity that historian Commager classes it a "notorious" decision.

haved in a civilized manner in America. Indeed, Americans did form mobs on occasion. These mobs did sometimes commit lynchings and other depredations upon the citizenry. But the remedy was ready at hand. Punish the individuals for their unlawful acts and, if conspiracy was involved, punish them for that also.

But Americans have broken radically from this tradition in the last eighty years. Today it is doubtful that there is any longer much of a tradition for civilizing groups. The break was most prominent in several directions. Sophisticates, assorted intellectuals, cynics, and aliens to the culture, along with the careless, undermined the supports to forms, rituals, and rules of order. The falling away from religion removed much of the underpinning from oaths, made prayer on public occasions empty or at least slightly ridiculous, and took away much of the support from forms. A determined informality in America, promoted by relativism, has made those who insist upon observing rules appear stodgy. It has been my misfortune to sit in meetings where the chairman addressed participants informally, thus removing the safeguards to individual dissent and making noisy dissent the alternative to mute acquiescence in what was proposed.

At another level, class theories began to occupy thinkers in the latter part of the nineteenth century. They began to describe labor as a class, business as a class, and farmers as a class. Socialists and assorted reformers were at the forefront of this class thought and the subsequent appeal to people as a class. Notions of the populace as consisting in the main of inert masses of people became prominent.

This development was followed by a thrust to the recognition and empowering of groups by law. The United States government virtually recognized the existence of economic classes by creating departments of agriculture, commerce, and labor. Progressives pressed to remove the safeguards against direct action by advocating the direct election of Senators, the recall of judges, and the initiative and referendum. Corporations were likened to individuals by court decision. Labor unions were given special exemptions by the Clayton Anti-trust Act, the Wagner-Connery Act, and others. Farmers were empowered to vote themselves price supports by various acts.[8]

Extra-Legal Grants of Power

However, much of the practical empowering of groups has not been accomplished by either constitutional amendment or legislative act. Instead, in many instances law enforcement officers have looked the other way while unions employed coercion and violence. Politicians have practiced a policy of divide and conquer on the American people. The Democratic Party has been most adept at this, though the Republicans have often attempted to compete. They have forged a party out of numerous minority groups, making promises and presumably providing favors for them. Many of these groups have become vested interests, legally and extra-legally.

As I write these words, Congress has just been engaged in providing *compulsory* arbitration for the railroads and the related unions. Negroes have gathered in Washington

---

[8] I have treated this development more fully in *The Fateful Turn* (Irvington-on-Hudson: Foundation for Economic Education, 1963), pp. 107-127.

for a massive demonstration. The pattern is repeating itself. The birds are coming home to roost. If the restraints are removed from group behavior by the grant of special privilege, if groups are empowered by law, if direct action is advanced because the end is "good," if the means for civilizing of groups are abandoned, compulsion and authoritarianism must be used to preserve order.

If anyone doubts that the situation is perilous, let him imagine this situation. Suppose the companies in a major American industry were to decide to operate without a union agreement, to throw their doors open and employ whom they would, and to announce this course as their policy in the future. Could anyone doubt that the violence that would ensue could only be curbed by violence? When groups become accustomed to having others submit to threats and pressure, they will become less and less willing to brook resistance. But there comes a time when social order requires resistance to the anarchy of contending groups. The road of resistance, however, leads to despotism in one form or another. Something analogous to the medieval way might be tried, of course, at the expense of liberty and equality. Or, we might begin the now difficult and forbidding task of the restoring of the American tradition of civilizing groups.

11.

Of Free Economic Intercourse

> Freedom of trade, or unrestrained liberty of
> the subject to *hold or dispose of* his property as
> he pleases, is absolutely necessary to the prosper-
> ity of every community, and to the happiness of
> all individuals who compose it.[1]
>
> —PELATIAH WEBSTER

THE PRINCIPLE which informed
American thought about economics during the period of
the forming of the tradition was that *each man should
have the rewards of his labor.* This was a moral ideal,
however, not in itself a tradition. But customs, practices,
laws, and institutions were developed which formed an
American tradition. The particular idea which informed
these latter was free economic intercourse. This phrase
is somewhat unwieldly, but its diminutive—free trade—
has been pre-empted for the more specialized function of
referring to trade among nations. Much more is involved
in economic intercourse than trade among nations.

Free economic intercourse was the means by which
Americans expected each man to receive the rewards of
his labor. How or whether he would get his due was his

---

[1] Quoted in Max Savelle, *Seeds of Liberty* (New York:
Knopf, 1948), p. 211. Webster was an American economic
thinker, among other things, who published a book in 1791
which contains the above declaration.

responsibility, of course. If he were free, he would have no one to blame but himself if he did not. This kind of freedom leaves every man at liberty to pursue his interests in whatever way suits him and implicitly places upon him the responsibility for taking care of himself and his own.

In theory, free economic intercourse embraces all the external conditions by which free individual action in economic matters may take place. It involves the right of the individual to dispose of his goods, his property, his services, and his time at whatever prices and within whatever conditions are agreeable to him. He may sell to or buy from whoever makes an offer which he can or will meet. He may produce goods in whatever quantity of whatever quality he can and will, and offer them for sale wherever it suits him.[2]

This appears so simple and to be so readily understood that we might be led to suppose that men would have perceived it all at the first dawn of consciousness. Yet so far as we know that was not the case historically. On the contrary, the nearest thing to examples of free economic intercourse appear to have occurred among peoples of high intellectual development. Such intercourse may even be a prerequisite of high civilization, or the two may go hand in hand. The explanation is not far to seek. The practices of free economic intercourse can be described simply, but the conditions within which they can regu-

---

[2] There are some obvious inherent limits on such action. If all men are to be free in this manner, none must trespass upon the property of another. There will be at least two parties involved in any trade, and every man is limited by the necessity of getting the agreement of the other parties to any transaction.

larly and predictably occur are most complex. The "mine and thine" of property must be carefully and rigorously distinguished by enforceable rules. Property protection requires an impartial force to prevent aggression by individuals and groups against property. Order must prevail generally. The citizenry needs generally to have learned to respect the possessions and rights of those in their midst. This depends upon a developed morality, sense of justice, and self-restraint. If free economic intercourse is to work tolerably well to the advantage of most men, the men must know how to look after their interests.

Knowing something of the delusions which men are wont to embrace, the passions which move them to unruly action, the frustrations to which they are subject, the disorders of soul and mind which plague them, it should not surprise us that approximations to free economic intercourse have been rare in history. Rape and pillage, wanton destruction and aggression, war and disorder have been much more common on this earth. Established freedom of contract, harmonious international relations, settled rules for economic transactions, political neutrality are artistic accomplishments of the highest order.

A Major Omission by Historians

We might suppose, then, that historians would celebrate in memorable prose the great moments of history when such accomplishments have occurred, that the people would remember and immortalize as heroes the men who fostered the developments, that we would look back in longing or with gratitude to the foundations of such an order. Yet it is not so today in America. Intellectuals reg-

ularly sneer at the "Puritan ethos," "laissez-faire" economics, and "rugged individualism," thus misnaming and mis-
understanding that which they would denounce. Most historians, having considerably more respect for accuracy
in dealing with the past and a somewhat better understanding of it, bog down in the details of long past contests or
read their unconscious assumptions about class conflict
and the "exploitation" of labor into their accounts of the
past. Though a multitude of books streams from the
presses, books which deal in some way with American
history, one searches among them in vain for a straight-
forward account of the development of free economic intercourse. Thus, a great tradition falls into obscurity.

There was, then, an American tradition of free economic intercourse. It was never perfectly realized, not
even as nearly as it might have been. Exceptions existed
at the height of its development, and some will be noted.
We should keep in mind, however, that exceptions frequently occupy the center of the stage in written history.
Students of American history of the nineteenth century
are likely to encounter frequent references to the national
bank and to tariffs. These are of some importance. They
did lead to dramatic debates and did occasion decisive action. It must be kept in mind though that they were islands of government intervention in an ocean of liberty.

It is very difficult to dramatize liberty, which may be
one of the reasons it gets so little play in many histories.
There may be exciting events by which it is won—legislative debates, oratorical flights in the courtroom, or decisive battles—but once won it takes its place among the
ordinary experiences of life. Liberty then becomes a matter of the routine enforcement of laws, the absence of op-

pressive action by government, the "uninteresting" civil suits in courts more often than the dramatic murder trial, and the millions of acts of self-restraint by citizens. Small wonder that we lose sight of it!

Liberty Seen by Contrast

The absence of restraint—which constitutes a major portion of free economic intercourse—can best be recognized by holding it up against restraint at some other time in history. This can be done in American history.

The American colonies were settled at a time when the relics of medieval restrictions were being absorbed into mercantilism, a new species of authoritarianism. The most salient feature of mercantilism was the attempt to use the governmental authority to direct the economic activities of a people toward the acquisition of national wealth. It was a highly nationalistic program, and it spawned many of the devices by which free economic activity has been hampered in the modern era. In the sixteenth and seventeenth centuries, when the ideas associated with mercantilism were first enunciated, wealth was visibly represented to most men as gold or, to a lesser extent, other precious metals. National wealth was sought by way of enhancing the gold supply of the nation. For most European countries, including England, this meant getting it from some country which already possessed it. In order to do this—since piracy was falling into disrepute, besides being dangerous—countries attempted to get a favorable balance of trade, i.e., to sell more to other countries than they bought from them. The balance would then be paid in gold.

Protectionism

Numerous restrictions were adopted to achieve this end.
Imports were discouraged by prohibitions and tariffs. Exports were stimulated by paying bounties for the production of staples that would be valuable in the export trade.
As one writer puts it, "the full panoply of protective tariffs
came early and quickly into existence—prohibitions on
the export of bullion, wool, and naval stores, bounties upon
the export of corn and some manufactured goods, duties
upon the import of foreign textiles and exotic luxuries."[3]
In the foreign trade, monopolies were granted to trade associations such as the Merchant Adventurers and to
joint stock companies such as the East India Company.
Prices and qualities of goods were subject to regulation.
"Labor, recognized as one of the essential factors of production, was subjected to careful control." There were
wage ceilings. "The training of the laborer was established
in the acts which governed apprenticeship."[4] There were
even attempts to control consumption, such as establishing fish days and prohibiting the importation of foreign
luxury goods.

The English colonies in America were founded mainly
for mercantilistic ends, so far as the English government
was concerned. If not in some cases, they were later used
in this way. Colonies were to contribute to the self-suf-
ficiency of the mother country by providing products
which could not be grown or produced there. They were
to buttress the export trade by producing staples which

---

[3] Philip W. Buck, *The Politics of Mercantilism* (New York:
Holt, 1942), p. 14.
[4] *Ibid.*, p. 17.

other countries wanted. Thus, the colonists were subjected to regulations with this end in view. Over the years, a great number of restrictions were placed on colonial trade and economic activity by England. The Navigation Acts attempted to restrict the carrying trade to English (or colonial) built and manned ships, as well as prescribing that certain goods must be sold only through England. The Staple Act of 1663 made it unlawful for the colonists to buy certain products directly from foreign countries. They had, instead, to be shipped first to England where duties would be collected on them. The exportation of specie from England was made illegal. There were other acts of the British Parliament prohibiting certain kinds of manufactures in the colonies, restricting trade among the colonies, and limiting settlement.

Mercantilism in America

It should not be supposed, however, that colonial governments were averse to mercantilism. Colonists chafed at restraints imposed from without, but wanted to use their own governments to advance the interests of the colonies by mercantile regulations. Indeed, most colonies had a multitude of regulations of their own devising. They had restrictions inherited from the Middle Ages. Land was likely to be encumbered by quitrents, entail, and primogeniture. There was some effort to perpetuate craft guilds along European lines in America. The apprentice system was much used. "As early as 1724 the master carpenters in Philadelphia had established a price or wage scale, and the practice soon spread to other towns. . . . In 1724 the barbers of Boston agreed to raise the price on shaves and wigs and to fine any member £10 who shaved a man on Sunday."[5]

The Puritans in New England even attempted to revive practices from the Middle Ages that had already fallen into disuse in England. John Cotton attempted to revive the doctrine of "just price."[6] At any rate, economic legislation abounded in the colonies. Blacksmiths were compelled to repair firearms, and weights and measures were regulated. "Inns, mills, and ferries were subject to control. Charges were limited by law, and the obligations of such institutions were legislatively defined. . . . Efforts were made to determine fair prices, fair wages, and reasonable profits."[7] The exportation of foodstuffs was sometimes prohibited, as was that of gold and silver. Some colonies attempted to develop manufactures by prohibiting the importation of certain commodities. Bounties were frequently offered by governments to stimulate the production of desired articles. Exemptions from taxation and monopolies were also granted. "Massachusetts granted a twenty-one year monopoly to the Braintree ironmakers, together with 'freedom from public charges. . . .' Virginia, in 1661-62, exempted tradesmen and artisans from the payment of tax levies."[8]

---

[5] Gilbert C. Fite and Jim E. Reese, *An Economic History of the United States* (Boston: Houghton Mifflin, 1959), p. 51. The "as early as" in the quotation is of doubtful validity. It probably should read "as late as," since these organizations appear to be relics of the medieval craft guild rather than modern trade unions.

[6] See E. A. J. Johnson, *American Economic Thought in the Seventeenth Century* (New York: Russell & Russell, 1961), pp. 8-9.

[7] *Ibid.*, p. 17.

[8] *Ibid.*, p. 29.

There were attempts to impose limits on land uses and on the amount to be held. Virginia tried to control the production and prices of tobacco, and made "repeated attempts to legislate into existence warehouses or even towns. . . ."[9] Import duties were levied in the seventeenth century primarily to regulate consumption. "Even in Virginia, where indirect taxation was favoured . . ., import duties were designed almost as much for sumptuary purposes as for fiscal. This was true, for example, of the law of 1661, which imposed duties on rum and sugar."[10]

Actually, however, much of this sumptuary, regulatory, and restrictive legislation is usually described as "attempts" to control economic activity. Frequently, it was not very effective, nor was it so pervasive as this random account of laws in various colonies might appear to indicate. Colonists resisted attempts to control their lives, evaded and ignored regulations, and persisted in going about their affairs as they saw best. From the outset, many of the medieval and mercantile rules did not accord with the possibilities of the situation in the New World. It was easy in the rather simple circumstances to trace out the consequences of actions; whereas, in more complex surroundings cause can be more readily separated from effect.

Failures at Plymouth and Jamestown

Specific examples may help to illuminate the point. Both the Virginia and Plymouth colonies were begun as corporate undertakings. The companies owned the lands,

---

[9] Savelle, *op. cit.*, p. 189.
[10] Johnson, *op. cit.*, p. 254.

and the settlers were to be servants of the companies. The produce went into a common storehouse; any surplus beyond what was needed went to the owners. In theory, all produce belonged to the companies. The consequences, we would say, were predictable:

> This plan did not yield good results. In Virginia the settlers "loafed on the job," since they got a living, irrespective of their personal efforts. They could receive but little, if any, benefit from the colony's surplus; hence a surplus was not produced. The Plymouth colonists became acutely dissatisfied for a number of reasons. The labor of unmarried men benefited other men's families; married men did not like to have their wives work for other settlers; the older men objected to being placed on a par with the younger; and the industrious workers thought it unjust that they received no more than the idlers.[11]

In short, the attempt at modified communism failed, and it was abandoned in a few years. Even before Plymouth gave up on it, however, a miniature instance of Lenin's New Economic Policy occurred. As one history tells it, "In 1623 a food shortage in the colony caused a temporary abandonment of the corporate method of farming. . . ."[12] The land was shortly sold or conceded to settlers as private property, and economic conditions improved greatly.

The trade monopolies of the companies suffered a similar fate. Once the colonists owned the land, the produce was theirs, and they insisted upon selling it to the highest bidder. The attempts to monopolize the fur trade fared

---

[11] Curtis P. Nettels, *The Roots of American Civilization* (New York: Appleton-Century-Crofts, 1963, rev. ed.), p. 223.
[12] *Ibid.*

little better. Several of the colonies attempted to control this trade for the benefit of the companies, proprietors, or governors, but to no avail. "Thus in New Netherland both the employees of the company and the patroons traded privately in defiance of its monopoly, while in Massachusetts, Virginia, South Carolina, and Pennsylvania local merchants and officials successfully resisted corporate or proprietary control."[13]

Trend Toward Private Enterprises

It is safe to say, in consequence of these experiences, that Americans became attached to private property and private trade, and that the powers over them recognized its importance for production. More broadly, the tendency was for attempts to regulate economic activity to break down over the years. The efforts to transplant the relics of medievalism in the New World, to impose mercantile and religious restrictions, usually failed. Even the British may have tacitly recognized this by their policy of "salutary neglect." One historian concludes his account of *American Economic Thought in the Seventeenth Century* on this note: "The futility of governmental control of wages in a dynamic society became increasingly apparent. . . . Freedom to buy and sell, freedom to establish mercantile or industrial businesses, occupational mobility, all these became inseparable phases of American economic liberty."[14]

Americans edged toward the formation of a tradition of

---

[13] *Ibid.*, p. 228.
[14] Johnson, *op. cit.*, p. 270.

free economic intercourse in the eighteenth century. Craft guilds lost their following, and the courts began to describe their efforts to control as a conspiracy. Restrictions upon land and property fell away. Customs and practices which augured an American tradition were taking hold. By the mid-eighteenth century, an intellectual outlook was gaining adherents, an outlook which was used to knit together experience and practices into a coherent philosophy.

The mainspring of this new outlook was the belief in a natural order for social arrangements based upon the nature of man, natural law, and natural rights. Many believed that it was imperative to act in accord with this natural order because God had set his stamp of approval upon it by building it into the universe. This belief spurred men to the discovery, proclamation, and adoption of a natural order in economics. The great codification of this order is Adam Smith's *Wealth of Nations*, published in 1776, the same year as the Declaration of Independence. Smith was an Englishman, but many American contemporaries could concur in his formulation, for they had already or were arriving at similar conclusions.

Many instances of a belief in free economic intercourse can be found in the writings of Americans in the latter part of the eighteenth century. Benjamin Franklin declared that "it seems contrary to the nature of Commerce, for Government to interfere in the Prices of Commodities. Trade is a voluntary Thing between Buyer and Seller, in every article of which each exercises his own Judgment, and is to please himself."[15] Pelatiah Webster

---

[15] Quoted in Virgle G. Wilhite, *Founders of American Economic Thought* (New York: Bookman, 1958), p. 308.

said, "I propose . . . to take off every restraint and limitation from our commerce. Let trade be as free as air. Let every man make the most of his goods in his own way and then he will be satisfied."[16] One writer sums up Webster's arguments thusly:

(1) Laissez-faire results in maximum production, because this yields the most profit. . . .

(2) Freedom of enterprise brings about production of the best quality of goods, because they will sell more readily and more profitably than goods of poor quality. . . .

(3) Unrestricted "liberty"[17] stimulates the production of the most needed and most scarce goods. . . .

(4) Natural liberty produces a contented and happy citizenry because the laws neither favor nor restrain any one. . . .

(5) Laissez-faire assures the frugal use of scarce and dear goods, because their high prices cause people to purchase and consume them sparingly.[18]

In a different vein, Richard Henry Lee declared: "Liberty, in its genuine sense, is security to enjoy the effects of our honest industry and labors, in a free and mild government, and personal security from all illegal restraints."[19]

Perhaps the most articulate spokesman over the years of free economic intercourse founded upon a natural order was Thomas Jefferson. In general terms, he observed

---

16 *Ibid.*, p. 172.

17 The author is hostile to this general line of reasoning, which explains the enclosure of liberty in quotation marks. He attempts to refute each of the points after he describes it.

18 Wilhite, *op. cit.*, pp. 173-74.

19 "Letters from the Federal Farmer," *Empire and Nation*, Forrest McDonald, intro. (Englewood Cliffs: Prentice-Hall, 1962), p. 138.

"that a right to property is founded in our natural wants,
in the means with which we are endowed to satisfy these
wants, and the right to what we acquire by those means
without violating the similar rights of other sensible beings; that no one has a right to obstruct another exercising his faculties innocently for the relief of sensibilities
made a part of his nature. . . ."[20] Moreover, he thought
that "the exercise of a free trade with all parts of the
world" was "possessed by the American colonists as of
natural right. . . ."[21] Specifically, "I would say, then, to
every nation on earth, *by treaty*, your people shall trade
freely with us and ours with you, paying no more than
the most favored nation, in order to put an end to the
right of individual States, acting by fits and starts, to in-
terrupt our commerce or to embroil us with any nation."[22]

The Break from Mercantilism

The general trend of thought, as summarized by one
historian of the eighteenth century, "was moving toward
a general ideal of economic freedom."[23] Thought, however,
is an auxiliary to rather than being a tradition. The tradition must be discovered from what the Americans established after they broke from England. Here, the record
is rather clear. They made great strides within a few
years toward the establishment of free economic intercourse. With the break, of course, they cast off an exter-

[20] *The Political Writings of Thomas Jefferson*, Edward Dumbauld, ed. (New York: Liberal Arts Press, 1955), p. 49.
[21] *Ibid.*, p. 19.
[22] *Ibid.*, p. 130.
[23] Savelle, *op. cit.*, p. 226.

nally imposed restraint on their trade. It should be reported, however, that some of the states adopted mercantilistic practices during the period of the Confederation. Several states even set price ceilings during the war. They failed, and in 1778 Congress recommended that they be suspended or repealed, with this interesting explanation:

> It hath been found by Experience that Limitations upon the Prices of Commodities are not only ineffectual for the Purposes proposed, but likewise productive of very evil consequences to the great Detriment of the public Service and grievous Oppression of Individuals.[24]

Even so, efforts along these lines were continued in the next few years in some of the states.

American trade with the rest of the world opened up rapidly in the 1780's, but the adoption of the Constitution of 1787 spurred even greater advancement. This new instrument of government took away from the states the power to levy import duties. It prohibited a tax on exports, gave Congress the power to regulate interstate commerce, and forbade states to lay import duties on goods coming from other states within the United States. Thus, trade was free within the United States and nearly so with the rest of the world.

The remainder of the restrictions upon property were removed: quitrents were no more; entail and primogeniture were abolished. An individual (at least a male over 21) could buy, sell, bequeath, and inherit property without let or hindrance. Indentured servitude disappeared. A market system for determining prices generally prevailed;

---

[24] Quoted in Fite and Reese, *op. cit.*, p. 110.

some cities may have retained a few regulations, but in general there were few, if any. White labor was free of controls; a man could sell his services at whatever prices he could obtain and work whatever hours were agreeable to him and his employer. He and his employer were protected by the courts from the use of coercion by such unions as existed. A writer in 1819 declared:

> In commerce and navigation, the progress of the United States has been rapid beyond example. Besides the natural advantages of excellent harbours, extensive inland bays and navigable rivers, it has been greatly in favour of their commerce, that it has not been fettered by monopolies or exclusive privileges. Goods or merchandise circulate through all the states free of duty, and a full drawback, or restitution of duties of importation, is granted upon articles exported to a foreign port. . . . Maritime and commercial business is executed with more celerity and less expense than in any other country. Vessels in the ports of the United States are laden and unladen in the course of a few days, whilst in those of other countries, as many months are required for the same purposes, owing to tedious regulations and less enterprise.[25]

Crevecoeur sang the praises of the American system of freedom and its consequences:

> The American ought therefore to love this country much better than that wherein either he or his forefathers were born. Here the rewards of his industry follow with equal steps the progress of his labour; his labour is founded on the basis of nature, *self-interest;* can it want a stronger allurement?[26]

---

[25] Quoted in Marvin Meyers, *et. al., Sources of the American Republic,* I (Chicago: Scott, Foresman and Co., 1960), 250.
[26] *Ibid.,* p. 282.

Freedom in Large Measure

It was a land of almost unbounded opportunity. "A man no longer needed a fortune of his own. If he had imagination, energy, and a good character in the community, he could buy land or stock, become a merchant or a manufacturer, with money borrowed from a bank or supplied by some well-to-do individual willing to gamble on a share of a future profit."[27]

A tradition of free economic intercourse had taken shape. The right of a man to the fruits of his labor was protected and respected. His right to use and dispose of what was his as he saw fit was virtually beyond question. Taxes were low; government was limited. There were, however, exceptions to freedom in nineteenth century America. Obviously, Negro slaves could not dispose of their time and labor as they saw fit. Women were still hampered by custom and law. State governments were inclined in the early part of the century to adventures in helping to finance such undertakings as the building of canals, activities which disturbed the workings of the market and probably accounted for overbuilding, unprofitable building, and speculative booms and busts. The United States government entered the field also with the national bank and protective tariffs.

Nonetheless, the general tendency was in the direction of the development of the tradition of free economic intercourse for most of the nineteenth century. The slaves were emancipated. Women got many of the rights that had formerly belonged to men. From the 1830's to 1860, the

---

[27] Charles M. Wiltse, *The New Nation* (New York: Hill and Wang, 1961), pp. 54-55.

governments tended to withdraw from economic affairs. In the latter part of the nineteenth century, governments gave considerable encouragement to industrialization, avoided regulation and control, created some instability by fluctuating monetary policies, and contributed to some unwise railroad building by grants and loans. Even so, freedom was the rule and interference the exception.

Unparalleled Economic Progress

The consequences of this tradition of free economic intercourse should be well known. Americans opened up a continent, built a vigorous merchant marine, cut down the forests and utilized the farm lands, discovered and utilized great quantities of minerals, made a multitude of inventions and entered the field of manufacturing vigorously, and developed an industry and agriculture of dimensions which could hardly have been imagined at the beginning of the nineteenth century.

What was the *cause* of this tremendous economic development? Undoubtedly, many conditions made it possible: there were land, natural resources, the bent of the people to utilize the resources, and much else besides. Many historians in the twentieth century have favored the view that the fabulous natural resources of America account for the prosperity of America. This, and the others mentioned, is a condition, however, not a cause of development. The resources had lain in America for millennia unutilized. People *caused* the economic development of America. Individuals provided the effort and labor which used the resources. What was the source of this effort? What released the energies of Americans? Above all else—and let it be writ large—it was FREEDOM. Anyone who doubts this proposition should make a comparison of the development of the Russian Empire in the nineteenth century with that of the United States. Many differences might be enumerated, but one that is ascertainable looms above the others—the difference in the amount and degree of liberty.

The Reasons Forgotten

One might suppose, then, that the blessings of liberty would have made Americans inseparably attached to it. It was not so, however. When men are at liberty to exert themselves as they will, some will accumulate and have much more than others. The increasing material prosperity, the abundance and variety of goods available, may have aroused envy in those who had less. The protective tariffs of the latter part of the nineteenth century did set the stage for talk of monopolies and may have protected industries to the disadvantage of consumers. Immigrants poured into America who had little understanding or appreciation of the American traditions. Above all, collectivist reformers implanted their ideas in the minds of intellectuals and the discontented. A campaign was waged against bigness in business, against "Wall Street," against the wealthy, against business itself. If they were not as well off as they would like to be, laborers were told that they were being exploited. If farmers were not getting as high prices as they would have liked, they were told that they were not getting their fair share. If artists and intellectuals were not appreciated in America as they were in Europe, it was because of the business motif in America. As for economic liberty, it was all very well in an earlier America, when there was land and opportunity available. But in a complex industrialized America "individualism" was outmoded. So people were told, and told, and told, until they began to believe it.

Thus, the stage was set for the departure from the American tradition of free economic intercourse. Despite the efforts of socialists in the late nineteenth and early twentieth century, however, Americans rejected the revolutionary road to socialism. It is unlikely that a people who have been acclimated to freedom would give it up all at once for the oppression of socialism. After all, our histories still told of the sorry experience at Jamestown and Plymouth. But people could be persuaded, by the skillful and devious use of language, to yield up their liberty bit by bit. But I would not be understood to be describing a conspiracy. Such evidence as I am familiar with indicates that most Americans who have fostered the reform programs which have diminished liberty believed that they were doing what was best for America, and that they could still retain "important" rights.

Back to Mercantilism

At any rate, economic intercourse is severely circumscribed in twentieth century America. The use of property is strenuously regulated in most municipalities. One must get permission to make an addition to his house. Laborers cannot sell their services at the prices at which they might be willing. There are minimum wage and maximum hour laws. Numerous regulations and restrictions apply to goods that are offered for sale. Most of those who work *must* contribute to Social Security. Graduated income taxes penalize the acquisition of wealth and reward the bearing of children. The courts have been so busy misinterpreting the meaning of that clause of the Constitution which gives Congress the power to regulate interstate commerce that they have hardly noticed the difficulties the states have been raising to discourage intercourse among them. I have in mind "use" taxes, particularly, but there are probably many other things of like character.

It would be a sanguine task for me to enumerate all the regulations, restrictions, and interventions which our governments are engaged in today. Our tobacco and liquor laws are a modern day version of sumptuary laws; our subsidies to the merchant marine, to air travel, to sundry "defense" industries are modern day bounties. One of the great ironies is that many of these programs have been pushed as being progressive. One might suppose that they were recent inventions to be utilized. It is not so. They are hoary with age. Paternalism, mercantilism, authoritarianism, have been the common lot of man through the ages. What was new and exciting about the age from which our legacy came was the experiment with and achievements that were fostered by individual liberty. Free economic intercourse was an important aspect of this individual liberty. It was once established as a part of the American tradition.

Today's reactionaries—i.e., "liberals," meliorists, socialists, and so forth—would close that gap in our history occupied by freedom and restore the controls, regulations, bounties, sumptuary laws, and limitations upon property which our ancestors shed with so much pain. They would do more, for there are new things in our age. The technology of our age makes possible an oppressive supervision that was not available to the agents of the English King. Totalitarianism *is* a modern phenomenon, but it is built upon presumptions which have a long history. The American tradition grew out of the resistance to giving those under the sway of these presumptions the unlimited force of government. It was a tradition of freedom—even of free economic intercourse.

12.

Of Internationalism

THE NOTION is widely prevalent that the United States followed isolationist policies in the nineteenth century. Students assert this "fact" with the kind of assurance that would stem from indoctrination. But a statement such as that the United States was isolationist in the nineteenth century is not even in the nature of a fact. It is an historical judgment, a judgment which would have to subsume a great many facts in order to be valid. Actually, "isolationist" is generally used as invective to denounce those who disagree with the policies which have been adopted by the United States since World War II— though the outline of these policies began to emerge some years before that. It is a key word in a language of argumentation, not a descriptive word.

In like manner, many assume that the trend of twentieth century American policies has been toward internationalism. Moreover, according to the prevailing ethos it is good to be an "internationalist," and it is bad to be an "isolationist." An "internationalist," judging by those who claim the title and the actions they promote, is one who favors reciprocal trade agreements, foreign aid, permanent alliances, involvement in the domestic affairs of other nations, government-to-government loans, managed domestic currencies, cultural exchanges under the auspices of government, and international monetary funds. It is often assumed, too, that those who support these programs are men of good will, while those who oppose them are at best misguided and at worst malevolent.

There should be no doubt that American foreign policy has changed in the twentieth century from what it was in the nineteenth. On this point, there appears to be general agreement. But changed from what to what is the question. How should the two different policies be described? More broadly, what was the American tradition regarding relations with other nations? Was the United States cut off from the rest of the world in the nineteenth century? Was the general tendency of the policy narrow, provincial, selfish, and inconsiderate? Have we broken out of our cocoon in the twentieth century to take up our rightful place in the world?

These are not questions which should be answered by the use of invective. They are historical questions which should be settled by a review of the evidence.

The first statement to be made on the basis of the record can be made categorically: *these United States were not isolated in the nineteenth century, nor did they follow isolationist policies.* On the contrary, among the early acts of the Second Continental Congress was to send representatives abroad. The Congress under the Articles of Confederation attempted to establish relations on a regular basis with as many countries as possible. The government established under the Constitution of 1787 attempted to operate in an international scene that was, to use a word commonly employed at the time, calamitous. For most of the first 25 years of the new Republic, Europe was disturbed and disjointed by the events surrounding and following upon the French Revolution. Nevertheless, the United States carried on diplomatic and trade relations with most countries most of the time and tried to use the influence of example to maintain sanity in a world where it appeared to be in short supply. The ideas of the Enlightenment, which informed the thought of the Founders, were cosmopolitan. Americans early wished the United States to become a nation among nations; the efforts of political leaders were usually bent toward accomplishing this objective.

George Washington's Advice

These statements should not be misunderstood, however: the American tradition of foreign relations was not internationalist as that term is *now* used. It *was* internationalist within the framework of the nineteenth century. To appreciate this, it will be helpful to look for and to try to recall the principles upon which American foreign policy was usually based. These can be approached by studying some of the important statements that were made by Presidents. George Washington's advice on foreign affairs in his Farewell Address is both the most famous of these and the most important for the formation of the tradition. It is worth quoting at length, because it became a guide for foreign policy makers through much of our history.

> Observe good faith and justice toward all nations. Cultivate peace and harmony with all. Religion and morality enjoin this conduct. And can it be that good policy does not equally enjoin it? It will be worthy of a free, enlightened, and at no distant period a great nation to give to mankind the magnanimous and too novel

example of a people always guided by an exalted justice and benevolence. . . .

In the execution of such a plan nothing is more essential than that permanent, inveterate antipathies against particular nations and passionate attachments for others should be excluded, and that in place of them just and amicable feelings toward all should be cultivated. The nation which indulges toward another an habitual hatred or an habitual fondness is in some degree a slave. It is a slave to its animosity or to its affection, either of which is sufficient to lead it astray from its duty and its interest. Antipathy in one nation against another disposes each more readily to offer insult and injury, to lay hold of slight causes of umbrage, and to be haughty and intractable when accidental or trifling occasions of dispute occur.

Hence frequent collisions, obstinate, envenomed, and bloody contests. The nation prompted by ill will and resentment sometimes impels to war the government contrary to the best calculations of policy. . . .

So, likewise, a passionate attachment of one nation for another produces a variety of evils. Sympathy for the favorite nation, facilitating the illusion of an imaginary common interest in cases where no real common interest exists, and infusing into one the enmities of the other, betrays the former into a participation in the quarrels and wars of the latter without adequate inducement or justification. It leads also to concessions to the favorite nation of privileges denied to others, which is apt doubly to injure the nation making the concessions by unnecessarily parting with what ought to have been retained, and by exciting jealousy, ill will, and a disposition to retaliate in the parties from whom equal privileges are withheld; and it gives to ambitious, corrupted, or deluded citizens (who devote themselves to the favorite nation) facility to betray or sacrifice the interests of their own country. . . .

Against the insidious wiles of foreign influence (I conjure you to believe me, fellow-citizens) the jealousy of a free people ought to be *constantly* awake, since history and experience prove that foreign influence is one of the most baneful foes of republican government. But that jealousy, to be useful, must be impartial, else it becomes the instrument of the very influence to be avoided. . . .

The great rule of conduct for us in regard to foreign nations is, in extending our commercial relations to have with them as little *political* connection as possible. So far as we have already formed engagements let them be fulfilled with perfect good faith. Here let us stop.

It is our true policy to steer clear of permanent alliances with any portion of the foreign world. . . .

Taking care always to keep ourselves by suitable establishments on a respectable defensive posture, we may safely trust to temporary alliances for extraordinary emergencies.

Harmony, liberal intercourse with all nations are recommended by policy, humanity, and interest. But even our commercial policy should hold an equal and impartial hand, neither seeking nor granting exclusive favors or preferences; consulting the natural course of things; diffusing and diversifying by gentle means the streams of commerce, but forcing nothing; establishing with powers so disposed, in order to give trade a stable course, to define the rights of our merchants, and to enable the Government to support them, conventional rules of intercourse . . .; constantly keeping in view that it is folly in one nation to look for disinterested favors from another; that it must pay with a portion of its independence for whatever it may accept under that character; that by such acceptance it may place itself in the condition of having given equivalents for nominal favors, and yet of being reproached with ingratitude for not giving more. There can be no greater error than to expect or calculate upon real favors from nation to nation. It is an illusion which experience must cure, which a just pride ought to discard.[1]

Washington's Views Upheld

These words of Washington's became (or were) a part of the consciousness of others, for those who came later to seats of power reiterated them. President John Adams resolved "to do justice as far as may depend upon me, at all times and to all nations, and maintain peace, friendship, and benevolence with all the world."[2] He said further, "It is my sincere desire, and in this I presume I concur with you [the Congress] and with our constituents, to preserve peace and friendship with all nations. . . . If we have committed errors, and these can be demonstrated, we shall be willing to correct them . . .; and equal measures of justice we have a right to expect from France and every other nation."[3] To which the Senate replied, "Peace and harmony with all nations is our sincere wish; but such being the lot of humanity that nations will not always reciprocate peaceable dispositions, it is our firm belief that effectual measures of defense will tend to inspire that national self-respect and confidence at *home* which is the unfailing source of respectability *abroad*, to check aggression and prevent war."[4]

Thomas Jefferson, with his usual felicity, states the

---

[1] James D. Richardson, *A Compilation of the Messages and Papers of the Presidents*, I (Washington Printing Office, 1896), 221-23.

[2] *Ibid.*, p. 232.

[3] *Ibid.*, p. 232.

[4] *Ibid.*, p. 240.

particular application of these general principles as he explains how the United States as a neutral nation should behave toward belligerents:

> In the course of this conflict let it be our endeavor, as it is our interest and desire, to cultivate the friendship of the belligerent nations by every act of justice and of innocent kindness; to receive their armed vessels with hospitality from the distresses of the sea, but to administer the means of annoyance to none; to establish in our harbors such a police as may maintain law and order; to restrain our citizens from embarking individually in a war in which their country takes no part . . .; to exact from every nation the observance toward our vessels and citizens of those principles and practices which all civilized people acknowledge; to merit the character of a just nation, and maintain that of an independent one, preferring every consequence to insult and habitual wrong.[5]

In more general terms, he declared himself in favor of "peace, commerce, and honest friendship with all nations, entangling alliances with none."[6] There are overtones of Adam Smith in this phrase: "to those who justly calculate that their own well-being is advanced by that of the nations with which they have intercourse. . . ."[7]

One more statement from an early President should indicate a general concurrence in some general principles. This is from the Monroe Doctrine:

> Our policy in regard to Europe . . . remains the same, which is, not to interfere in the internal concerns of

---

[5] *Ibid.*, p. 361.

[6] *Ibid.*, p. 323.

[7] *Ibid.*, p. 369.

any of its powers; to consider the government *de facto* as the legitimate government for us; to cultivate friendly relations with it, and to preserve those relations by a frank, firm, and manly policy, meeting in all instances the just claims of every power, submitting to injuries from none.[8]

Principles of Foreign Policy

From these primary policy pronouncements some general principles emerge. They can be reduced to a few heads and stated as imperatives in the following manner:

The United States *should*

1.   Establish and maintain a position of independence with regard to other countries.

2.   Avoid *political* connection, involvement, or intervention in the affairs of other countries.

3.   Make no permanent or entangling alliances.

4.   Treat all nations impartially, neither granting nor accepting special privileges from any.

5.   Promote commerce with all peoples and countries.

6.   Cooperate with other countries to develop civilized rules of intercourse.

7.   Act always in accordance with the "laws of nations."

8.   Remedy all just claims of injury to other nations, and require just treatment from other nations, standing ready, if necessary, to punish offenders.

9.   Maintain a defensive force of sufficient magnitude to deter aggressors.

The question arises at this point as to whether the

---

[8] Henry S. Commager, ed., *Documents of American History*, I (New York: Appleton-Century, Crofts, 1963, 7th ed.), 236-37.

statements quoted earlier are anything more than ideal-
istic pronouncements, piously proclaimed. In our times,
we are all too familiar with the protective coloration of
rhetoric under which politicians and nations conceal their
thrust to power. These words must be tested by the actions which followed them. Moreover, the American tradition must be discovered in the customs and practices,
not in the ideas.

Did the American tradition conform to the above principles? In answering this question, it should be clear
that I am not ascribing an invariable rectitude to American behavior. Americans have probably been no more
nearly perfect than have any other peoples. Furthermore,
they lived in a world where other nations were not perfect
either. Nevertheless, for the first 109 years of the existence
of the Republic Americans developed and maintained a
tradition that was in keeping with the above principles.
During the early years, when Europe was embroiled in a
succession of wars, vigorous efforts were made to steer
clear of foreign entanglements. The United States adopted
a neutral position, attempted to maintain friendly relations with all the countries, and steadfastly clung to independence. Jefferson went so far in his efforts to maintain peace at one point that he invoked an embargo on
American shipping. (For a period of a couple of years the
United States *was* isolated, technically, from most of the
rest of the world.)

For the whole of the nineteenth century the United
States made no permanent or entangling alliances. Generally speaking, intercourse was promoted and advanced
with all countries. Goods entered America from around
the world with only minor duties upon them until well

past the mid-nineteenth century. Export duties were prohibited by the Constitution. People could enter America freely for most of the nineteenth century; immigrants were welcome, and naturalization was easy. Cultural exchanges took place regularly, under the protection but not the auspices of the government. The United States cooperated with other countries to open trade with Asiatic countries.[9]

No single instance comes to mind of interference in the internal affairs of another country during the first hundred years of the Republic. There were, of course, boundary disputes, and there was the expansionist war with Mexico, and the latter may well have been a departure from principle. The Monroe Doctrine did not claim for the United States the right to intervene in any country's internal affairs. It proposed rather to prevent further European colonizing in America. The Monroe Doctrine was a unilateral undertaking which did not commit America to the policy determination of other powers. In short, American independence was iterated and preserved by it.

A Century of Peace and Trade

We can say with confidence that the United States established a tradition of foreign relations in keeping with the principles laid down by the Founding Fathers. The diplomatic history of the nineteenth century is filled with examples of treaties of amity and commerce with other powers, with cooperative efforts to establish rules of intercourse, with the sending and receiving of ministers and ambassadors, with the opening of trade and com-

---

[9] See Dorothy B. Goebel, ed., *American Foreign Policy* (New York: Holt, Rinehart and Winston, 1961), p. 108.

merce with distant powers, and with negotiations to settle peacefully real or imagined injuries which citizens of one country had done to those of another.

It follows that the United States was neither alone nor acting alone in the world. The American tradition blended with and was a part of the Western tradition of international relations. This greater tradition embraced numerous means for facilitating and maintaining harmony among nations, such means as treaties, congresses, ambassadors exchanged between countries, respect for the nationals of one country in another, and so on. However, at the time of the birth of the Republic respect for the tradition was in a sorry state. European countries had been embroiled in a series of "world wars" in the eighteenth century, involving the land and naval powers of the world. These appear to have culminated in the cataclysmic struggles which we associate with the French Revolution and the era of Napoleon. These latter developments signify a huge assault upon the corpus of traditions by which Europeans lived. It was a vital question whether any tradition could survive the onslaught.

Yet much of the diplomatic tradition did survive the holocaust; the zeal of the French revolutionaries succumbed to the guillotine; Napoleon was made an unemployed despot. Britain outlasted France; tradition triumphed over ideology. But the England that emerged victorious in 1815 was not the England that had gone to war in the 1790's. England made great headway in industrialization in the intervening years. Men and ideas were having an impact also. The political ideas of John Locke, the economic ideas of Adam Smith and David Ricardo, the conception of continuity with the past advanced by

Edmund Burke combined to buttress tradition, to revitalize the inheritance from the past, and to give a new, and liberal, direction to the future. Order was restored to Europe, trade commenced to heal the wounds of martial enmity, and some measure of decency and justice began to characterize the relations among nations. By the mid-nineteenth century Britain had become a momentous influence in the world for peaceful harmonious relations and free trade.

Golden Age of Western Civilization

It is common nowadays to find the period from the Congress of Vienna (1815) to the onset of World War I (1914) referred to as the Golden Age of Western Civilization. The reason for this characterization is not far to seek. Wars were few, brief, and limited. When the peace was threatened, a concert of powers usually met in a congress to avert war. Private property was usually respected, and the boundaries of nations usually enjoyed the protection which stemmed from this respect. The barriers to trade, travel, and intercourse were falling. Country after country adopted or revitalized representative government, and the rights of civilized men enjoyed the defense of a vigilant press and the protection of far-flung navies.

Some despotisms remained, sorry and largely ineffectual relics of the past. In these circumstances, "there emerged a multiplicity of international organizations. All the 'civilized' nations of the world joined the Red Cross society. . . . Thirty formed a Universal Telegraph Union (1875). Twenty-three agreed to make common use of the metric system . . . (1875). Sixty adhered to a Universal Postal

Union, created in 1878. . . . Nineteen ratified a convention of 1883 for the standardization of patent laws. Fif-
teen signed another convention of 1887 providing for practically uniform copyright laws."[10] It is worth pointing out
that these developments took place within what propa-
gandists are now apt to call "international anarchy."

If the nineteenth century was a Golden Age, and it certainly was in relations among nations at the least, what
made it so? First, a system of nations existed in the world.
These nations were jealous of their independence of one
another but were equally devoted to the maintenance of
the general sanctity of the nation-state, its established
boundaries and perquisites. Second, within these nations
there was a mounting devotion to liberty and opposition
to state tyranny. Demands arose from every quarter for
changes in this direction. As one historian says, "In one
country precedence was given to liberation from a foreign
domination or to national unity, and in another to the
change from absolutism in government to constitutionalism. Here it was simply a question of reform of the franchise . . ., while there it was a question of establishing
a representative system. . . . And over all of them [these
demands] rose one word that summed them all up and
expressed the spirit which had given them life—the word
liberty."[11] Third, leading nations, particularly Great Britain
and the United States, worked to open up the world to
trade, commerce, and intercourse. In the circumstances

[10] Carlton J. H. Hayes, *Contemporary Europe since 1870*
(New York: Macmillan, 1958, rev. ed.), p. 307.

[11] Benedetto Croce, *History of Europe in the Nineteenth Century*, Henry Furst, trans. (New York: A Harbinger Book, 1963),
pp. 4-5.

that resulted, gold served as the medium of exchange. Goods could be readily exchanged around the world, and prices and production were determined by "the workings of private markets. . . . Likewise, the task of distributing the gains from trade and the opportunities for growth among national economies was substantially left to the world market. . . ."[12] To put the matter another way, politics and economics were kept at a decent distance from one another in important affairs.

In more general terms, a scholar has described the workings of this order:

> What first strikes us in considering this order is the respect it enjoyed, which is only accentuated by the bad conscience or apologetics accompanying cases of infringement, which made it possible for international law to be regarded as a genuine law . . .; for the world to be united through a network of long-term agreements which therefore made for the stabilization of international relationships; for tensions between large and small states to be continually adjusted—the unjustly suspected "balance of power"—and for a high degree of agreement to exist regarding legal conceptions and national standards of justice.[13]

The consequences of this order ought to be well known: peace, and a mounting and spreading prosperity. The order was invigorated by regulated competition, ordered by some common conceptions of justice, vitalized by its consonance with liberty, and dependent upon the determined independence and the balance of power among nations.

---

[12] William Y. Elliott, *et. al.*, *The Political Economy of American Foreign Policy* (New York: Holt, 1955), p. 9.

[13] Wilhelm Röpke, *International Order and Economic Integration* (Dordrecht-Holland: Reidel, 1959), pp. 74-75.

American Leadership

What was the relation of the United States to this order? As I suggested initially, the American tradition of
foreign relations was an integral part of the Western tradition. From the outset, the United States participated
heartily in the diplomatic, commercial, and cultural customs and practices which make up that tradition. There
is more to it than that, however. The thought will not
down that the United States contributed much to the sal-
vage of the remains of the tradition in the early nineteenth
century and to the development of a more vital one later
in the century. The point is difficult to prove because if
influence be conceived only in terms of power, it must
be admitted that the United States was not a world power
to be reckoned with in the early nineteenth century.

But is the thrust of power always more influential than
that of example without the benefit of physical force? It is
not clear that it is. Let it be noted that during the time of
Europe's madness (1790's-1815) America remained an island of sanity, trying to maintain a neutral position, in-
sisting upon the respect for the rights of neutrals, holding
to the concept of the laws of nations, attempting to establish peaceful intercourse with the rest of the world.
Nor should it be forgotten that in the wake of the French
debacle few responsible Europeans believed that republican governments could be moderate in their actions and
stable in their course. The behavior of the United States
reversed that judgment in the course of the century, as
more and more countries turned to constitutional repub-
lics. Moreover, the central principles governing relations
among nations which were the guidelines of statesmen

during the Golden Age were the same ones advocated by Washington, Adams, Jefferson, and Monroe. However, I ascribe not originality but the influence of example to the Americans.

At any rate, one of the questions posed at the beginning of this article can now be answered. That is, how should American foreign policy in the nineteenth century be characterized? An unequivocal answer can be given: IT WAS INTERNATIONALIST. Thus, the American tradition was one of internationalism, within a framework of a Western tradition of internationalism. It envisioned the existence of independent nations which would carry on a great variety of relations with one another according to established rules. This system permitted a rich diversity of practice, custom, and law within countries, in keeping with their desires and traditions, while encouraging a uniformity of practice in matters that would facilitate peaceful intercourse. Internationalism on the negative side can be called NONINTERVENTIONISM. This, too, was at the heart of the American tradition.

Twentieth-Century Departure

There can be no doubt that the United States has departed from the earlier tradition in the twentieth century, a departure that was preceded, accompanied, or followed by many other countries around the world. Indeed, the initial departure was so abrupt that it can be fixed with near certainty. The year was 1898, the occasion the Spanish-American War, the outcome overseas expansion and the acquisition of empire.

But there were developments which prepared the way

for this departure. The most notable of these was the establishment of a policy of protectionism. The United States, of course, had tariffs from the beginning. At first, they were conceived as revenue measures. But from 1816 on they were frequently advocated and adopted as protective measures. Even so, until the 1860's they were very limited in their coverage, adopted as temporary expedients to protect infant industries, and vigorously opposed by a considerable portion of the politicians, and presumably the electorate, of the country. Still, the matter should not be glossed over. There were overtones of economic nationalism in Henry Clay's American System, set forth in the 1820's. Nationalism can be and has been used to undermine internationalism. The royal road to this development has been the protective tariff. It intertwines politics and economics, supports the notion that the economic well-being of a nation is opposed to that of others, and promotes discord and jealousies. More, it sets the stage for national expansion and imperialism.[14]

This last point deserves some elaboration. Critics of private capitalism have ascribed imperialism to capitalistic industrialization. It is true that industrialization requires markets and raw materials, facts which have been offered as the basis of an economic explanation adduced for colonialism and imperialism. The internationalism of the nineteenth century, however, afforded the opportunity for markets and materials without imperialism. Free trade was the acceptable means to this end. But in the latter part of the nineteenth century many nations began erecting trade barriers by adopting ever higher tariffs. As one

---

[14] See *Ibid.*, parts 1-2.

historian aptly describes this development, "the *laissez-faire* principle which had been regarded as a natural and ideal accompaniment of industrial progress in Europe during the era from 1830 to 1870 was replaced to a large extent during the era from 1870 to 1910 by neomercantilism, by governmental attempts to treat industry and agriculture, commerce and labor, as 'national interests.' "[15]

Prelude to War

The effect was to close off markets and materials from the general trade of nations, and for a single nation to attempt to monopolize whole areas. (It is worth noting also that these practices tended to promote domestic monopolies as well.) As protectionism shut off access to markets and materials, nations moved to acquire their own exclusive sources. Hence, the surge of imperialism, the carving up of choice areas of the world into spheres of influence, the territorial expansion which culminated in the first great cataclysm of the twentieth century—World War I. Much else was involved in these developments, of course. For example, the idea of survival of the fittest, borrowed from Darwinism and applied to nations, played a part. But the protective tariff can be usefully conceived as the forbidden fruit in the nineteenth century Garden of Eden.

For the United States, the acquisition of Spanish colonies in consequence of the Spanish-American War can be understood, then, as a logical culmination of protectionist policies which had been established from the Civil

---

[15] Hayes, *op. cit.*, pp. 36-37.

War onward. Having departed the American tradition by intervening in the affairs of Spain, the United States speedily became embroiled in all sorts of foreign undertakings and adventures. Two years after the Spanish-American War the Marines were helping to put down rebellion in far-off China. By the end of Theodore Roosevelt's nearly two terms in the presidency much of the remainder of the American tradition of internationalism was in shambles. There was the sorry episode by which the Canal Zone was leased from the bogusly created Republic of Panama. This was followed by the proclamation of the Roosevelt Corollary to the Monroe Doctrine, by which the United States claimed the "right" to intervene in other American countries, given certain conditions. Matching words with deeds, Marines and customs agents began putting in appearances in various Caribbean ports. Woodrow Wilson talked of reversing many of these trends, but some of his policies succeeded in getting the United States more embroiled in world affairs.

Compulsory Collectivism Spreads

Much more was involved by this time in the departure from the American tradition than economic nationalism. Collectivist ideas had become a part of the intellectual equipment of many intellectuals, and they were spreading a new conception of reality and of internationalism. Karl Marx was certainly the fountainhead of a new "school of internationalism," and socialists in general were billing themselves as the "true" internationalists. This is one of the great ironies of history. On the one hand, socialists have vehemently denounced nationalism. On the other hand, wherever they have come to power, or begun to come to power, they have thrown up "iron curtains" around the nation, and put all sorts of obstacles in the way of intercourse.

All of this is very confusing, but it has an explanation. Socialists proceed toward their goal, or they imagine that they do, by way of a planned economy. In order to plan the economy they have to control all the factors involved in it. They cannot have free intercourse of people, goods, or ideas, for any of these would introduce unknowns that could not be controlled. They cannot permit their effort to be subjected to a world market. But the existence of independent countries threatens their existence, or so they think quite often. There is always the invidious comparison with other countries, for socialist experiments have resulted in miserable failures. Besides, they need the materials if not the markets (for they have trouble supplying their own markets) in the rest of the world. The only possibility for achieving this is by the creation of a world socialist state. All independent nations would be gone. Then, socialism would work, or, if it did not, there would be nothing left with which to compare it, to prove that socialism was not the "wave of the future." Lest some think that history would pose a problem, it should be pointed out that history has largely been rewritten in the twentieth century to accord more or less with the socialist vision. Brainwashing (or "psychiatric treatment") should take care of the rest.

What has all of this to do with the United States? Let us note the general outlines of the course of developments in the twentieth century, and we shall see. American leaders have discarded one by one, or in bunches, the principles of the Founders upon which the American tradition of internationalism was based. They yielded up a portion of independence by joining the United Nations. The United States has intervened in, become involved with, and has her destiny connected with other countries by way of the sending of armies, the giving of foreign aid, and by mutual assistance policies. We have made permanent and entangling alliances, beginning with the North Atlantic Treaty Organization. We seek special trade privileges by way of reciprocal trade agreements. The United States supports some foreign governments and opposes others, not on principle quite often but for expedient reasons. Even those few principles which have not been discarded—such as, to cooperate with other countries to develop civilized rules of intercourse—are being pursued in dubious ways. The United States left the gold standard, so far as Americans are concerned, in the 1930's, has long ago thrown up formidable barriers to immigration, and has to a considerable extent substituted government-to-government loans in place of the activities of private lenders.

Welfare States at War

The major characteristics of our policies in the twentieth century have been economic nationalism (particularly in the 1930's), interventionism, and the turning to collective security. At home, we have established what is commonly called the welfare state; abroad, we are following policies antithetical to our own independence and that of other countries.

Enough has been said now to choose a word to characterize our policies. I nominate INTERVENTIONISM. "Internationalism" and "isolationism" as they are now usually employed are propagandic appellations for advancing intervention, whether knowingly so used or not. The American tradition was one of internationalism. We are now devoted to a course which will eventuate in a world state, chaos, or both, if it is not reversed. A world welfare state would be nearly as close to socialism as most "moderates" would now wish. Anyone who doubts any of these propositions should restudy the history of the last forty years and review current proposals being advanced by world leaders and advocated by intellectuals.

But is the older American tradition a viable alternative to the current course? Who can say with certainty? Conditions have changed somewhat. Not as much as some imagine, however. Communism is a menace today on a scale which I would not minimize. But this Republic was born amidst turmoil that would equal that of our day. Washington's Farewell Address was delivered shortly after the terror had swept over France. Jefferson took his position when Napoleon was at the height of his power.

Think what a field day the advocates of collective security would have had advising Washington, Adams, and Jefferson. They could have argued, with much force, that the United States was too feeble to go it alone. It was "necessary" to get the protection of one of the great powers, to align themselves with one or the other contending groups. Independence is all well and good, but it would have to wait until fairer times.

Let it be noted that this was not the course followed. Despite the temptations to follow such a course, the United States followed a resolutely independent course, even to the fighting of an "independent" war against Great Britain, disdaining allies (the War of 1812). They must have known what we have forgotten, that independence yielded up for expedient reasons is hardly recovered. We know something of the consequences of the American tradition of internationalism; we are fearful of the end product of interventionism. But it is for the historian to tell the story, not to determine the course.

13.

Of Virtue and Morality

Writers in the twentieth century have often entertained themselves (and presumably their readers) by taking potshots at their particular *bête noire*, the despised Puritan. If Americans are not so spontaneous in their sex relations as some writers would like, it is ascribed to repressions inherited from Puritanism. If they are stingy or ungenerous on occasion, that too must come from their Puritan heritage. If they lack the French *joie de vivre,* it can be blamed on Puritanism.

In vain, I suspect, some scholars, notably Samuel Eliot Morison and Perry Miller, have shown that the Puritan of the seventeenth and eighteenth centuries was not that way. In reality, he was not always stern, joyless, and forbidding. However valuable such work may be, it could not be expected to stem the torrent of adverse criticism manufactured by "imaginative" writers and journalists. Most of them probably could not care less what *the* Puritan of earlier times was like. They were after more consequential game. For Puritanism as it is popularly conceived and described is none other than the American tradition of virtue and morality.

The historical confusion engendered by such oversimplified misappellations can be passed over for the moment. The point is, Puritanism was used as a symbol of distaste; and, since the characteristics ascribed to Puritanism were in reality characteristic of American ways, the assault upon this symbol was an assault on the American tradition. The discrediting of the one tended to undermine the other.

There was, then, an American tradition of morality and virtue. It is most difficult to delineate, however. Morality and virtue have usually been associated with religion. Indeed, they may be inseparably joined in some way. George Washington maintained that they were. In memorable words, he declared:

> Of all the dispositions and habits which lead to political prosperity, religion and morality are indispensable supports. In vain would that man claim the tribute of patriotism who should labor to subvert these great pillars of human happiness—these firmest props of the duties of men and citizens. The mere politician, equally with the pious man, ought to respect and cherish them. A volume could not trace all their connections with private and public felicity. Let it simply be asked, Where is security for property, for reputation, for life, if the sense of religious obligation *desert* the oaths which are the instruments of investigation in courts of justice? And let us with caution indulge the supposition that morality can be maintained without religion. Whatever may be conceded to the influence of refined education on minds of peculiar structure, reason and experience both forbid us to expect that national morality can prevail in exclusion of religious principle.[1]

Yet the United States did not have an established religion, nor was Washington advocating one. There were already

---

[1] James D. Richardson, *A Compilation of the Messages and Papers of the Presidents,* I (Washington: Government Printing Office, 1896), 220.

a considerable variety of sects, and more would arise or come in the future. However, traditions are not laws, as I have already pointed out. It is possible to have a tradition of morality and virtue—which, in turn, is dependent upon religion—without its being legally prescribed. Indeed, America had one.

Individualism and Morality

This was made possible by the fact that morality was primarily an individual matter. To put it more directly, only individuals could be moral according to the prevailing ethos. For action to become moral it meant that individuals should have made choices. Thus, prescribed morality was antithetical to the tradition. The corollary to individual morality was individual responsibility. When an individual chose his course of action, he became responsible for its consequences. If he affronted the community codes of behavior, he would be made to feel the contempt and displeasure of that community. If he violated laws, he would be held responsible by punishment. In like manner, individuals received the rewards of their endeavors. This was facilitated by provisions for private property, by definite distinctions between what belonged to one man and what to another, and by community approval of those who justly acquired wealth or fame.

To my knowledge, no one has attempted to rank the virtues which were admired in the American tradition. It is doubtful that it could be done, for Americans did not go in for hierarchies. But certain virtues were prominent. According to one historian, the following were the

leading virtues in the middle of the eighteenth century:
"patriotism, public service, industry and frugality, justice, and integrity."[2] Another historian, writing of the
nineteenth century American, attributes these virtues to
him:

> The American had a high sense of honor and would
> not tolerate acts dishonorable by his standards. Words
> like truth, justice, loyalty, reverence, virtue, and honor
> meant much to him. . . . He admired industry, temper-
> ance, sportsmanship. . . . He recognized the sovereignty
> of the individual conscience, consulted it on most mat-
> ters, and yielded the same privilege to others.[3]

But a random listing of virtues does not do justice
to the tradition. After all, virtue and morality were the
mortar which held the bricks of the American tradition together. These virtues were not chosen at random; they
were an integral part of the structure of the life of a people. Liberty, individualism, voluntarism, personal independence, and individual responsibility can only be made
to work by a people who have developed virtues which will
buttress these ideas and practices. For people in general
to concur in practices by which each man receives the
fruits of his labor, they need to have a set of values in
keeping with these practices. These values must exist in
intricate interrelation, not in careless disarray.

High on the list of American virtues were industry,
thrift, and frugality. Hard work was not only a practical
means to acquiring goods but also a positive good itself.

---

[2] Clinton Rossiter, *The First American Revolution* (New
York: A Harvest Book, 1953), p. 230.
[3] Henry S. Commager, *The American Mind* (New Haven:
Yale University Press, 1954), pp. 30-31.

Undoubtedly, many believed that an idle mind was the
devil's workshop, but there was also the consideration
that a man who had worked hard all day could sleep the
sleep of the just. Work was the sovereign prescription for
sorrow, for heartache, and for vague discontent. It kept
the young out of mischief and filled the long hours of the
aged. Work was not so much a curse to be avoided as a
blessing to be sought. It was the means by which an individual assumed responsibility for himself and his own,
achieved independence, and showed himself to be a man.

Thrift, too, was a positive virtue. If capital accumulation
was the aim, a penny saved was indeed a penny earned.
Waste not, want not, was the negative way of justifying
frugality, but the practice had deeper sanctions. That
which we hold is a gift of God, held in stewardship from
him. To treat it casually or carelessly would be to hold the
giver in contempt. The counter vices to these virtues were
laziness, extravagance, and wastefulness. These vices were
universally condemned in an earlier America. Indeed, it
was generally held that those who were deprived in some
way were usually to blame because they had yielded to the
vices and not practiced the virtues.

The Virtue of Simplicity

Simplicity was much admired by Americans. This probably reached its peak, so far as public affairs were concerned, during Andrew Jackson's time. But republican
simplicity had been advocated and practiced by Jefferson also. Simplicity of manners, directness of approach,
straightforwardness of action were the standards Americans applied to behavior. They disapproved of pomp,

"putting on airs," an undue complexity, and deviousness. Rhetorical flourishes were all very well in a public speech, but ordinary business should be conducted without obscurity.

This preference for simplicity can be understood; it had an important role in the ethos. If men are to look after their own affairs, if each man is to be responsible for himself, if he is to make choices, the alternatives must be clear. Questions must be raised above the level of complicating circumstances. In effect, this means that they must be posed as moral alternatives, in most cases.

Many twentieth century writers have derided the tendency of Americans to turn questions into moral problems. Yet it is not at all clear how they would propose alternatives to most men. Moral choices can be and are made by simple men who could not hope to understand all the factors in a complicated situation. Indeed, it is doubtful that anyone knows all the particulars of a given situation, or that they could reach a decision if they did. Simplicity is required for individual responsibility and for choice.

Self-respect was another of the major virtues in the American tradition, along with its corollary, respect for others. To be self-respecting meant that one was self-supporting, independent, dependable, conscious of the good opinion of his neighbors, honest, and able to contribute in some way to common tasks. Somewhat of disgrace was attached to falling short of any of these. In his own eyes, a man lost stature by failing to provide for himself. To his neighbors, his virtue was at least suspect. Respect for others involved a consciousness of distance between you, a distance to be bridged only when both parties desired. This meant that another's property was something you used only at his invitation, his time you imposed on at his behest, and his religion, beliefs, and habits you tolerated so long as they did not too grossly offend the taste of the community. American communities were apt to uphold moral standards, not so much by laws as by informal reproval of undesired conduct.

Christian Heritage

These virtues were knit together and given force by the religious and philosophical heritage which most Americans shared. Most Americans have been and are Christian, nominally, devotedly, or haphazardly. Within Christianity, the tone was set by various Protestant sects, at least until the twentieth century. Moreover, these were distinctly colored by English Protestantism, which was heavily suffused with Calvinism in the sixteenth and seventeenth centuries. The Puritans contributed to the American ethos the conception of each man having a calling, of the importance of work, of the practice of thrift and frugality. From the Quakers came the emphasis upon the individual conscience, upon an inner light, and upon the command to obey its promptings. The Baptists insisted upon religion being freed from political control and upon the right of a man to choose how he would worship.

Many of these sectarian beliefs were fused or transcended by revivalists in the Great Awakening, which occurred in the middle of the eighteenth century. Thereafter, most of Protestantism came to share a common ethos. One writer lists the characteristics of American Protestantism in the early nineteenth century, and follows them with these comments:

It is notable that each of these characteristics emphasizes the free decision of the individual will. Christianity in America has emphasized these expressions of a change of heart and of the conversion of the individual: the pious practice of the believer, the revival in the society, and missionary effort to the unconverted. Fundamental to all of this is a fresh grasp on a free and inward decision of the spirit as essential to real religion, and a corresponding rejection of any coercion in religious belief.[4]

The personal piety which religion promoted was evinced in the moral life and the practice of those virtues enumerated above, and others.

But this is to affirm what has not yet been demonstrated, i.e., the connection between religion and morality. To make this demonstration, it will be useful to raise some ultimate questions. Why is self-respect a virtue? Why should men be honest? Why should they tell the truth? Is it good to be independent? In short, what makes those things virtues which men have so denominated?

In our day, there are many intellectuals who doubt that there is any necessary connection between religion and morality. They profess to see no need for a metaphysical realm in which the physical must subsist and have its being. For them, the above questions can be answered pragmatically, so far as they need to be answered. Thus, they might say that it is important that people be honest in order that society may function smoothly. If people did not tell the truth, they would stop trusting one another,

---

[4] William L. Miller, "American Religion and American Political Attitudes," *Religious Perspectives in American Culture*, James W. Smith and A. Leland Jamison, eds. (Princeton: Princeton University Press, 1961), p. 89.

and relationships would deteriorate. In brief, they argue that human reason and social needs form a sufficient base for rules of behavior.

It is not for the historian to answer these ultimate questions that have been posed. His task is completed when he has described what men believed and did—and what the consequences were. Thus, so far as the questions are philosophical or theological, they fall outside the area of my competence. But so far as the actual beliefs that men have held and the relationship of these to the practices of morality and virtue are concerned, these are very much historical questions.

There is no doubt in my mind, then, that American morality was closely connected to religion and philosophy. Nor do I wish to imply that this was merely a fortuitous nexus. Powerful sanctions usually accompany the taboos and imperatives which a people accept. The rationalist may conclude, for example, that murder is an obvious evil, that all men will readily concur with him in this opinion. Surely, he might think, there is no need for supernatural sanctions against murder. The matter may be otherwise, however. Remove the sense of awe and mystery which men have before God and who is to say that you do not contribute to the removal of the awe and mystery which envelops human beings and protects them from one another ordinarily?

Moral Order Established by God

At any rate, the American tradition of virtue and morality had deep religious sanctions. These religious beliefs can be set forth in philosophic terms, though it must be understood that most Americans could not have articulated them in this way. Generally, Americans believed that they lived in a created universe. They believed in a Creator, God transcendent, who stood outside the humanly conceived dimensions of time and space and who made this world.

The common appellation for God in the eighteenth and nineteenth centuries was Providence. God as provider meant different things to different people, of course, depending upon the amount of learning and depth of thought about it. In general terms, though, it meant that he had provided whatever existed in nature—i.e., the universe, its laws, man and his nature, the materials with which men worked. President John Adams captured this conception in the closing words of his Inaugural Address:

> And may that Being who is supreme over all, the Patron of Order, the Fountain of Justice, and the Protector in all ages of the world of virtuous liberty, continue His blessing upon this nation and its Government and give it all possible success and duration consistent with the ends of His providence.[5]

The great support of morality in these religious beliefs was the conviction that this created universe was pervaded by a moral order. By the eighteenth century, many thinkers interpreted this moral order in terms of natural laws. From this point of view, to say that there is a moral order in the universe means that this universe works according to laws. But whether it be understood as natural law or Divine injunction, the belief in a moral order made morality and virtue imperative. Those acts are morally good

---

[5] Richardson, *op. cit.*, I, 232.

which are in keeping with the moral order; virtues are those principles of action which are consonant with the order.

Let us revert to an earlier question. Why is it good to be independent? Because this universe is pervaded by a moral order. Because man is a moral being. Because choice is essential to morality. Because independence is necessary to free choice. How may a man become independent? He may do so by practicing industry, thrift, and frugality. Industry, thrift, and frugality lead to independence because there is an order in the universe, an order in which rewards are likely to be proportioned to effort, in which possessions may be augmented by careful husbandry, in which thrift will be rewarded by increased savings. It may appear a quibble, but let it be noted anyhow: these actions are not good because they have good consequences; they have good consequences because they are good—i.e., that they are in keeping with the moral order. Self-respect begets respect for others; honor begets honesty; fidelity begets faithfulness.

Faith in Freedom

The belief in the existence of a moral order had many attendant results for Americans. It meant that the triumph of right was established and certain. There could be no ultimate tragedy: right would win; justice would triumph; goodness would overcome. Observers have often remarked that Americans were optimistic. Recent interpreters have tended to ascribe this to their experience and environment. Let us suggest a deeper source, the belief in an ultimately triumphant moral order.

This belief served as a profound basis for freedom for Americans. In the first place, it was conducive to faith. The man who lacks faith will be easily inclined to the view that he must do everything himself, that if men are not compelled they will not act in desired ways, that someone or a group must provide a master plan else society will come to pieces, and chaos will reign. The man with faith in an order higher than himself can be content to leave other men to their devices, secure in his knowledge that God is not mocked, that right will triumph, and that his major task is to see that he is not destroyed in the process. He can believe that an economic order may work justly without society's intervention by way of a master plan. There is an order in the universe that brings a harmony out of the diverse activities of men if it is not interfered with by rules devised by men and promulgated in the society, if aggression is estopped, and if freedom prevails in the market.

Second, such a belief in a moral order can serve to promote liberty because it is to the advantage of men to come to know the order. They can do so most adequately if the greatest liberty prevails. The consequences of actions are not obscured; the rewards of endeavors can be viewed without obstruction. In this view, no amount of human effort can thwart the moral order, of course, but human intervention can greatly confuse the onlooker. For example, he may ascribe his prosperity to human agency, or his discoveries to invention. It is extremely important for men to discern cause and effect clearly, for their actions will tend to be predicated upon conclusions about this. Liberty is an important condition of such discernment.

Third, the individual responsibility that follows from living within a universal moral order is essential to the working of liberty. If each man is to have liberty, he must assume responsibility for himself. If he does not, or if society does not impose it upon him, he will suffer, and he may use his suffering as an excuse for compulsory social action.

Reliance on Voluntarism

A tradition of virtue and morality took shape in America, then. It was supported by religion and buttressed by philosophy. It was made manifest in numerous customs and practices: in individualism, in voluntarism, in limited government, in extended liberty, in laws which placed the primary responsibility for his actions upon the individual. Individuals were impelled to work, to strive, to accomplish, because they assumed the responsibility for their well-being. Above all, the belief in a moral order was demonstrated by the things which Americans did not attempt to do by compulsion: by permitting voluntary religious associations, by leaving the individual free to work out his own salvation in his own way, by *not* planning the economy, by *not* presuming to control the behavior of other nations, by resting the government on the free choice and activity of the citizenry.

This system was not founded upon the notion that men are naturally virtuous or morally good, though some could be found who would subscribe to such propositions, but upon the view that there is a moral order in the universe, that all men's schemes will come to nought if they are in opposition to it, and that it is better to remove the tempta-

tion for interfering as far as possible from men by checking power and limiting its legitimate use by government.

There should be no doubt that long strides toward the
abandonment of this tradition have taken place in the
twentieth century. According to much of current economic
thought, those who practice thrift are enemies of prosperity because they lower consumption and slow the
wheels of production. Hard work may be a virtue in some
circles, but the good life is portrayed in America as a play
life. As for frugality, articles have actually appeared sug-
gesting that waste is necessary to full production and
employment. My impression is that self-respect and personal independence are not highly rated today. Sociability
is a much higher virtue. At any rate, less and less is left
to the individual and more and more power is assumed by
governments.

Undermining the Foundations

The philosophical props have been knocked from under
the American tradition; theologians and preachers have
long since ceased to support it with one voice. Intellectuals,
many of them, have come to doubt that there is any order
in the universe, much less a moral one. The Darwinians
promulgated a constantly changing universe, one in which
the only enduring quality was change itself. The Marxians
turned the old order upside down, made technology rather
than man the mover in this world. They and other socialists thingified society (with help from some conservatives),
and reduced the individual to a cog in its giant wheel.
Environmentalists denied the freedom and responsibility
of the individual, and pragmatists proclaimed that these

were meaningless questions. Nietzsche declared that "God
is dead," and his disciples attempted to raise man in His
stead. Preachers of the Social Gospel emphasized the reform of society and worked for the Kingdom to come, a
kingdom which bore a striking resemblance to the mate-
rialistic utopias advanced in the nineteenth century.
Meliorists set out to create their own moral order, one at
considerable variance from that made by the Creator.
In short, the older beliefs were turned upside down. The
tradition was undermined.

The Master-Planned Economy

These intellectual developments set the stage for many
twentieth century practices and attitudes which are by
now familiar. If there is no moral order in the universe,
the economy must be planned, else chaos will result. Man,
or society, must plan and do everything. If the United
States does not exert its power and influence in the world,
great harm will presumably result. Who knows what
France might do with atomic bombs? If men are left to
their devices—are left at liberty—what might be the
consequences? Children must be propagandized, adults
kept at work, the aged supervised or provided with suitable tasks. Lacking a faith in a moral order, men must
engage in frenetic social activities to maintain order.
Lacking a working belief in a transcendent God, men will
play at being gods. They cannot accept freedom because
they cannot predict the consequences of freedom. Hence,
they are driven to more and more controls in order to
have a predictable condition. Lacking a belief in immutable law, judges presume to make their own law.

Could George Washington have been right? Is there a connection between religion and morality? More, is there a connection between these and the possibility of maintaining liberty? In the American tradition, there was. Can it be that this connection subsists in reality? Those who maintain otherwise, or who act otherwise, need to demonstrate how they, of their own efforts, will maintain freedom without a moral order. The consequences of their experiments thus far are not such as to inspire faith in man's unaided abilities. One wonders if any more journeys into the twilight zone of humanistic meliorism are warranted! The residues of the American tradition of virtue and morality point in another direction.

14.

To Agree To Disagree

It is customary nowadays to list all sorts of things as social problems. If children are disobedient to their parents, if deaths occur on the highways, if some people lack housing that suits their taste, these are not only likely to be described as social problems but also, if the incidence is widespread at all, "national problems," or, better still, "international problems." Having described the problem, having given it the largest possible scope, then the standard operating procedure is to name "fact-finding" committees, distribute lurid and imaginative accounts of it to the press, and to prepare "stop-gap" legislation to deal with the emergency, pending more nearly definitive solutions. Our politicians have come to resemble hordes of Dutch boys, rushing from hole to hole to stem the tide of an ocean of "problems" by sticking their fingers in the holes. Even the millions of bureaucrats who are hired to stand with their fingers in the holes, though it is not always clear whether they are plugging or making holes, have to be continually augmented.

It is my belief that many of these "problems" are the products of an ideological orientation. The symptoms are often distressingly real, but the diagnosis only aggravates them. Undoubtedly, there are problems which transcend the scope of individuals and of families. There may well be some that could be more effectively dealt with by communities, or even larger social and political units. But to extend the scope of all problems to the utmost limits is the result of an elemental failure to distinguish among them. Most of those that are now called "national problems" could be readily reduced to individual and family problems. If all the misconduct of children is lumped together as "juvenile delinquency," it assumes massive proportions. But parents can discipline their own children, regulate their hours outdoors, and call them to account for their misconduct. Our dikes are not stemming an ocean tide; they are only hard put to contain all the dirty water we persist in emptying into a common pool, encouraged by many intellectuals and politicians.

Enduring Problems

The great social problems do not change much, if at all, with the passage of time. Our ways of defining them may change. The conditions within which they make their appearance change, and the symptoms will vary depending upon the direction that is taken to solve them. The problems remain the same because they arise from enduring facts of life. Namely, each one of us is different from every other person. Each of us is endowed with a will to have his own way. We have desires, preferences, values, needs, wants, beliefs, prejudices, and customs which are always, at the least, potential sources of conflict. Most of us desire the company of others—are social beings—yet prize our privacy and independence. The sources of conflict are quite often further increased by our attachments to particular cultures, countries, classes, churches, rituals, and habits. We live in danger of assault by others and are ourselves prone to intrude in the affairs of other men. There are undertakings which we like, even if we do not need, to do with others. We are so constituted, and are so situated in the world, that we must have the help of others in protecting ourselves.

The social problems which arise from these facts about people and the universe can be stated in the following manner: How can people, who are potentially in conflict with one another, live together in peace and harmony? How can they achieve sufficient unity for protective, social, and economic purposes? How can room be left for the development and fulfillment of the individual without giving license to the aggressive wills of these same individuals? To put it another way, the problems are to find ways of maintaining both order and liberty, of harmonizing unity and diversity, of permitting both social cooperation and individual independence, of protecting people from aggression without crushing their initiative and creativity.

The history of the world is dotted with the graveyards of city-states, nation-states, kingdoms, and empires which have failed to deal with these problems effectively enough to survive. Peoples have yielded up their liberty for national glory, been bedazzled by the splendor and pomp of monarchs, sold their independence for the promise of security, concentrated power to subdue anarchic groups, suppressed differences which they believed threatened their social organization. Peoples have tended to vacillate between the extremes to which the *demos* is given and the confining autocracies of monarchies.

From this viewpoint, the American experience is particularly significant. Of course, Americans did not *solve* the problems described above. Nor is it likely that any people will ever solve them. It is a prominent superstition of our age that problems which arise from the nature of man, of human relationships, and the nature of the universe can be finally solved. Such solutions could only be achieved by getting rid of all people. The most that we can hope and work for is to provide a social framework within which these problems can be kept to manageable proportions, within which there can be a tolerable degree of harmony, a maximum of liberty with a minimum of friction, and an adequacy of unity for security against aggressors without choking out diversity.

The Unique American Experience

There was an American tradition for such a framework. I am calling it here the tradition to agree to disagree. By these words, I mean to describe the essence of the tradition, to sum up the many aspects of a whole tradition. It sums up, too, the only way that I know of that offers much hope of satisfactorily dealing with the problems of human existence enumerated above. The matter should not be put in a pessimistic tone: the American tradition was a creative and artistic rendering of human experience into a way for securing both order and liberty. It was an exhilarating vision which our forefathers had, and an inspiring example which Americans set for a time.

Disagreement was not, of course, the goal or ideal. No one but a sophist could take pleasure in disagreement. Certainly, Americans were quite often people of conviction and given to enthusiasms. And, men of conviction find it extremely difficult to understand why others do not agree with them. To agree to disagree may even be called an expedient, for that is what it is and was. It was a very practical expedient when Americans began the United States. There were in America people from many lands, accustomed to diverse practices, and zealously missionary in spreading their ways. There were several races, a multitude of religious sects, people of an independent and adventurous spirit alongside those who wanted to live in communities separate from the "world." There were Puritans, Quakers, Mennonites, Baptists, monarchists, democrats, slaveholders, abolitionists, establishmentarians, disestablishmentarians, physiocrats, mercantilists, Germans, Jews, Scotch, English, Dutch, Swedes, Negroes, alcoholics, and total abstainers. There were those who would base the elective franchise upon property or wealth, while others favored only the arrival at manhood. There were individualists and communitarians, and many other persuasions with vigorous advocates. A "United States" was only possible if men could agree to disagree about a great many things.

What was expedient for them is, however, an essential of liberty. Theoretically, it might be desirable for all men to agree on everything, though I doubt it. Practically, such agreement would only be possible if all individual wills were crushed and subjected to a single will. The effort to do this is always in the direction of the well traveled road to despotism. The alternatives are agreement to disagree or despotism.

If men simply agreed to disagree, however, there is great likelihood that disorder, chaos, and oppression would follow. The strong would oppress the weak. Men would form bands to prey upon and subdue others. Disagreement would soon be something bought at a high price. Far from being something simple to achieve, free disagreement must be provided for by subtle and creative social arrangements and protected by powerful inner sanctions of the individual. These things the American tradition provided. It is from this point of view that I would like to sum it up.

Governments Must Be Limited

The first essential for effective disagreement is that governments be strictly limited in what they are to do. Governments *are* necessary to the maintenance of order and protection of the individual, but they may easily become instruments of oppression and use their powers to produce unwilling assent. A written constitution was the device adopted by Americans to contain and limit government. Many current "liberals" hold the position that, except for the rights of certain "pet" minorities, disagreement is adequately provided for by allowing freedom of speech and press and maintaining a voting mechanism by which the actions of governments may be altered or reversed. But insofar as the agreement to disagree encompasses liberty, the provision for mere verbal disagreements does not begin to be enough. And, it is by no means all that the United States Constitution established. The Constitution attempted to limit governmental action by listing matters beyond the jurisdiction of the federal government, by denying certain powers to the states, and by providing that all those powers not specifically granted to the federal government were reserved to the states or to the people. Thus, it provided for substantive liberty as well as verbal disagreement.

The most important political provision for disagreement was the federal system of government. By this system, powers were not only dispersed, thus further limiting the governments, but also a way was opened for following quite different policies locally. Thus, if the people of a state decided to do so, they might have laws and customs quite different from an adjoining state or from any other state. Variety and diversity were possible. But the free movement of people (excepting slaves, when and where slavery was established) and goods placed practical limits upon what could be done by a state. If a state passed oppressive laws, the chances were good that it would lose population and wealth. If it had higher taxes than neighboring states, its merchants would lose trade to those of other states, particularly along the border. If any group were given special privileges to the disadvantage of other citizens, these citizens might retaliate by leaving the state.

Republican Form of Government

Agreement on some essentials is necessary to providing conditions within which people can be at liberty, develop their own ways—in effect, disagree. They must agree upon the establishment of a framework for liberty. Obviously, constitutionalism and federalism must be widely accepted in order to survive. The Founding Fathers thought one other structural condition was necessary: republican forms of government. The Constitution not only

established a republican form for the central government
but also prescribed that all states must have governments
that were republican in form. Basically, this meant that
the actions of government stemmed initially from the
electorate, and that the people would act through representatives. Such governments would have a popular base,
but, it was hoped, the worst effects of direct government
would be prevented by the necessity of acting through
representatives. Efforts were made, also, to prevent or
delay precipitate majority action by representatives. By
having two Houses in the national government, each of
which had to pass legislation by majorities, by providing
for presidential vetoes, by requiring that legislation passed
over vetoes be passed by at least two-thirds of each House,
by creating an independent judiciary which would apply the laws, the Founders hoped to prevent all government action which did not have widespread support. In
short, there was an effort to limit government to that action upon which there was general agreement. The effect of this should be to limit to a few matters the action
actually taken. This would keep the area of individual liberty large while satisfying the requirement that government be by agreement.

Those who have written about American traditions have
usually paid far too much attention to the political (or
governmental) tradition and far too little to the customs,
habits, folkways, and beliefs which lay outside the political realm. For in the American tradition most things were
left to individual and voluntary group decision. But it was
in the area outside of legal imposition that agreement to
disagree really worked. It was here, too, that the underlying support for tradition lay. The belief in and prac-

tices which we associate with individualism were not the least of these. The tradition of individualism embraced private rights, individual responsibility, respect for the individual, and the belief that the individual is the only thing of final importance. Herein lies the final significance of the agreement to disagree. If individuals are to be held responsible for their acts, if these acts are to have moral content, individuals must be free to choose their courses of action. This means that they must be permitted to disagree. Choice is the important thing, but the possibility of disagreement is necessary to choice.

Equality Before the Law

The corollaries of individualism are equality before the law, voluntarism, and some means of civilizing groups. If the individual is to assume his responsibilities to look after himself and his own, if he is to exercise his rights, he needs to be legally equal to all other men. To put it negatively, he needs to be free of any imposed disabilities. When the law acts impartially toward all individuals, all will not fare equally, of course. But they will have mainly themselves to blame for such inequalities as exist. Some individuals will not be able to look after themselves, however, because of disabilities inherited or acquired. In the American tradition, they were supposed to be taken care of mainly by the voluntary activity of individuals and groups. All sorts of voluntary groupings were permitted and promoted for doing things which individuals could not do alone, charitable, educational, business, and so on. Groups are potentially dangerous to individuals, however, not only because groups differ in their nature from individuals but because they can overpower and suppress the individual. In America, there was a tradition for civilizing them. Mainly it consisted of denying them the right to use force to have their way, of avoiding direct political action by groups, and of breaking them up into individuals to deal with them.

Free economic intercourse was a very useful adjunct to individualism; indeed, it was a corollary of equality before the law and an essential condition to disagreement in economic matters. People differ greatly from one to another as to what goods are wanted, in what quantity and of what quality they should be made, whether they should be produced by hand or by machines, how labor should be employed and paid, and so forth. If economic intercourse is free from control, these matters will be settled by the customers, each man deciding for himself so far as it lies within his power and by agreement with others when more than one person is necessary to the decision. If men want to make money, and many appear to, the market will provide many of the answers to otherwise unanswerable questions. Men may disagree, even with the market, but they will pay heavily for their disagreement.

The American tradition, then, was one of liberty for men to seek their own well-being as they saw fit, to do so alone or in the company of others, to exert their wills in their own behalf, perchance for self-expression and individual fulfillment. But such liberty does not dispose of all social problems; it even raises some. Both individuals and groups, when they are free, are apt to exert their wills upon others uninvited, to oppress them, and to seek their personal or group interest at the expense of others.

The American tradition provided for these eventualities also, in two important ways. First, the American tradition was one of government by law. This meant that all men were under the law, and that they must act in accordance with certain rules, or be punished if they were caught. They must not use force on another who has not first provoked the act by use of force. They must live up to the terms of their contracts. They must not commit fraud or practice willful deceit.

A Tradition of Competition

Second, there was a *tradition of competition* in America. I have not discussed this elsewhere in detail, but it was probably the most important tradition for bringing harmony out of potential conflict. So far as we know, many men *are* aggressive by nature. They are capable of committing aggression upon others. Some have believed that the way to handle this bent is to suppress it, to close off all outlets to express it. The American way, however, was to channel and direct it through competition, to permit a legitimate mode for the expression of the desire to best others. Indeed, this was the mode of American progress. Through competition, conducted according to rules, men were striving continually to do something better than anyone else had done or would do, to build a better product, to write a better book, to invent, to discover, to create, to accumulate, to originate, to perfect, to overcome, to outplay, and to excel. The competition motif pervaded American business, education, arts, charity, games, social life, and religion. The consequences were the achievements for which America became known around the world.

But competition was the cornerstone of the agreement

to disagree. The very disagreement and difference spurred the achievement, but the underlying agreement was expressed in this aphorism: "May the best man win." Each man could pursue his own interest, but the result of this was often more and less expensive goods, new and improved products, more comfortable transportation, swifter communication, more alert teachers, more zealous ministers, more vigorous athletes, and so on. True, there would be those who would not be captivated by many of these achievements, or even reckon them to be achievements, but so long as they were not forced to contribute to them by government, their disagreement was protected, and their opposition as effective as their powers of persuasion.

This whole tradition to agree to disagree was knit together and given inner vitality by a tradition of virtue and morality. The belief in a moral order in the universe gave metaphysical support to the American way. It made liberty an imperative, for choice was the mode for the individual's participation in this moral order. It supported, too, the virtues—i.e., industry, thrift, frugality, self-respect, independence, respect for others—which made the system work. In the final analysis, the belief in a moral order in the universe made the agreement to disagree acceptable, for the final triumph of righteousness would not be thwarted by differences among men. Men would suffer, if and when they were wrong, but not the moral order.

The agreement to disagree was facilitated in relations among nations by the system of nation-states and the tradition of foreign relations in the nineteenth century. Internally, the peoples of a nation could pursue whatever ways suited them. Externally, they could carry on relations with others, so long as they did so in a civilized manner. The

condition of dealing with others was the agreement to do
so in a regular and civilized manner, to respect the nationals of other countries within their borders, to see that
their citizens honored contracts, to concur in those practices which would facilitate trade, commerce, and intercourse on equitable terms.

It is not my contention that this tradition made men
perfect, that it removed all abrasiveness from human relations, or that it solved all problems. It did, however, provide a framework for people to live in harmony with one
another, offer opportunities for the fulfillment of individuals, impose checks upon the licentious wills of individuals, arouse the devotion of the populace so as to make
unity possible, permit a great degree of diversity, and have
a basis for establishing order. It did not do what no system
is likely to do: banish suffering from the world, provide
perfect justice for every man at every moment, or solve
all the "problems" which men could conjure up. Perhaps
it succeeded so well that some men, viewing the accomplishments under it, believed that utopia was possible.

The Search for Utopia

At any rate, nineteenth century intellectuals were pro-
lific in devising plans for "solving" the remaining problems of human beings. Communists, socialists, anarchists,
perfectionists, communitarians, and ideologues of every
imaginable persuasion vied with one another for the prize
of having *the* perfect plan. But these ideologies were at
war with the whole Western tradition, or, for that matter, with any tradition. The wisdom of the ages might
proclaim that human nature was flawed, but it could not

be so if perfection was to be achieved. Indeed, it would be better if there were no human nature, only plastic human beings. To make such conceptions believable, Marx, Nietzsche, Darwin, Freud, James, and Dewey, among others, stood the world of traditional belief on its head.

Many are confused today because they hear familiar words used in unfamiliar ways, and unfamiliar words used to describe familiar things. But this is the consequence of standing the world of belief on its head. Black then becomes white; freedom becomes unfreedom. For example, to some—Marx prominent among them—freedom came to be identified with an absence of tension or conflict. Thus, even competition becomes an intolerable evil, for it regularizes and gives approbation to that which should be removed. To others, the bent to aggression sets up intolerable frustrations if it is not relieved directly, i.e., by physical combat in war.

Those of us now living have behind us some of the catastrophes that resulted from the ideologies which would solve all problems. We know of the fascist attempt to achieve social and economic accord by the empowering of groups organized as syndicates, and the forging of an irrepressible unity in the fires of war. We know of the Nazi attempts to achieve an earthly paradise on the unity which arises from blood and soil, and of the unspeakable atrocities they committed against those who were disruptive of that unity. Then there have been the Russian communist experiments, the massive efforts to alter human nature, the persecution of dissidents, the reigns of terror, and the predictable famines and shortages. On a world scale, the agreement to disagree has dissolved, melted in the fires of catastrophic conflicts and nearly

permanent civil disorders. Almost everywhere the tendency
has been to replace it with the forced concurrence to concur, the tendency to coerce into obedience.

America No Exception

Happy the nation that should be spared such trials!
Would that I could report that Americans had stood apart
from all this, weeping with those who wept and mourn-
ing with those who mourned, but determined to stand by
a tested and proven tradition, a tradition to agree to disagree. But it is not so. American soil has been spared
thus far the bloodletting that has followed upon the ideological attempts to turn the world upside down in this
century. But many Americans, too, have succumbed to
the lure of utopia. They have traded in the old tradition
and wait, impatiently and even riotously sometimes, for
the paradise which ideologues have promised. If there is
still unemployment, it is not as bad as it once was, we are
told. If there is still intolerance, it will end upon the
"completion of the revolution," we are promised.

My point is this, however: the agreement to disagree
is disappearing from America also. It is not going in the
revolutionary way it did in Nazi Germany or Communist
Russia. Rather, it is disappearing step by step and stage
by stage. The belief in a Higher Law is undermined by a
relativism which admits of none, and constitutionalism
ceases to impose limits on government as the Constitution
is reinterpreted in the light of changing conditions. Republican government loses its vitality because of the attempts to make it into a direct democracy and to have it
act in ways for which it is not suited as a form. Localism

is swallowed up by an all-embracing centralism, and the federal principle falls by the way. Government by law is superseded because the welfare state must be imposed by a government by men. Individualism loses ground to collectivism. The area for voluntary activity is diminished as the area of compulsory activity is expanded. Equality before the law is obscured by the efforts to make men equal by law. Minute regulations are imposed in an attempt to regulate groups which have been empowered by law, and we forget how to civilize groups. Free economic intercourse declines before a mounting tide of regulations, and we drift toward neofeudalism and neomercantilism. Internationalism has largely been replaced in foreign relations by interventionism. Ideologues attempt to envision a man-made order which will serve in the stead of the moral order they have displaced, and struggle mightily to obscure immorality by denying its existence.

The Welfare State

These tendencies have not yet resulted in the complete obliteration of the tradition. A saving remnant of Americans have clung to the tradition. Moreover, many "liberals" have attempted to preserve some of the tradition to agree to disagree, particularly that part of it they call "civil rights." They have pressed for the concentration of power in a central government, for the planned economy, for the regulation of business, for foreign intervention, for collective responsibility at home and abroad. On the other hand, they have attempted to forestall some of the consequences of these actions for liberty. The result is what is now generally called the welfare state. According to the mythos of the "liberals," a way has been found to preserve the best of the American tradition while avoiding what they conceive to be the onerous consequences of individual action and responsibility. It is the middle way of the welfare state.

Many Americans apparently believe that there is truth in this myth. What they do not perceive is the illusory character of what is said to be preserved and the very real uses of power which have been introduced. Thus, we are told that there is no need to fear the concentration of power in government so long as that power is checked by the electoral process. We are urged to believe that so long as we can express our disagreement in words, we have our full rights to disagree. Now both freedom of speech and the electoral process are important to liberty, but alone they are only the dessicated remains of liberty. However vigorously we may argue against foreign aid, our substance is still drained away in never-to-be-repaid loans. Quite often, there is not even a candidate to vote for who holds views remotely like my own. To vent one's spleen against the graduated income tax may be healthy for the psyche, but one must still yield up his freedom of choice as to how his money will be spent when he pays it to the government. The voice of electors in government is not even proportioned to tax contribution of individuals; thus, those who contribute more lose rather than gain by the "democratic" process. A majority of voters may decide that property cannot be used in such and such ways, but the liberty of the individual is diminished just as much in that regard as if a dictator had decreed it. Those who believe in the redistribution of the wealth should be free to redistribute their own, but they are undoubtedly limiting the freedom of others when they vote to redistribute theirs.

Effective disagreement means *not doing* what one does not want to *do* as well as saying what he wants to say. What is from one angle the welfare state is from another the compulsory state. Let me submit a bill of particulars. Children are *forced* to attend school. Americans are *forced* to pay taxes to support foreign aid, *forced* to support the Peace Corps, *forced* to make loans to the United Nations, *forced* to contribute to the building of hospitals, *forced* to serve in the armed forces. Employers are *forced* to submit to arbitration with labor leaders. Laborers are *forced* to accept the majority decision. Employers are *forced* to pay minimum wages, or go out of business. But it is not even certain that they will be permitted by the courts to go out of business. Railroads are *forced* to charge established rates and to continue services which may have become uneconomical. Many Americans are *forced* to pay social security. Farmers are *forced* to operate according to the restrictions voted by a majority of those involved. The list could be extended, but surely the point has been made.

Force and Compulsion

That the compulsory character of the welfare state is not always apparent has a variety of explanations. Political demagogues call our attention to the benefits and make no mention of the compulsion by which they are to be acquired. "Liberal" ideologues have constructed a language for discussing their programs which hides the force and coercion that is involved. Americans continue to obey the laws willingly, in keeping with the habits drawn from tradition, unaware that the tradition has been undermined. The more thoughtful may read the fearful penalties attached to disobedience of federal laws: $10,000 fine or ten years in prison or both. Many are undoubtedly convinced that what the government is doing is what we *should* do in any case. They may be right, but they should understand that however desirable the programs, they are programs imposed by force or the threat of force, that disagreement with them may be only verbal, and that each such extension of governmental authority is at the expense of individual liberty.

Let us draw the unavoidable conclusion. The welfare state *cannot* be instituted without destroying the agreement to disagree. There cannot be a nationally planned economy without taking from individuals the right to plan their own economic activities. Groups cannot be empowered without giving them coercive powers over individuals. We cannot have a federally imposed homogenized and integrated society without at the same time destroying diversity. Competitiveness may be discouraged and squelched, but the smoldering aggressiveness of individuals which has been denied constructive outlets will erupt in the violence of "rebels without a cause." There is no denying the ingenuity of "sophisticated" intellectuals who can fabricate endless explanations for the failures of their programs, explanations which will leave the programs unindicted. If reality were entirely plastic, if it consisted only of mental "constructs," I have no doubt they could devise a world in which men might agree to disagree and yet always act in a unified manner on everything. Unfortunately for them, and fortunately for us (for I am unwilling to admit that they could build a better universe), their phantasies are pitted against a concrete reality, and the consequences of their programs will come whether they recognize a language that would describe them or not.

Room for Disagreement

For those who believe in liberty, there is still room for hope. The universe will still bring to nought the conceits of men, though all may suffer in the process. Men have sometimes learned a little from their experiences. The American tradition is still sufficiently alive that the language drawn from it kindles a warm response in the breasts of some men, and many "liberals" are still inhibited by it from pressing their programs to their logical conclusion. The verbal disagreement that is still possible by way of freedom of speech may still be used to persuade men to acknowledge the compulsion of the welfare state. The electoral process can still be used to reverse these tendencies. Congress still sits, and many men there have the courage to stand against executive authority and even to talk back to the Supreme Court. There can be no possibility of getting all men to agree to the multitude of positive governmental programs involving compulsion, but it may still be possible to recover the tradition to agree to disagree.

15.

The Restoration of the American Tradition

CAN the American tradition be restored? Supposing it were desirable to do so, has the time not passed when it might have been done? Once embarked upon a course, must a people not pursue it to its end? Anyhow, would it not be a revolutionary undertaking to attempt to restore the tradition? Appearances would indicate that a new tradition has been erected upon the remains of the old in America, that the reformers have succeeded in developing a tradition of positive governmental action, of collective security, of intervention in the economy, of integration of the population, of government by men, and of direct group action. They have created numerous institutions—Interstate Commerce Commission, Federal Communications Commission, welfare and education agencies, and so on—and the bureaucracy which operates these certainly has become a vested interest. It looks as if the task of restoring the American tradition might be akin to the effort to put Humpty-Dumpty together again—in a word, impossible.

My opinion is that this way of formulating the problem greatly exaggerates the difficulties of restoring the tradition. The difficulties are two-fold, not manifold. They consist, in the first place, of convincing a sufficient portion of the American people that it would be worthwhile restoring. Second, it would involve overcoming the tenacious and determined resistance of the vested interests (that is, those who stand to gain personally by a multitude of governmental programs and practices) who will raise a deafening hue and cry at every effort to pry them loose from their privileges, perquisites, and benefices. As things now stand, they will be given the maximum aid, comfort, and coverage in their outcries by the press and other media of communication. The resultant noise might frighten the timid into supposing a revolution was going on, but a resolute Congress should be able to undo in short order what it has done in decades.

Some might suppose that the above vastly oversimplifies the problems. But I am not attempting to maintain that the two things mentioned above will be easy to do. They will require a resoluteness in politicians and populace that has not been in much evidence lately. What I am saying is that the restoration of the tradition does not involve any deep social revolution or profound metaphysical difficulties. There is *no tradition* of interventionism to be uprooted, only forcefully imposed restraints to be removed.

The belief that the twentieth century innovations in America constitute a tradition stems from a confusion of ideology with tradition. Throughout this work, I have tried to keep clear the distinction between the two. An ideology, as I understand it, is a completed version of reality. It is a product of the mind of a man or of the minds of several men. It may begin with some facts drawn from experience, though it is more apt to start with an *interpretation* of these facts. One might, for example, start with the observed facts that some people do not have as many clothes as others, nor are their houses as warm, their salaries as high, their cupboards as well stocked, and so on. So far, so good, but at this point the ideologue usually begins to intrude assumptions and value judgments, whose validity he has not tested, if they are testable.

The ideologue will say, to continue the example, that everybody *ought* to have the necessities of life. He may insert the notion that the universe was created in such a way that these things would be provided, if no one interfered. Things are not the way they *should* be. He casts around for a villain. The villain, of course, is whoever is doing the *exploiting*, and that will be those who have more than others, possibly those who have the most. Depending upon his predilections and his patience or spare time, the ideologue may spin out his interpretation to embrace a philosophy of history and a vision of what things will be like when *injustice* has been removed and utopia has arrived. Indeed, it is the essence of ideologies that they are utopian and that they have an implicit philosophy of history. At least, this has been so since around 1850, and not many ideologies go back before this time.

Ideologies Always Collectivist

Ideologies, then, are the products of intellectuals. But so, possibly, are ideas, philosophies, theologies, artistic creations, inventions, discoveries, and so on. It is a mistake to confuse even a collection of ideas which has been rounded out into a philosophy with ideologies, however. Ideologies have distinguishing features by which they can almost always be recognized. (1) They contain a *completed* version of reality. Everything that has or will happen is already explained. (2) They are utopian, and Marx's protestations to the contrary should mislead no one as to the heady utopianism of Marxism. (3) They have a *plan* for the realization of utopia. Marxism is confusing again because he apparently believed that the change would come automatically. But his disciples have had to devise plans. These plans involve centralized control and planning of the social and economic life of a people, or all people. (4) Ideologies must always be *imposed* upon a people and maintained by force or threat of force. Some of the people may cooperate in their own enslavement, but there will always be dissidents, and the realization of utopia requires that everyone participate, willingly or not. (5) Ideologies are always *collectivist* in character. This is made necessary by the other characteristics.

On the contrary, a tradition arises out of the lives of a people. It is *not imposed* from above; indeed, it is not ordinarily imposed at all. Whereas an ideology is operative in the area where force is used, traditions stem from the area of freedom available to a people. They are the customary ways a people develop for carrying on relationships with one another, the habitual forms for conduct and activity, the usual means for going about doing something or other. Ideas may contribute to the development of a tradition, theologies may buttress it, philosophies may comprehend it, but it can no more stem from these than ideas can exert force without the instrumentalities of men. Many traditions probably take shape in the same fashion that a path through a wooded area will in the country. Someone discovers that a certain route from one point to another is the nearest one which will encounter the fewest obstacles. He customarily takes this course until his tread has begun to shape the path. Others follow it, and in time this path becomes the way from one point to another.

The Natural Growth of Tradition

Traditions are apt to lie close to the nature of things and to be constantly modified by experience. Thus, it is easy to understand how a tradition would be formed of a family consisting of a man and a woman and their progeny. By nature, it takes a man and a woman to produce a child. It does not appear to conflict with any reality that they should assume the responsibility of rearing the child. The chances are good that they will become devoted to the child, and it may well be that they will sacrifice for its benefit. These practices may be, and usually are given social and religious sanctions, in addition to legal support, but they accord well with the experience of mankind.

Traditions, then, take shape by the efforts of men to cope with circumstances and conditions in regular ways. They exist whether men have a word to stand for them or not. No law is necessary, ordinarily, for them to be observed, though a law running contrary to them will be hardly enforced. The whole of them, in their complexity and variety, constitute the paths which men follow in leading their lives in a given society. Any large-scale disruption of the traditions will result in the disorientation of the populace. In the modern era, the great revolutions— i.e., English, French, Russian, Chinese, and so forth— have been the efforts to overturn traditions by the use of force under the guidance of ideology.

My point is this: the reverse does not appear to occur.

When ideology is abandoned or discarded, revolution does not occur. When force is removed from behind it, ideology collapses, and people resume the tenor of their lives, following old and developing new traditions. I have in mind Germany and Italy after World War II, or England after the collapse of the Puritan regime.

Of course, two conditions are probably particularly important to a smooth transition from ideology to tradition. Law and order would need to be maintained after the collapse of the forcefully imposed ideology. Second, the extent to which the tradition had been disrupted would determine how readily it might be resumed. For example, if private property had been outlawed, there might be considerable difficulty in re-establishing property. Even so, when force was removed, this is likely to be one of the first things to which most people would attend today. Of course, Americans do not face any such difficulties in restoring their tradition.

Ideology Plus Force

The validity of two propositions needs to be established before the above analysis can be made relevant to the present American condition. First, it must be shown that Americans have been guided by an ideology in reforming the government and its relation to the populace. Second, it must be clear that the practices informed by this ideology have been imposed by force.

It is easy to show that the Soviet Union was founded upon an ideology imposed by force. Lenin made no secret of the fact that he was a communist. The bloody imposition of their programs upon the Russians should have left no doubt that brutal force was used to implement the programs. But Lenin and Stalin were proclaimed revolutionists. The vast assault upon the body of traditions of the Russian people could not have been covered up, if the leaders had desired to do so. They acted too swiftly and decisively for that.

In America, however, things have been quite different. There has been no proclaimed nor bloody revolution in the twentieth century. Instead, changes have occurred gradually, in an evolutionary manner, with the possible exception of a short period in the early New Deal. Efforts have usually been made to show how each departure from it was really in keeping with the American tradition. When President Franklin D. Roosevelt made his court reorganization proposal, for instance, he maintained that he was attempting to revitalize the "true" American tradition. Moreover, reformers have sought to use the institutional framework for their changes rather than simply destroying it. They have even managed to use such institutions as the Supreme Court, whose authority rested upon a profound tradition, to advance their programs. The ideology has usually been obscured behind a scientistic and pragmatic cover.

In consequence, both ideology and force have been rather well hidden from the view of an idle onlooker. Nonetheless, there was and is an ideology. It has almost always been just beneath the surface in the speeches of the reform politicians, the writings of the theorists, and the fulminations of the discontented. Their "four" (or "eight") year plans even burst into view and became a part of the language of the people under such interesting names as Square Deal, New Freedom, New Deal, Fair Deal, and

New Frontier. Back of these, the ideology is more difficult to discern, but it is there.

The Ideology Outlined

There is not space here to explore the ideology in detail, but it should suffice to call attention to its outline. Where such ideologies as the Marxist, socialist, and fascist were set forth in detail and considerable distinctness, the ideology of the American reformers is fuzzy, blurred, implicit, and lacking in clarity. It is quite possible that some of the most ideological of the reformers today are unaware that they are ideologues. Several reasons can be given for this state of affairs. Many of the progenitors of present-day reformers subscribed to rather explicit ideologies; they were socialists, Marxists, devotees of the Social Gospel, or "sociocrats." But they were usually repudiated by their American contemporaries, and for various reasons they or their disciples got out of the organizations and parties by which they could have been identified. Too, the decay of language and the decline of philosophy have made it possible for ideologues to hide from themselves and from others the fact that they are. There are advantages, too, in avoiding explicit affirmations of the ideology. Most of the assumptions upon which it is based have been discredited, and if the doctrines were openly affirmed they could be debated. No such difficulties are raised when the ideas are kept conveniently beneath the surface. Ideologues can operate from day to day—"pragmatically and experimentally," as they like to claim—advancing their ideology without having to defend it.

The ideology is made up of a composite of ideas drawn

from progressivism, meliorism, utopianism, pragmatism, collectivism, with overtones of the class struggle, elitism, egalitarianism, and scientism. The name for them all taken together is "democracy," or so its proponents would have us believe. Those who advance this ideology in America are usually called "liberals." The elements of the ideology are loosely linked together and some of them are, in fact, antithetical to one another. For example, egalitarianism and elitism are patently in conflict with one another, on the surface anyhow. Beneath the surface where they operate, however, they are made compatible by scientism. Thus, the society would be supposed to move toward equality, but this would be done by an elite of "scientists." This explains the myriad experts, brain-trusters, and college-trained bureaucrats who are employed by the politicians to develop and advance their programs. It should be noted, too, that the great variety of "isms" in the ideology permits a continual shifting when the programs come under attack. If the "elite" comes under attack, it can take shelter under progressivism. That is, it maintains that its programs are progressive. Those who attack them are reactionary.

Skin-Deep Inconsistencies

We might suppose, then, that there would be a general lack of consistency in the programs advanced by the "liberals." It does not appear. True, there appears to be confusion quite often, and they do like to have debates on what they are pleased to call "issues." But what they usually debate is whether or not the federal government should do this or that at this time, whether the minimum wage should be raised to $1.15 or $1.25 an hour, whether more federal aid should be given for urban renewal or education, whether foreign aid should be reduced in order to build more federal housing projects, whether foreign aid should be economic or military, whether strings should be attached to foreign aid or not, and so forth. In short, much of the apparent confusion is window dressing. There is sufficient consistency in the general direction to conclude that their programs are informed by ideology.

Programs almost invariably call for more central government activity, more centralization of power in the federal government, more power in the hands of the President and of "independent" agencies, more spending by all governments, more deficit financing, more aid to the "underprivileged," more benefits under Social Security, more control and regulation over the economy, more uniformity of practice throughout the country, and more integration of the population. The direction is always toward a diminution of property rights and a redistribution of wealth. We move further and further away from individual responsibility toward collective responsibility for everything. The direction is almost always away from government by law toward the arbitrary decisions of judges, boards, commissions, committees, and administrators. The press reported that Attorney General Robert F. Kennedy was unconcerned with the drawing of a precise bill for Civil Rights. Let it be a very general measure, and let the courts determine its scope and limits.

The result of all these tendencies is arbitrary and authoritarian government. It is arbitrary because the powers are vested in administrators to exercise as they see fit, each case decided according to its "merits." It is authoritarian because the decisions are usually made by authorities, i.e., experts. It is ideological, because the above have been found to be the conditions for moving toward collectivism in this century, and the programs themselves are collectivist. It is antitraditional because the programs come from intellectuals rather than taking shape out of the lives and habits of the people. It is even anti-intellectual because it lacks a coherently articulated philosophy which could stand the test of reason.

Founded on Force

That this ideology has been and is advanced by force or the threat of force should not need demonstration. But it does. The programs, and the force that is used to impose them, are supposed to be legitimated by being "democratic." Now modern "liberals" are majoritarians when it suits their purposes, but they do not feel bound to even this requirement of "democracy." Present indications are that if a Supreme Court decision went contrary to the wishes of over 90 per cent of the populace, and if the decision pleased them, they would favor it. Moreover, many "liberals" have no compunction about belaboring the taste of the great majority of Americans, their taste in automobiles, consumer goods, recreation, and so forth.

Even if they were consistent majoritarians, however, it would not change the fact that force is used to impose the programs. Any positive use of government is predicated upon the use of force upon someone. This is not altered by the number who would vote for it or the desirability of the object sought. If everyone would willingly contribute to the program or participate in it, no purpose would be served by enacting a law. If everyone would willingly give of their substance and time to Social Security, to the Tennessee Valley Authority, to foreign aid, to the support of the Peace Corps, to the redistribution of the wealth, to the support of education, it would be superfluous to make laws about it. The fact that it is made a law means that force or the threat of force is going to be used to make those comply who would otherwise be unwilling. Those who persist in passing positive legislation proclaim their failure at persuasion, their lack of faith in freedom, or their devotion to the use of force.

The evolutionary manner of the imposition of the ideology by force in America has not made the reformist way into a tradition. It is true that many Americans have acquired habits of dependence upon the government, that parents have come to expect that the populace collectively will pay for the education of their children, that some foreign governments have come to rely on foreign aid, that many groups have become accustomed to privileged positions. But none of this can subsist without the support of the state. Repeal the legislation, maintain law and order, and the façade of the reformist "tradition" will collapse, revealing nothing behind it.

Remove Privileges and Restraints

Let me be more specific. Remove the welfare and unemployment program, and nature will take over shortly. For men grow hungry in only a brief interval, and this will be a sufficient prod to drive them to seek remunerative employment. Repeal the minimum wage laws, and the onerous bookkeeping imposed on employers, let the hungry man make himself attractive to an employer, and the "unemployed" will soon be busy doing the millions of jobs that are not now done because it is too expensive or too troublesome to hire someone to do them. Remove the exemptions and protections from labor unions, rigorously and impartially enforce the law, and they will no longer be able to create crises in the nation.

There has been much talk and writing since World War II about the "placid decade," the lethargy and conformity of youth, the lack of creativity and imaginativeness of people. This can be readily cured. Remove the restraints upon people, the government guarantees of security, and people will soon be inventive once again. Many a youth will begin shortly to improve his "image," and some will even learn to say "yes, sir" once again. There is no greater spur to invention, to imaginativeness, to creativeness, than the realization that one is responsible for his own well-being. The pressure of circumstances is an invaluable stimulant to human ingenuity.

Voluntary Charity Restored

But—and at this point the reformer plays his ace—what will happen to those who cannot provide for themselves, to the education of the young, to the care of the sick, to the support of the widows and orphans, to the aid of the destitute, to the handicapped and the unfortunate? That so many should ask the question should be the answer to it. Surely those who are so concerned that it be done would be willing to contribute to it themselves. If they devoted all of the energy they put into advancing government programs to the care of the needy, the needy should be well cared for.

There would be some differences, of course. Those who evince such deep concern might be expected to put their money where their mouths now are. Recipients of charity might be expected to show some gratitude for it, rather than accepting the property or the fruits of the labor of others as a right. The virtue of giving would replace the compulsion of taxation. Professional welfare workers would have to convince the populace, not just lawmakers, that they were doing a good job. Those who believe in foreign aid could pour their money into other countries, with or without strings attached. All of this will not work perfectly to relieve all undeserved suffering. No program would. What government programs do is to remove the distinction between deserved and undeserved suffering, take away the right of the individual to the disposal of his property, and relieve him of the responsibility for managing his affairs well.

Consequences Revealed

What I am saying is that if we remove the forcefully imposed ideology, tradition will be reasserted and redeveloped. This does not even depend upon the memory of the tradition, but it might well be aided by it. When individuals are responsible for their well-being once more, thrift, frugality, and industry are almost certain to become virtues again. The consequences of practicing the vices which are their opposites would be apparent even to many simpletons. No one would be likely to fall error to the notion more than once that he could spend his way to prosperity by spending his substance on consumer goods. Those who did so would be marked by the community as wastrels.

It is not for me to say what particular forms will be devised in the reassertion of the tradition, what will be reborn from the past, and what will be developed for the first time. No one need trouble himself to think of all the ways people of a like mind might act to accomplish things, what might be developed as aids to the individual in protecting him from the unscrupulous, how much and in what ways religion may be needed to support virtues and condemn vices. Ideologues have to plan their programs in infinite detail. Their programs always suffer from the deficiencies of a single mind, or of a few minds. Their foresight needs to be good indeed, for they involve huge populaces in their calculation. A society resting on tradition and devoted to liberty does not suffer from these drawbacks. Every individual may have a plan of his own. Most, if not all, of the whole population contributes to the provision of goods, services, ideas, customs, and habits. The failures of foresight hurt most directly the individual who has made them, but the benefits of his plan, if it is a success, may reach to all mankind.

The restoration of the American tradition does *not* depend, then, upon elaborate plans for the ordering of peoples lives, for what their folkways, customs, patterns of behavior, and habits shall be. These will be taken care of by people themselves, when they are let alone. It *does* depend, however, upon the restoration of a framework for liberty, so that people can act freely once more. It is in this realm that general agreement would be needed to restore the American tradition. Undoubtedly, there are, or have been, other ways for protecting the liberty of the citizen than those developed in America. But they are not viable alternatives for Americans, nor has it been demonstrated lately that another system would be better. America had a system of constitutionalism, of local government, of government by law, of private rights, for the civilizing of groups, and so on.

The Framework Still Stands

Perhaps *had* is not the right word. Most of the American political tradition is still there. There is still a Constitution, only significantly altered in two or three instances so far as language is concerned, though greatly altered by misinterpretation. The United States is still a Republic, still has a federal system of government, still has much of the framework for liberty intact. The major task of restoration is to get men to read, understand, and observe the Constitution once more, to limit and balance the powers of the state and central governments once again, to heed the rhetoric and forms of the tradition. This is an educational problem more than anything else. However, more direct action can be taken by unseating those who show no understanding or appreciation of the tradition by the electoral process. If judges persist in ignoring the provisions of the Constitution, they can and should be impeached. In like manner, administrators can and should be impeached if they will not stay within the bounds of the Constitution. Indeed, my guess is that it would not take many impeachments to make even Presidents cautious of exceeding their authority. Congress might contribute much by cleaning its own house, resuming its constitutionally granted authority for appropriations (in the fullest sense, not in the nominal manner it frequently does today), and by dismantling the boards and commissions which it has created to evade constitutional and legal limitations.

By these and similar means the tradition might be restored, without revolution, without severe dislocation, without violence, and it might be that the unemployment of ideologues would be only temporary. On the positive side, it would be a return to the path of liberty which our Founding Fathers marked out for us.

16.

Building upon the American Tradition

THUS FAR, I have touched but light-
ly upon changing circumstances in American history. Yet
this point is the cornerstone of the "liberal" position.
"Liberals" usually maintain something like this: Conditions have changed greatly since the time of the founding of the United States. America was largely an agricultural land then; now it is an industrial one. Technological
innovations have been the means for changing the character of America. The mass media of communication, the
developments in transportations, mass production and
automation, the tremendous increase in industrial and
white collar workers, have transformed the country. The
position of America in relation to other countries has
been radically altered. Once the ocean was a great bar-
rier to travel between Europe and America; now it can
be spanned in a few hours. The military exigencies of a
world drawn close together by developments in transportation and communication and threatened by atomic
bombs are much more pressing than those of the past.
The number of people in America has vastly increased,
and the way of life of Americans has undergone momentous changes.

From a cataloguing of these and other changes, the
"liberal" (and, for that matter, almost all intellectuals

and opinion makers) goes on to conclude certain things about American society and institutions. Not many years ago, reformers were arguing that the Constitution was all well and good for an agricultural society, but an industrial society requires vastly expanded governmental activity. County and other local units of government may have served very well for rural communities, but in the day of urban complexes they are outmoded. More "advanced" thinkers have argued that the separation of powers is positively dangerous in these days of split-second decisions. In short, they ascribe the alteration and discarding of the American tradition (without so denominating what they are talking about) to the pressure of changing circumstances.

Changes certainly have occurred since the time of the adoption of the Constitution. Certainly, some of these changes have bearing for the American tradition. On the surface, at least, it is doubtful that there has been another period of such rapid change to match that of the last 175 years.

But the significance of any given change is not usually self-evident. Before changes result in altered institutions, they are winnowed through the minds of men; they are interpreted. From these interpretations come our understanding of the meaning of new conditions. In the nineteenth century, it was customary for thinkers to develop philosophies of history, i.e., comprehensive and all-embracing interpretations of change, how it came about, where it was headed, and what it signified at the time. G. W. F. Hegel constructed perhaps the most famous of these. Sometimes a philosophy of history was the center piece of an ideology. This was and is so in the case of

Marxism. Philosophies of history, however, have fallen into disrepute in the twentieth century, along with philosophies of almost everything else. Most American historians today imagine that they make do with *ad hoc* interpretations, if they make any at all.

In fact, however, an *ad hoc* interpretation of history is almost as unsatisfactory as an *ad hoc* religion, and just about as unlikely. Let it be noted that there are many scholars today who gather their facts and arrange them in chronicles, interpreting only very narrowly, if at all. In such cases, they may well have dispensed with any philosophy of history. But before historical studies can be brought to bear upon social change, they must be interpreted by someone. Before an interpretation can have the coherence and consistency to support or advance social programs, it must have a philosophical or ideological framework. Many historians have *not* ceased to interpret American history, and these interpretations *do* say something about social change. It follows, then, that they must be based upon either implicit or explicit philosophies or ideologies.

They Planned To Change History

An examination of the histories that are reckoned to have been important for social change would show that this has been the case. The works of such men as Frederick J. Turner, Charles A. Beard, and Vernon L. Parrington are filled with formulations drawn from philosophy or ideology. These works, and those popularizations which drew their sustenance from them, certainly did support and advance social change in certain directions.

My point is that the prevalent notions of the significance
of change are not drawn simply from changes themselves, nor from histories of them. That governments
must grow larger and larger, that industry must be ever
more minutely regulated, that more and more activities
must be done by collective compulsion, is the product of
interpretation, not raw circumstances. The belief that the
American tradition is outmoded belongs in the same
category. In short, Americans have departed from their
tradition and headed in new directions because some men
have wanted to change America, or because they believed
on the basis of untested assumptions that America must
change. Circumstances do not tell us what to do; they are
only mute conditions within which we operate.

Circumstances certainly have changed. The context of
our lives has been altered by skyscrapers, atomic bombs,
automobiles, jet airplanes, computers, and communists.
But none of these, nor any others that could be named,
have told us to change our goals or our ideals. Some of
these may have made life more sweet, but none of them
has made liberty less desirable. Independence and morality were not changed in the scale of human values by
circumstances. The passage of time has not made politicians less likely to resort to oppression, and the invention
of the jet airplane did not make it desirable to yield up
national independence. The American tradition *is* outmoded if we want to use the government to look after the
intimate needs of the population. It is *not* outmoded for
those who still value liberty and independence.

The belief that changed circumstances have altered
the direction of America is shielded from exposure and
refutation by the failure to distinguish between the ephem-

eral and the enduring. Some things indubitably change, and will continue to change from time to time. Nations grow stronger or become weaker, and the power situation changes in the world. New tools for producing goods replace old ones, and men change their methods of producing the goods, though many of the products are as old as civilization. Beliefs, ideas, and values have been known to change from one time to another.

Some Values Endure

Other things endure and remain, unchanged so far as we can tell. So far as we can make out, man has a nature that is little altered, if at all, by the passage of millennia. All men are mortal, and all the medical advances have not made a dent in this fact of existence. Man lives his life against a stop watch, as it were. If his life is to have meaning, it must be gained in a limited time. Men still eat food, sleep for a number of hours each day, get a sense of well-being from activity, take pleasure in the simple things of life—the smell of coffee brewing, the joy in the arrival of friends, the stimulation of conversation, the sense of achievement in a job well done—if they have not been entirely corrupted. Men are still torn between good and evil, as they have been so long as we have records of them, self-seeking on the one hand, and selfless on the other. The garments by which he shields both his physical and inner self from the world change, but the man remains much the same as he ever was.

Nor is there any evidence that the laws which govern the universe change. True, we may view them from different perspectives, gain new insights and lose sight of old

ones, but the laws of gravity, of flight, of inertia, of
human relations, of supply and demand, still operate.
Jet flight may depend upon newly discovered principles,
but older principles were not proved wrong by them. The-
ology and philosophy may be thrust aside, but there are
no new discoveries which disprove the belief that this
universe is sustained by an underlying metaphysical realm.
Individual liberty is still the area within which the individual can operate free from restraint. Discoveries, developments, inventions, innovations, trends do not alter
the fundamental and enduring character of reality, though
they may hide us, temporarily, from it.

Let us assume that many Americans are still devoted
to their traditions, that they have not knowingly consented to the departures from them, that they still value
liberty, that they cherish national independence, that they
are concerned to preserve the moral dimensions of life by
allowing for choice, that they believe in private rights
and individual responsibility. Let it be agreed that much
endures, and that which does is the most important for
human life, beneath the surface of the most drastic
changes. When there is agreement on these things, it is
possible to go on to the meaning of change for the American tradition.

Laws Build Obstacles

The fact of changing circumstances bears upon the
traditions in these ways: First, it means that habits, customs, and ways of doing things should be alterable in
order for people to deal effectively with new developments
and conditions. The most formidable obstacles to such

flexibility are the legalizing and institutionalizing of patterns of behavior. Governments are almost always the villains of this piece. This is so in part, for America anyhow, because governments are supposed to act by law. Thus, in any undertaking overseen by government, there will be numerous rules and regulations which have the force if not the form of law. Those who enforce the rules, those who live by them, become attached to them; and because government action is usually slow and apt to be circumvented, rules which were conceived as temporary expedients tend to become rigid and fixed.

Bureaucracies have long been notorious for their inflexibility. But any positive government action usually results in the construction of some rigidity. A good case in point is the railway labor unions. They were permitted and supported by the United States government to draw up and enforce rigid work rules. New locomotives, new safety devices, new types of freight cars were introduced, but the unions clung to the established rules. It is not that private undertakings cannot tend to inflexibility also; the difference is that the consequences are much more immediately visited upon the inflexible in private affairs.

If changes are to be dealt with effectively, flexibly, and creatively, governments should be severely limited in the number of things that they do. I am aware that Americans have attempted to introduce flexibility in government by giving discretionary powers to boards, commissions, and government agents, but this has succeeded in making government action arbitrary and authoritarian without notably improving flexibility. It would appear, again, that individual freedom and responsibility are the best means for assuring adjustability to changing circumstances.

Second, the passage of time has provided us with experience with our institutional framework of liberty. The bent of some men to oppress others has not changed, but they have found ways over the years to usurp power and use innocent instrumentalities for oppressive purposes. To be more plain, certain shortcomings and weaknesses in the Constitution are now apparent. A Constitution which was conceived to limit the government it created is being circumvented. Analysis shows some of the particular ways this has been done.

The "General Welfare" Clause

Two innocent phrases in the original Constitution have been employed for the vast extension of the powers of the central government. One of these is the reference to the "general welfare." The phrase appears both in the Preamble and the body of the Constitution. We know with certainty that it was not interpreted at the time as a grant of power. If it had been, the Constitution would not have been adopted. It is quite possible that it was intended to *limit* governmental action. General welfare can be conceived as the welfare of everyone; and if legislation has to benefit every individual, there will not be very much of it. It was also a rhetorical device; its use suggested that the government was to be for everyone, not for special classes or interests among the people. It has now been misinterpreted, however, to give a plenary grant of power to Congress to do anything which congressmen can stretch their conception of the "general welfare" to cover, whether they do so by the route of the "greatest good for the greatest number" or by their personal feelings and inclinations. Far from limiting governmental action, it has opened the floodgates to unlimited action.

In view of these developments, references to the "general welfare" should be removed from the Constitution by amendment. It would be profoundly in keeping with the American tradition to do so. Moreover, such action would be a constructive response to notions and circumstances which have changed.

The Power To Regulate Commerce

Another phrase which has been used to extend greatly the sway of the national government is the one which gives to Congress the power "to regulate Commerce . . . among the several States. . . . " The records of the time indicate that it was intended "to facilitate" commerce among the states. Under the rubric of the "power to regulate interstate commerce," however, reformers have used it as an opening wedge to regulate and control any activities of Americans which they can bring under it by any stretch of their fertile imaginations. Moreover, it is not even being used very effectively to accomplish its original object, as states pile up rules and taxes which effectively obstruct the free movement of peoples and goods.

It is quite possible that the Founders put the phrase in the wrong place. Rather than granting power to Congress in this respect, the chances are good that the object could have been achieved by prohibiting the states from obstructing commerce. If law and order were then maintained by all governments, commerce should be effectively facilitated throughout the United States. This change could be made by constitutional amendment, felling a great complex of

dubious or harmful regulation, and helping to restore
the tradition.

Experience has shown, too, that the powers of the states,
and of individuals, were not sufficiently safeguarded by
the original Constitution. The defect lies in leaving the
final decision as to constitutionality to the federal courts.
In short, a branch of the government affected by the decision makes the decision as to its powers. It should not surprise us that they would frequently have a generous view
of these powers. Something along the lines of the "Court
of the Union" Amendment now under consideration should
help to remedy this imbalance in the federal system.

The Role of the Judiciary

Even so, the jurisdiction and authority of the federal
courts need to be more adequately defined and circumscribed. It needs to be made clear that the courts do *not*
make law; they only *apply* the standing law to particular
cases. The reason for having a written constitution was
so that every literate person might have recourse to it, and
see for himself what action was constitutional and what
was not. This idea has been so badly subverted today that
no one can be sure what the law is in many instances.
John Marshall's argument (in *Marbury* v. *Madison*) can
stand, but his position was that when there is a conflict
between the Constitution and acts of legislature, the court
is bound by the Constitution. So are we all! Every officer
of the government is bound to defend the Constitution.
It is a written document. Where its language is vague, it
should be made clear. Then when any public official acts
contrary to its provision, he should be impeached. Indeed,

the exceeding of authority granted there or the violation of its provisions should be considered so heinous an action that the person who did it would be effectively ostracized from the society, if not by law, at least by social consent. The Founders did not fully realize how much sanction must support constitutionalism for it to work effectively to limit government.

The powers and prerogatives of the President now exceed what was envisioned in the Constitution. The changes have occurred by precedents, usurpations, grants from Congress, and by the creation of the notion that the President is and must be the Leader. Peoples appear ever and again to drift toward monarchy, toward the charismatic leader, toward the single man who will rescue and save them. If this is a tendency of people in general, this tendency has been aided and abetted in America by reformist intellectuals who sense, if they are not fully aware of it, that their programs require a single mind to direct them. Note this pronouncement of a contemporary intellectual:

> Concrete and timely assessments of specific complex questions will not of themselves combine to form "an image of national purpose." That can be done only by a man, and only one man can do it. Elements of a general policy can come from hundreds of sources. . . . But the national purpose in the world can be crystallized and communicated, at any given time, only by the President of the United States.[1]

---

[1] McGeorge Bundy, "Foreign Policy: From Innocence to Engagement," *Paths of American Thought*, Arthur M. Schlesinger, Jr. and Morton White, eds. (Boston: Houghton Mifflin, 1963), p. 308.

When the growth of power and prerogatives of the presidency are combined with the adulation of the leader, as they have today, the stage is set for caesarism.

Again, we can learn from experience how these departures from the constitutional tradition have taken place, and get some clues as to how they might be prevented in the future. A precedent can have no standing in constitutionalism. The fact that President Eisenhower sent troops to Little Rock, and that this action was not effectively challenged, does not establish the legality of the action, though the action may have been legal in this case. To reason in such fashion is the same as for a thief to reason that because he was not caught and punished for robbing a store that this establishes the legality of the action. A President may guide his action by precedents, just as most of us tend to do, but this only indicates an expectation of legality, not a guarantee. Whether it is necessary to spell this out in the Constitution, I do not know. If there were a real return to constitutionalism, it should not be necessary.

Growth by Usurpation

A good example of the growth of presidential power by usurpation is the so-called "executive agreement." President Franklin D. Roosevelt apparently invented this "power." There is no grant of any such power in the Constitution; thus, there is no need for an amendment. The increasing grandeur of the office, with its helicopters, jet airplanes, limousines, Marine bands, numerous advisers, attachés, physicians, press agents, protocol, tax exemptions, contingent funds, indicates departures from republican simplicity rather than the Constitution. It might be well, however, to place additional constitutional limits on the prerogatives of the office. To do so would certainly be in keeping with the American tradition. Those who serve in public office in this country are rewarded financially out of tax moneys taken from Americans by force, or the threat of force. In view of this rather hard fact, it behooves them to live in a rather austere fashion. What is more important, however, is that public officials not be allowed to shield their thrust to power behind the grandeur of the surroundings.

Congress, too, has made signal departures from the tradition. They have yielded up much of their prerogative for initiating legislation to the President. They have turned over lawmaking responsibilities to "independent" boards and commissions. Much of the increased power of the executive department has been granted by Congress. Many things might be done, but one thing appears essential to a return to government by law. There needs to be an amendment to this effect. *No one shall be punished for the violation of any federal law except it shall have been specifically enacted by Congress in all its details.* In one stroke, this would take away from the courts, tax collectors, boards, and commissions the arbitrary powers they now exercise over Americans.

Limited Power To Tax

Experience has shown, too, that there need to be limits upon the taxing power of governments in order to secure to the people the right to the fruits of their labor. To this end, the first step to be taken should be the repeal of the

Sixteenth Amendment. There are many possible directions to take after that. One would be to require that all taxes upon income or property be levied in proportion to their amount or value. This would prohibit progressive taxation. It might be well, too, to prohibit any exceptions or exemptions from the rate. It might be useful, also, to establish some limits upon spending, but my guess is that if taxes are proportional the great lure of redistribution, which is the lure of the spending programs, would be effectively removed.

It is not my intention, however, to set forth a complete program, in all its particulars, for restoring and building upon the tradition. Rather, I have only wished to indicate the outline of such a program. My major purpose, however, was to demonstrate what constructive use can be made of experience gained from changing circumstances, from trends, and from particular events. These can be used creatively to indicate what action needs to be taken to preserve and build upon the tradition.

There is a third way in which changing conditions bear upon the American tradition. Inventions, discoveries, new ideas, and changes in situation pose new problems and offer new opportunities for liberty and progress. For example, there have been many inventions since the drawing up of the Constitution—radio, television, movies, automobiles, to name a few. At the time of the framing of the Constitution, the only general media of communication was the press. Thus, the First Amendment to the Constitution provided, among other things, that "Congress shall make no law . . . abridging the freedom . . . of the press. . . ." Why not include the other media—radio, television, movies—under this injunction? It would be in keeping with the

American tradition to do so. Action could be taken to establish property rights in certain frequencies, and the full protections of property could be extended to them.

Government as Propagandist

New dangers from government have arisen, too, from the use of new inventions and from the development of new techniques. Propaganda, for example, is not new, but the extent to which it is used, the technological devices for spreading it, and the knowledge of psychology which is used in employing it have increased so much that governmental use of propaganda is a problem on a quite different scale from what it was in 1790. Surely, everyone should be aware in this day of the extent to which governments use the press, radio, television, movies, outdoor advertising, and public relations experts to manipulate people. Government controlled schools and universities extend this influence until it is virtually all pervasive.

Governmental agencies turn out reams of "information" to influence the public. The difficulty here is not that *propaganda* is being employed. The resort to propaganda by anyone is something that we might all deplore. But there is no way to prevent private individuals from using propaganda without destroying freedom. The case is different, however, with government officials. When governments employ propaganda, they are using moneys extracted by force or the threat of force for illegitimate purposes. That is, they are using our money to persuade us of what they want us to believe. The remedy for this should be found in constitutional amendments prohibiting all informational activity by appointive officers, and all use of tax moneys by elected officers for propaganda or informational purposes. Anyone who wants to use his own time and money to convince others of his way of thinking should be free to do so, but it does not follow that governments should be able to do so.

Other examples could be given, but these should suffice to illustrate how a tradition may be sustained and built upon in view of changing circumstances. Conditions do not change the goals of a people, nor do they make them outmoded if these goals were of an enduring kind. So far as I can see, it is just as sensible to be devoted to liberty in 1964 as it was in 1776. Many of the difficulties in the way of preserving liberty and order are the same today as they were in 1776. To deal with these, the established tradition is relevant. New difficulties have arisen in the meanwhile, or have been caused by usurpation and intentional change. The American political tradition provided means for dealing with these, by constitutional amendment, by impeachment of usurpers, by defeat of politicians at the polls, by the separation and limitation of the powers of government officials. To build upon the tradition, it is necessary to keep the tradition in mind, to note dangers to it and departures from it, and to take note of what conditions have changed that require action. In short, history and experience can be constructively used within the framework of tradition.

The Case for Saying No!

Anyone familiar with the current "liberal orthodoxy" should be aware that my suggestions, if they were even entertained by "liberals," would be described as "negative."

Let the charge be accepted. They are negative in that they attempt to prevent the use of force and violence upon the innocent. They are negative in that they are aimed to prohibit the use of arbitrary power by government officials, negative in that they would deny the use of tax money for political demagoguery, negative in that they would restrict the obstructive activities of states and local governments, negative in that they would reduce publicly financed grandeur, negative in that they would attempt to estop the forceful redistribution of the wealth.

But their *positive* side is as an ocean compared to a brook. They are aimed to protect and defend the life, liberty, and property of individuals, to extend and maintain the area of individual choice, restore individual responsibility, allow full room for the fulfillment and realization of the individual, open up our vision to a moral order in the universe, advance prosperity, restore charity and gratitude to human relations, and help to relight the beacon of liberty so that the light can go forth from America once more to the confused and oppressed peoples of the world.

All of this is what I understand to be THE AMERICAN TRADITION.

Index